CROOK COUNTY

CROOK COUNTY

Racism and Injustice
in America's Largest Criminal Court

NICOLE GONZALEZ VAN CLEVE

STANFORD LAW BOOKS
An Imprint of Stanford University Press
Stanford, California

Stanford University Press

Stanford, California

© 2016 by Nicole Gonzalez Van Cleve. All rights reserved.

Printed in the United States of America on acid-free, archival-quality paper

Library of Congress Cataloging-in-Publication Data

Names: Van Cleve, Nicole Gonzalez, author.
Title: Crook County : racism and injustice in America's largest criminal court / Nicole Gonzalez Van Cleve.
Description: Stanford, California : Stanford Law Books, an imprint of Stanford University Press, 2016. | Includes bibliographical references and index.
Identifiers: LCCN 2016003706 (print) | LCCN 2016004894 (ebook) | ISBN 9780804790437 (cloth : alk. paper) | ISBN 9780804799201 (e-book)
Subjects: LCSH: Discrimination in criminal justice administration--Illinois--Cook County. | Racism--Illinois--Cook County. | Criminal courts--Illinois--Cook County. | Minorities--Legal status, laws, etc.--Illinois--Cook County.
Classification: LCC KFI1799.C62 C728 2016 (print) | LCC KFI1799.C62 (ebook) | DDC 345.773/010890097731--dc23
LC record available at http://lccn.loc.gov/2016003706

Typeset by Bruce Lundquist in 10/14 Minion Pro

To my loving sons,
Dylan Salvatore Van Cleve and
Micah Gonzalez Van Cleve.
May you someday dust off this book, read it
and learn how justice used to be.

Thus grew up a double system of justice, which erred on the white side by undue leniency and the practical immunity of red-handed criminals, and erred on the black side by undue severity, injustice, and lack of discrimination . . . It was not then a question of crime, but rather one of color, that settled a man's conviction on almost any charge. Thus Negroes came to look upon courts as instruments of injustice and oppression, and upon those convicted in them as martyrs and victims.

W. E. B. Du Bois, *The Souls of Black Folk*

TABLE OF CONTENTS

PREFACE

THE U.S. SUPREME COURT RULED that "justice must satisfy the appearance of justice."[1] We expect our criminal courts to be legitimate, fair, and race-neutral. Most legal scholars, practitioners, and the general public presume that racism exists adjacent to our courts (if at all), in legislation, policing, and incapacitation. In fact, the violent deaths of Eric Garner, Michael Brown, Tamir Rice, and Laquan McDonald punctuated the harsh reality (which most people of color know too well) that there are two systems of justice in America: one for upper- and middle-class whites and another for the poor and people of color. When many of the officers involved in these cases were not indicted on criminal charges by local prosecutors and when justice came excruciatingly slowly, the public, media, and policy-makers began seeing the courts as part of this double system of justice: justice with a white side and justice with a black side.

While these high-profile cases began dispelling the myth of a colorblind criminal justice system, most Americans still do not expect racism to embed itself with impunity in our American criminal courts. How could it, given the myriad due process protections, legal safeguards, and a courtroom record supposedly holding judges and lawyers accountable? This book is the long-overdue explanation.

Imagine the classic images from the Jim Crow era. Signs over water fountains, doors, bathrooms. One sign from the Jim Crow Museum is poignant. It reads:

No dogs,

No Negroes,

No Mexicans

This sign publicly identified and separated black and brown people into separate spaces and punctuated the principle that people of color are at the level of animals, specifically dogs. Imagine the justice system having a similar sign outside the courthouse doors, where there is a type of backdoor justice that the poor and people of color enter, while whites enter from the front, or perhaps enter just to govern the system from which they are generally exempted. Imagine the cultural persistence of decades of patterned segregation to the criminal justice system, of cultural practices that minimize, marginalize, and abuse the backdoor entrants to criminal justice in America. Eventually, you could take down the signs and let the system run on its own racialized momentum. If there are two criminal justice systems, they are two systems that are separate and *unequal*—one with a front door and one with a hidden back door where the majority of citizens—the poor and people of color—experience America's failed promise of fair and equal justice.

This is not what I expected to find when I began a study of the criminal courts in Cook County–Chicago, the largest unified criminal court system in America. I found the criminal courts serving as a crucial gateway where racism and discretion collide, with dire effects for both the experience and the appearance of justice. These findings assault our expectations of justice and our notion of racial equality in an era of supposed colorblindness.

Michelle Alexander's book, *The New Jim Crow: Mass Incarceration in the Age of Colorblindness*, is one of the most recent works that has generated public and scholarly interest in mass incarceration and its dire effects on communities. There, she takes readers on a critical journey through history, policy, and politics to argue how mass incarceration is the new "Jim Crow." While her book is eloquent, accessible, and an important effort to harness all the empirical work of other social scientists, Alexander, admittedly, paints with a "broad brush" how race and racism explain mass incarceration. She asks the poignant question "How exactly does a formally colorblind criminal justice system achieve such racially discriminatory results?" She provides a pessimistic response by saying that evidence will "never be available in the era of colorblindness."[2] Ironically, she says that one can "close the courthouse doors" to any claims of bias in a colorblind era.

This book is an empirical answer to that paradox; it is an opening of the courthouse doors. I detail how the "doing" of colorblind racism transforms the gateways of criminal justice, our criminal courts in particular, from *central sites of due process* to *central sites of racialized punishment*. I show how extreme racial punishment embeds itself in processes, not just in sentencing outcomes or in locations of punishment like prisons, but in due process procedures that appear infallible to legal scholars, policy-makers, and the general public. More specifically, this ultimately impacts reform issues that explicitly address the public defense system in America. Pretrial abuses and procedures are punishing defendants before they are found guilty, while defense attorneys acknowledge a system that does not afford dignity to their clients. Reforming indigent defense must start with a lens that focuses on the entire courtroom workgroup of legal professionals (judges, prosecutors, and defense attorneys) who create the quality and experience of justice for the mostly minority and impoverished offenders.

A law professor in Chicago discouraged me from examining the culture of the courts—asserting that Steve Bogira's *Courtroom 302* had already told all the "stories" from the trenches of justice in Cook County–Chicago. The goal here is not to provide a series of stories, but instead to show these stories as part of a sociological account of justice in an era of mass incarceration. In other words, I seek to provide an empirically based, theoretical framework to understand how these "stories" aggregate to a larger sociological account of how our courts operate and how racism serves an essential function.

This research began fifteen years ago as an ethnographic study of both the prosecutor's office and the public defender's office where I clerked and participated in their respective cultures. I later returned to this field site and supplemented my ethnography with 104 interviews with judges, prosecutors, and public defenders and another 1,000 hours of additional observations from 130 "court watchers" trained in collecting qualitative data in the courthouse. This ambitious "court watching" effort took two years to complete. It is upon this robust dataset that I build an empirical account of racism in our criminal courts. While the book assumes a narrative style, let it not distract from the data and careful analysis required to come to the conclusions in this study.

In addition, this work assumes the vantage point of court professionals and provides an account of how *they* see defendants, victims, families, and other consumers of justice. The stories of defendants, victims, and families are the backdrop of this account, but they are omnipresent. While the defendants themselves could have testified to these abuses and often have, it is powerful to see these stories unfold through the professionals whose actions define the experience and appearance of justice in our courts. Plenty of ethnographic accounts turn the lens on marginalized populations. My goal is to turn the lens on those in power as they do the marginalizing. My hope is that this work will encourage other ethnographers to do the same: identify the marginalization and then shift the lens to those who create the conditions. That being said, it is important to note that protecting the anonymity of those described in this book—be they attorneys, judges, or defendants—is imperative. Pseudonyms are used; courtrooms, locations, and exact dates and years are masked; in some cases, identifiable features of cases, attorneys, and defendants are changed to avoid the risk of revealing the subjects as they are described in this book.[3] However, I will reveal an entire culture of racialized justice that is larger than any individual judge, prosecutor, or defense attorney. As we shall see, this social system of racialized justice has deep roots and certainly many branches.

It is with deep reverence and respect that I acknowledge the families, defendants, and victims whose stories are profiled in this research. Some are still serving time in Illinois prisons as a result of the decisions and practices recounted in this book. Some are now free and coping with the consequences of being "marked" and marginalized by a criminal record. Others have died in prison. While their identities remain anonymous, their collective story is no longer invisible. *I remember and saw your story. And now others will as well.*

CROOK COUNTY

INTRODUCTION

Opening the Courthouse Doors

THE GANG CRIMES UNIT of the State's Attorney's Office in Cook County–Chicago was where the most bullish state's attorneys worked. Many were nicknamed for their ferocity, sounding like their own gang of sorts—"Dirty Dog" Richardson, "Beast-Man" Miller, William "Billy Club" McManus, to name a few. These were the types of men who comfortably put both feet up on their desk and welcomed you to their office with the soles of their shoes.

Nameless mug shots of a stream of black and Latino defendants acted as wallpaper for their office—a visual souvenir of convictions and conquests. This wallpaper provided a striking, racialized backdrop to the practice of criminal law and was my introduction to the criminal courts and criminal justice. Nearly all the prosecutors who built and exhibited this showpiece were white; in contrast, nearly every mug shot in the mural was a person of color. I moved backward several steps so that I could see the entire wall, and then I paced reverently along it, as though I were scanning a memorial of the dead.

I was the only person of color in the room; I was the prosecutor's unlikely new law clerk—a person who looked more like someone from the mural than an aspiring attorney in the office. Truth be told, I felt like a little girl playing dress-up in a power suit. I tried to keep my head down and fit in, but I was visibly stunned at the scale of the mural and the undeniable color line of "color-blind" criminal justice. Sensing my awe, my supervising prosecutor narrated the environment: "You see the scum we have to deal with?" The mural provided a vivid, symbolic picture of who the "other" was in this dynamic.

Court professionals—prosecutors, defense attorneys, and judges alike—often used the phrase "working in the trenches" to distinguish their work in the criminal justice system as separate and different from more cushy or elite aspects of the law. The "trenches" implies a warlike dynamic, a place to hide under hostile fire, and begs the question *Who is the enemy?* I scrawled this note, and many others, in a small corner of my legal pad that became my first ethnographic field observations at this site. Nameless mug shots of a stream of black and Latino defendants provided a collective racial caricature of the prosecutors' central mission as courtroom professionals. In the words of this prosecutor, they were taking this kind of "scum" off the street.

This book exposes the myth of colorblind criminal courts and examines how racial meanings become ingrained within the administration of justice despite procedural protections. Incarceration in the United States has grown seven times over the past forty years.[1] This growth is concentrated among blacks and Latinos and has transformed our social and political landscape, including the racial composition of our courts and prisons. The black-white difference in incarceration rates is particularly astounding. By all other social indicators of inequality, incarceration is unmatched. "Racial disparities in unemployment (two to one), nonmarital childbearing (three to one), infant mortality (two to one), wealth (one to five) are all significantly lower than the eight to one black-white ratio in incarceration rates."[2] Furthermore, racially disproportionate incarceration contributes to a cycle of poverty, growing structural inequality, and higher (rather than lower) crime rates.[3]

Numerous works examine the collateral consequences of mass incarceration on poverty, crime, and inequality within communities of color and even on daily life,[4] yet few works discuss the impact of racial disparity on the criminal justice apparatuses themselves. In fact, had I not ventured into the courthouse as a budding ethnographer assuming the role of a law clerk, I would not have seen the striking parade of black and brown defendants through courts managed by mostly white attorneys and judges. This book represents my journey to understand how the racial and social divides that manifest in the era of mass imprisonment affect the experience of justice in our criminal courts and the due process procedures that appear to be race-blind.

Inheriting Racism

Criminal courts are transformed by the patterns of segregation created by mass imprisonment. As such, the lawyers processing defendants tend to be white, educated, and upper-middle class and those being processed tend to be minority, uneducated, and poor.[5] In the supposedly "post-racial" era of Obama, America's purportedly colorblind racial ideology[6] and racism manifest in more-covert, institutional, and structural ways. For attorneys working in criminal courts defined by racial segregation between defendants and decision makers, such obvious racial inequality in spaces intended to be race-neutral creates a cultural dissonance among the professionals who inherit this heightened racialized social system.

This book shows how professionals reconcile the cultural dissonance of racial segregation with the moral and institutional imperative to process cases and people, en masse, in the criminal justice system. It is about how criminal justice professionals in a main gateway of mass incarceration participate in the incarceration "machine" despite obvious racial divides, uncertainty with the meaning and morality of what they do, and conflict about what real "justice" means in a punitive era of being "tough on crime." I explore how attorneys cope within the courts and how the racial divides between defendants and decision makers transform our courts into central sites of punishment, the likes of which legal scholars and reformers have failed to anticipate and interrogate. This book raises questions about modern forms of colorblind racism and the claim that they are kinder, gentler, and different from the overt forms of the past. As I show, imbued with the institutional authority of the state, hidden in the organizational contours of due process procedures, and normalized into insular cultures, colorblind racism transforms into state-sanctioned racial violence.

It took years of revisits to this field site (by myself and with other researchers) to understand how the enigmatic features of colorblind racism were not only operative but central to the efficiency of the system. The segregated, structural divides created by mass incarceration inform a type of racialized, legal habitus of ideologies and practices internalized in the production ethic of court procedure—the cultural engine of an entire assembly line of criminal justice. This habitus is like a "feedback" loop created by the broader trends of mass incarceration, the punitive turn in penology and punishment,[7] and the intensification of surveillance and policing that impacts the lives of the poor and people of color.[8]

Consequently, these trends in mass incarceration and the lingering cultural and racial stigmas they reproduce become incorporated as "embodied history, internalized as a second nature and so forgotten as history."[9] It is as though attorneys inherit a culture of racism that has existed "a priori" (before) their participation. The *a priori racism* that defines the courthouse culture and the legal habitus existed long before they arrived at the courthouse, and it will sustain itself long after they retire.[10]

From an institutional standpoint, the cultural beliefs and practices of this habitus drive all the taken-for-granted assumptions that define discretion in the criminal courts.[11] These discretionary actions are the gaps between the formal rule of law and how attorneys interpret these rules in practice. From how to comport oneself as a courtroom "insider" to the very norms of practice that define the legal community, this embodied history aids in the categorization of cases and people that professionals manage as case flow. This habitus shapes the sharp moral boundaries between the mostly white professionals who process cases and the minority offenders who are being processed.

Traditionally, one thinks of colorblind racism as an enigmatic type of racism that codes racial difference as moral difference, thereby obscuring racial divides and the social inequalities they produce. Coded racial language makes the expression of colorblind racism a "slippery, apparently contradictory," "rhetorical maze" with whites concealing racial beliefs with rhetorical moves and verbal strategies.[12] Haney-López extends this concept with the term "dog-whistle politics" or the political use of coded racial appeals that manipulate hostility toward nonwhites.[13] As he argues, the resonance of these racialized appeals pushes the political tides toward policies that reproduce white, elite advantage and amplify social inequality among middle-class whites and nonwhites. Studying the criminal courts brings these theories into the realm of everyday practices where white advantage and racial violence are reproduced in our most sacrosanct legal institutions.

Scholars of race contend that racism is more than simply ideology, that it is part of an entire system of institutions and structures that organize society.[14] However, in research, the "doing" of colorblind racism is observed as a linguistic sleight of hand—"seen" and heard only through its verbal expression and linguistic maneuvers or in the macro-level, political realm.[15] As Eduardo Bonilla-Silva argues, these racial practices operate in a more subtle, "now you see it, now you don't" manner, yet, as Ian Haney-López shows, the effects on inequality and politics are dire.[16]

Accounts of structural racism acknowledge that racial inequality is rarely produced by acts of blatantly identifiable racism; it is systemic, institutionalized, and frequently functions without the active participation of any one bigoted decision maker.[17] Yet, critical race scholars note, such theories depersonalize how racial prejudice, racial inequality, and racial power are experienced between people or within institutions.[18]

Missing is an empirical account that advances colorblind racism as more than just a "doing" of rhetoric, but a type of complicated habitus that informs institutional exchanges.[19] Racism is done *not* just "out there"—in traditional measures of inequality like education, income, job prospects, and the creation of racial stigma—but also in the everyday workings "in here"—in the interaction and social exchanges that define the experience of institutions. Examining the criminal courts and the procedural exchanges required to process what has become a racialized underclass of marginalized offenders reveals how colorblind racism is practiced within institutional boundaries—even aiding in the efficiency of the system itself.

Criminal Courts and the "Doing" of Racism

In criminal courts, lawyers, especially prosecutors and judges, are forced to deliberate on the morality and criminality of others (on behalf of the state). As such, morality is a central currency wielded by professionals. By the nature of being held accountable by the courts, the defendant is labeled as immoral to the point of criminal.[20] The professionals who process defendants, especially prosecutors who are at the helm of these legal proceedings, draw sharp distinctions between themselves and the defendants they process. These labels are dichotomous and absolute, and they rigidly delineate the prosecutor from the prosecuted, the judge from the judged, the defender from the defended—all distinctions that sharply demarcate the moral from the immoral.

Similar to moral boundaries maintained in criminal courtrooms, morality is a currency wielded in the "doing" of modern racism and is instrumental in drawing boundaries between whites and blacks while feigning colorblind ideology. As the logic goes, disdain for people of color is based not upon racial difference or inferiority as sets of biological features, but upon the moral inferiority that minorities embody. Often these immoral labels reference the historical stigmas, stereotypes, and controlling images associated with blackness and brownness—the supposed tendency to be lazy, hypersexual, and undermotivated, for example.[21]

These distinctions about morality and criminality, on the one hand, and morality and racism, on the other, meddle within the context of our criminal courts; there, one's moral status is conferred by both legal categories and racial categories. As such, the "immorality" of defendants is both a criminal distinction and a racial one. In this logic, disdain for defendants is not based on the color of their skin but on the moral violations they embody. With the authority of the law, a host of racialized abuses are not only allowable in public spaces but are seen as deserved and justified. Because a moral rubric supersedes racial difference, professionals maintain that court processes are "race-neutral" or colorblind.

A constant threat of violence patrols these courthouse arrangements. Armed sheriff's officers police boundaries in the courtroom—boundaries that separate minorities from the court proceedings and, periodically, inflict random and cruel abuses on courthouse visitors as examples of how to "stay in line." There is little outside accountability from the public or from other areas of the legal profession. The professionals practicing in the criminal courts operate in an environment where abuse, threats to defendants and their families, and policing of racial arrangements is normalized as part of community culture that informally governs the courts and allows professionals to valorize the moral purpose of their work. Without accountability and oversight, the criminal courts are their own social system, governed violently, with race underscoring a "grotesque caricature of due process and the rule of law."[22]

A Journey into the Trenches of Justice

When I began this research on the criminal courts in 1997, I never intended to write a study on punishment and race. I anticipated examining traditional concerns of jurisprudence; perhaps a revisiting of Malcolm Feeley's classic work *The Process Is the Punishment*, in which he looked at the pretrial costs of punishment imposed upon offenders before they pled guilty.[23] I suppose it is a sad irony that my hypothesis was partially correct. I found racial punishment before, during, and after conviction. This style of punishment was not inflicted just on defendants. It was inflicted on their families or anyone, even victims, with black or brown complexions who happened to walk into the courthouse.

When I began writing my first field notes in the courts, I was only a nineteen-year-old undergraduate student. I was granted leave from traditional classes, and my field site was a training ground for the ethnographic study of a culture. I chose the Cook County–Chicago courthouse as my field site because

I had ambitions of going to law school and eventually becoming a prosecutor. I assumed a participatory role at the site, working as the prosecutors' law clerk.

Like many Americans, I anticipated a "law and order" arrangement: "tough on crime" rhetoric dominated my perceptions of our court. Yet, in those first days on the job as both a clerk and a young ethnographer, I found my senses assaulted by the number of blacks and Latinos on the list of detainees in the lockup. One by one, they paraded in bright orange jumpsuits, numbers written on their arms, some in shackles, their hair unkempt and unclean from the Cook County Jail, many of them younger than I was. Most were too poor to retain counsel, and I watched as their families, longingly and tragically, watched their sons, daughters, husbands, and boyfriends being taken back into custody to await trial or being sentenced to five, ten, twenty-five years or more. Rather than being charged with violent offenses, most were charged with possession of drugs, theft, intent to sell drugs, or other nonviolent offenses. The majority were pretrial detainees—offenders too poor to pay their bond, so they languished in the overcrowded jail—unable to work, parent, pay rent, provide child support, or any number of other daily tasks that if not done could tear apart one's family or livelihood. What I was witnessing was the demographics of mass incarceration in action—a central gateway for mostly poor people of color to enter or cycle through a system of punishment.

Naively, on my first day, I began tallying the number of minority defendants on my legal pad. During one court call, all but four of the thirty defendants were black or Latino. Those defendants who were white were often immigrants who needed language translators to understand the proceedings. I asked my supervisor to help me make sense of the disparity, but I was too scared to overtly ask about race. Instead, I mustered the courage to ask her about her views on crime and poverty—a question that could proxy race. She snapped at me for asking such a question, responding with a paternalistic trope about welfare dependency. Like my introduction to the Gang Crimes Unit, I stood intimidated by the response and realized, especially as the sole person of color among the professionals in my courtroom, that it was better to stand quiet and try to fit in.

No doubt my own racial identity allowed for this access. I am Chicana but not dark-skinned. I came from a blue-collar Chicago neighborhood. I pronounce "Chicago" like a Chicagoan (shi-KAW-go). Accordingly, I could talk the slang with the insiders and could code-switch with the rough-around-the-edges prosecutors, defense attorneys, and even the cops.[24] When I needed to interact with the judges, I wielded my affiliation with Northwestern University, which was perceived as "elite." I hid the fact that I was actually too poor to pay for my tuition, room, or board (a wealthy alumnus did that for me).

I was a young woman, and I realized that my age and gender could work to my advantage. I could feign ignorance and ask experienced prosecutors to explain their practices and beliefs. I often started my toughest question with, "This is a really dumb question but . . ." and they were often eager to teach me the ropes.

Balancing these numerous identities was strategic and allowed for access to a court culture known for its insularity. Most importantly, the heart-wrenching experience of racially passing in the eyes of the white professionals gave me cultural access: a chance to hear and observe white professionals as they talked outside of the frameworks associated with the veiled niceties of colorblind racism. I had access to a place where whites were allowed to stop being nice and start acting racist. I often contemplated the privilege and research access that my lighter skin afforded me and made a commitment to turn the ethnographic lens upon the white professionals doling out racial abuse.[25]

My time in the field was an indoctrination: the prosecutors, judges, and defense attorneys took me under their wings. It was through this process that I learned the rules of the racialized court system—rules that included both how to process cases efficiently and the proper moral and professional justifications for such practices. Often I reflected on that role, averted my eyes from defendants and their families, and hoped that I did not see anyone from my neighborhood. I would speak Spanish to the *abuelitas* who came into court and tried to help in marginal ways that only made me feel worse about my role. But mostly I felt fear. Fear to talk about abuse, fear to stop it, and fear to ask questions about it. In one instance, a judge who knew that I could sing asked me to perform in open court for a wedding that he was officiating as a favor. I thought the judge was joking and viewed it as unprofessional and even disrespectful to the families, defendants, and possible victims who were having their day in court. I whispered to the prosecutor and asked her how to say no. She said, "If the judge asks you to sing, you ask, 'What song?'" There I was, like the judge's and prosecutor's marionette, singing in open court, "Wind Beneath My Wings," shortly after defendants were sentenced to prison time. What little decorum was left of open court was shattered in this circus-like charade. My field notes acted as the one expression—the one place—where I could bear witness to all that I saw.

It took periodic revisits to my field site and field notes to fully see how these patterns emerged in their persistent and pervasive forms. This is not surprising given the enigmatic and "slippery" features of today's modern form of racism, which ignores or denies the existence of discrimination and often shifts its concerns to moral rather than biological inferiority. What was surprising was that racism, in the context of the courts, was pervasive, direct, and violent. Day after day, I noted grave abuse—on and off the record—in front and backstage environments. There were times, dark times, when the callousness with which prosecutors and defense attorneys talked about dead victims, babies, mothers, and violence against blacks and Latinos was too much. I would have nightmares; I would stop eating; I went for on-campus counseling to talk about what I had seen. At one point, I vowed never to come back to my study or my field site. But, over time, perhaps like the professionals themselves, I became numb to the abuse; I observed it but did not question it. I disapproved of it but was not shocked by it. Perhaps this numbness was not unlike how many of the attorneys in this study were co-opted into being complicit in the cultural code of the courts. Or, perhaps, my pursuit of objectivity scared me into avoiding words like "morality," "humanity," "justice," "redemption," and other human rights principles that extended beyond this location.

In graduate school, I returned to the same courthouse and clerked in the public defender's office to get an alternative point of reference, and I observed defense attorneys "coping" with the culture that I had noted five years earlier. Defense attorneys whom I interviewed admitted to racialized courtroom work-group practices, acknowledged their disdain and complicity in this culture, but admitted that these practices were long-standing and persistent. Over time, this pervasive culture came to seem like "business as usual." In fact, making a big deal about the treatment of defendants, their families, or any courtroom outsiders was a sign among courtroom insiders that you were a little "wet behind the ears." Certainly, acknowledging racial divides was met with silence, confusion, and hostility—informal sanctions so harsh that you never made the same mistake twice.

Five years later while revisiting these observations in graduate school, I developed a partnership with the Chicago Appleseed Fund for Justice—a social advocacy nonprofit—to create a court-watching program to police the professional standard of courtroom behavior. As an experienced ethnographer, I was charged with designing this program, which included the training materials and rubric by which court watchers would evaluate professionals. Court watchers were systematically trained and instructed to examine court procedures, professional norms, and the overall professional decorum of the court. In all, 130 court watchers observed all twenty-five felony courtrooms—both on- and off-the-record practices. Ultimately, it was through their eyes that I began to see race again.

I assumed that I would receive accounts of the courts' effectiveness, accessibility, and administration. As the court watchers' detailed forms and written narratives came back for review, their outsider accounts of racial disparity and their stories of abuse along racial lines matched my initial impression of the courts. When I debriefed these researchers, many of them were shocked by their experiences, feeling either abused because they themselves were people of color or unsettled because they felt privileged and protected for being white. These data, which amounted to 1,000 hours of observations by court watchers with "fresh eyes," rejected the "business as usual" explanations of courthouse practices.

I began revisiting my field notes for similar patterns. I reread my notes from the first day I walked into the court, the first image of the gang unit and their mug-shot mural, and I began merging my impressions with the more than 1,000 hours of observations from court watchers. The result was not just a stream of interesting "stories," but a sociological account of a criminal court system defined by racial divides and meanings.

Armed with these data, I examine some of the classic questions about how our criminal courts function culturally and organizationally by engaging race and racism as a central variable overlooked by seminal works on criminal courts published after the "Due Process Revolution."[26] Specifically, how are courtroom workgroups and local legal culture affected by the racial divides that separate white professionals from minority defendants?[27] What role do racial categories play in streamlining processes and maintaining efficiency? How do criminal courts reproduce racial politics—a particular social order divided along racial lines? How does this arrangement reproduce itself through bureaucratic practices that are defended as "colorblind" to the mostly white professionals governing it?

Racialized Justice in an Era of Colorblindness

In addition to providing an improved understanding of the racialized nature of the criminal courts, this book makes three central contributions to the sociological conception of racism and the broader dialogue regarding modern forms of racism and punishment. First, it addresses how the larger trends in mass incarceration—namely, the racially disproportionate effects of punitive policies and laws—affect the criminal justice institutions tasked with maintaining the system. Segregation and racial inequality ultimately shape and inform institutions despite myriad due process protections, purported colorblind ideology, and bureaucratic formality that appear to protect against racism and racial bias.

Second, this case contributes to an understanding of how modern forms of racism are practiced within institutions. While scholars of race generally agree that racism is more than just "ideology" or a product of a few "bad apples," here I address how racism can be practiced within institutions. In fact, racism is even emboldened by institutional rules and laws. Rather than a kinder, gentler brand of racism that hides in enigmatic ways, "doing colorblind racism" within institutions sanctifies racial abuse, as the immorality of one's racial category is confounded with one's criminal category. This raises questions about whether colorblind racism is, in fact, kinder, gentler, and more enigmatic than the overt racism of the past.

Finally, these findings speak to an important shift in the scholarship on punishment and social control. In an era of mass incarceration, defined by intense segregation and racial inequality, our criminal courts are transformed from central sites of due process into central sites of racialized punishment. This development has far-reaching implications for how we understand procedural justice, rule of law, legal ethics, legal consciousness, and ultimately, policies targeted at reform.

While this book demonstrates how racial punishment is wielded in the context of the criminal justice system, these effects could be operative in other segregated systems that claim to be race neutral, like social welfare offices, schools, hospitals, and other systems managed by whites who are mobilizing narratives about morality and governing the outcomes and the well-being of poor people of color. This is not just a story about the criminal courts or the law; this is a story about racism in action, culture in isolation, and the effects that both can have on an institution. Alarmingly, I chose to study a criminal court—a social institution that is supposed to be the bedrock of justice, impartiality, and fairness. Consider this field site selection the ultimate litmus test of how racism can infiltrate seemingly race-neutral institutions protected by the most stringent due process procedures, a court transcript—and even the Constitution. What we will see is that these protections are often transformed into tools of punishment, giving new meaning to Malcolm Feeley's classic work *The Process Is the Punishment.*

To examine these themes, I will take you into the courthouse where seg-regation is endemic and divided along racial lines, where people of color are forced to sit behind bulletproof glass as they watch their cases managed by an all-white cast of attorneys and judges. Here, we will journey in the hall-ways, dirty corridors, and isolated culture of a large urban courthouse defined by racial divides and policed through violence and fear. These scenes will be animated by the insiders who taught me the cultural rules of the courts, my own indoctrination into this culture, as well as the observations of outsiders or court watchers as they react to and retell the experience of viewing a space that has the look and feel of the Jim Crow era.

Dismantling Court Culture

To understand how professionals make sense of such racial disparities and even defend them as colorblind, I will pull apart this court culture piece by piece, as the prosecutors and judges narrate and teach the moral rationales for racialized justice. This close study will address how racialized scripts become hidden in the contours of justice—living in the "off-the-record" strategies and the prac-tices of plea bargaining. As we will see, this book does not unearth rogue at-torneys or racists, but it reveals court culture that thrives on racism to function efficiently—a complex culture that exists as its own social ecosystem, far from the oversight and accountability of the legal bar and the city at large.

I also provide evidence of how criminal defense attorneys construct a defense within the boundaries of a racialized court culture, and I show how criminal defense is more about navigating the cultural laws that govern the courtroom workgroup than about a sophisticated management of legal evidence, trial work, or the pursuit of legal motions. As a result, defense at-torneys admit to becoming complicit in a racialized system that they find reprehensible.

While this culture of racialized justice is pervasive, it is not one-dimensional. I will delve into the complex notions of justice and law as seen by the two cen-tral adversarial players that define our criminal courts: the prosecution and the criminal defense. Classic accounts of criminal courts portray prosecutors and defense attorneys as interdependent, co-opted players sharing the same beliefs and organizational imperatives. Instead, we see how both prosecutors and de-fense attorneys can possess both normative notions of justice and racialized no-tions of justice. I argue that while racialized cultural logics govern and legitimize how attorneys sort and dispose of cases, they retain thoughtful critiques and frameworks of fairness, justice, and reform.

Many prosecutors express a desire (and capacity) for race-neutral justice—even creating boundaries between themselves and police officers when overt bigotry becomes apparent in the system. Prosecutors identify what I describe as a "thin blue line of bigotry," and locate racial bias as adjacent to (rather than within) their professional culture. And the defense attorneys, despite their expressed sympathies for defendants and their disdain for being complicit in a system that abuses their clients, often act as willing ambassadors of racialized justice. They use the rubrics and logics of racialized justice to determine which defendants are "worthy" of their time and resources while helping to translate the cultural laws of the workgroup to their clients.

Finally, I examine the implications of these arrangements on law, justice, and the consumer experience of our courts. I argue that coupled with institutional authority, the promise of procedural justice, and the guise of bureaucratic protocols, colorblind racism is anything but subtle or polite. I end with a call to action on holding our American criminal courts accountable.

Crook County and the Code of the Courts

Elijah Anderson's book *Code of the Street* takes the reader on a journey to understand what, for some, is a foreign culture of morality and decency in the inner city. While writing this book, I decided to revisit Anderson's text and was stunned by the parallels of our ethnographic accounts. For Anderson, inner-city life is governed by a moral code: a code of civility, on the one hand, and a code of conduct regulated by violence, on the other. I extend this construct to the criminal courts as an analytic tool to understand another inner-city community—a court community. Like the code of the streets, there is a notion of civility that is *written into formal law*. This stands in stark contrast to the "cultural code" that defines the *practice of criminal law*—one that more accurately doles out violent pretrial abuses the likes of which redefine the notion of pretrial punishment. The criminal courts have become a type of "street law" for "street people." This statement speaks to how racialized justice bastardizes the practice of law, how well-intentioned practitioners become co-opted and often coerced into its culture, and how marginalized people become its primary consumers—whether as defendant, victim, witness, or family member lending support. This is ultimately an account of marginalized lawyers, practicing marginalized law for marginalized people. This book opens the courthouse doors and reveals the indignities of justice as defined by the civility and violence of a culture. This is America's brand of justice for the poor and people of color— a brand of justice that the local community calls "Crook County," if only to mock the system's legitimacy and redefine the attorneys as the true "crooks," who dole out racialized justice like the pain of punishment.

1

SEPARATE AND UNEQUAL JUSTICE

TO DRIVE TO THE NATION'S BIGGEST and busiest courthouse, take I-55 South from the "Loop"—the center of the city—as though you are making your way to Midway Airport. Drive toward poverty; until the neighborhoods get more racially homogeneous, more black and brown; until the regal Chicago skyline is small but visible in your rearview mirror. Exit at California Avenue, just a few exits shy of Cicero, and start navigating by artifacts of concentrated poverty: look for trash, broken glass, discarded hubcaps on the side of the road, worn gym shoes thrown over electrical wires, and bars on the windows of homes. Look for storefront churches advertising salvation and redemption for a modest fee adjacent to liquor stores offering another type of escapism. Look for graffiti on brick walls of buildings; spray-painted murals memorializing the honorable deaths of young men, women, and children who died in local violence—sacred shrines depicted upon the profane markers of deterioration and disadvantage.

The criminal courthouse is situated in a predominantly Mexican neighborhood with concentrations of violence, gangs, and drugs. Storefront lawyers' offices are among the few businesses in sight. With bars on the windows of their offices, even the few local lawyers who set up shop here seem imprisoned. Mothers push babies in worn umbrella strollers, and the elderly cart groceries home against a backdrop of cement walls, spiked barbed wire, and chain-link fences that surround the adjacent jail. Daily life goes by these fixtures of incarceration.

On my first day driving to the courthouse on 26th and California Avenue (Leighton Criminal Court Building), the Chicago weather served a brutal bite.

It was ice-raining horizontally so that the rain transformed into painful BB pellets that relentlessly and percussively pounded on the windshield of the car. The ice-rain crystallized a perimeter of separate and unequal arrangements that may have been ignored if the sun had been shining or if my first visit had been on a warm spring day.

Beyond the white structure of the Greco-Roman courthouse was what looked like a Depression-era breadline. Umbrellas were tilted and angled, making the breadline appear like a shantytown fortress in defense of the weather. Those without umbrellas huddled under newspapers and jackets, extended in contorted directions like a modern sculpture, to protect themselves from the wind and ice. It was the 8:30 a.m. courthouse "rush hour" and the breadline was the security queue for the general public—a line that included defendants, families, witnesses, and children. This group, which stretched far outside the building, was almost entirely comprised of people of color.

Adjacent to this line was a separate entrance for attorneys and personnel who had identification badges. While the general public was left to withstand the elements, the flow of professional traffic moved swiftly through, flashing credentials with sheriff's officers nodding and helping to expedite and to avoid inconvenience. The personnel and professionals in this group tended to be white.

Such adjacencies of a black and brown breadline braving the elements and a VIP lane for white professionals instantly demarcated a Jim Crow–style social arrangement on the outside perimeter of the courthouse. This visual of a black and brown entrance and a separate entrance for whites was my first clue of a double system of justice—one for people of color and the poor, and one for wealthy whites.

The Chicago cold heightened the visibility of racial inequality and made such waiting not just inconvenient or racially segregated but particularly cruel, and perhaps unusual in a modern era where we are culturally trained to ignore racial difference. Silently, I watched from a warm, leather-seated sedan, driven by my supervising prosecutor. The windshield wipers acted like a metronome, keeping time of the oppressive duration of the public's wait.

In these early days of visiting the courts, my supervising attorney drove me to the courthouse in that leather-seated sedan from one of the wealthiest North Shore suburbs in Chicago. She said it was for my own safety. On the surface, such a gesture was kind, but it also encapsulated the prevailing stigma held by professionals about where they do justice and whom they do it for: in their view, their commuting to "26th and Cal" was a journey into the trenches of justice where they dealt with the underbelly of society.

Introducing the All-White Cast

A small population of mostly white attorneys must commute to this space and manage a system foreign to their personal lives and communities. Cases in Cook County are handled by an "all-white cast."[1] Eighty-four percent of state's attorneys (SAs), 69 percent of public defenders (PDs), and 74 percent of trial court judges are white.[2] This is in stark contrast to the cases and people they process. In 2004, 86.2 percent of felony defendants were male, 69 percent were African American, 17 percent were white, and 11.2 percent were Latino.[3] The Public Defender's Office represents about 23,000 indigent defendants each year. These individuals are determined by a judge to be too poor to secure private counsel.[4]

Such an imbalance quickly presents in visual terms as racial segregation in and around the courthouse. Even outside the building, I observed that segregation was not just spatially arranged but extended to separate and unequal rules and practices between white professionals and the people of color who defined the consumers of criminal justice. On the east side of California Avenue (facing the courthouse) is a five-story parking garage known for the aroma of urine and for being the only free parking in the area. This lot is restricted for jurors, lawyers, cops, and courthouse employees. An older sheriff sits at the gate. On some days, the security gate is propped up and you can find the sheriff napping. Like the courthouse entrance, white drivers with flashy cars are assumed to be lawyers and rarely get stopped—except if the driver chooses to stop. Usually, those who stop are "outsiders" or jurors who *believe* the posted sign that states that a courthouse badge is necessary for entry.

Courthouse insiders will tell you a separate set of rules. If you drive with authority and give a wave to the sheriff, you should have no trouble passing through to the garage—regardless of what the sign says. Such advice travels through social networks of mostly white attorneys, interns, and students. This tip speaks nothing of race, but the unspoken privilege is delineated along a racial divide. The professionals who give out the tip tend to be educated and white. The jurors and outsiders who stop, then pass through the gate with little scrutiny, are also white.

The outsiders who may or may not be aware of these unspoken rules tend to be black, Latino, and poor. Where does that leave them in this urban landscape in and around the courthouse? Unlike the white professionals, blacks and Latinos arrive at the criminal courthouse on foot, travel by city bus (which may take several transfers), or get dropped off in front of the courthouse by a friend or relative.

For the lucky few who have cars, metered lots play a cruel joke on the unsuspecting. High-priced meters have a maximum time limit that barely allows for the time it takes to stand in the security line and find your courtroom. Because leaving the courtroom to feed the meter may cause a defendant or victim to miss his or her case (thereby, forfeiting bond and causing a defendant, in particular, to go to jail), a parking subculture emerged to cope with this cruel catch-22. Some relatives, neighbors, and friends wait in well-worn cars for friends and strangers alike. The cars have rusted paint and loud mufflers that rattle and bark when the car is turned on to idle for warmth. The occupants periodically feed the meters on behalf of friends and strangers—creating a makeshift parking arrangement for the poor. In contrast to the mild indignity of the parking garage smelling of urine, this parking charade has a circus-like feel, with children playing outside the cars while adults chat and compare notes. What is obvious to outsiders and first-time visitors to 26th and Cal is that this charade is racially defined. These separate and unequal structural divides between white and black are firm boundaries that are rigid, unbending, and policed by white courtroom insiders— especially Cook County sheriff's officers. Such rigid boundaries extend inside and around the building—delineating black, brown, and poor from educated, privileged, and white. It is an isolated ecosystem that thrives on segregation.

Criminal Courts as a Complex of Punishment

Once you've driven to 26th and Cal, an impressive white Greco-Roman courthouse casts an imposing presence upon the surrounding desolation. Vacant lots, railroad tracks, and abandoned industry define what appears to be a post-apocalyptic landscape. It's difficult to comprehend that you're only six miles from the center of the city, but far from the view and access of most Chicagoans, tourists, and downtown lawyers. This is not the mayor's Chicago: the pristine version of a metropolis with glorious fountains, museums, and the Magnificent Mile. And it's not Obama's Chicago, which extends beyond Hyde Park's mini-mansions all the way to Grant Park, the site of Obama's Election Day speech—a place synonymous with an emotionally searing visual of the hope of a post-racial America. No. This part of Chicago is built like Alcatraz Island, a prison of justice encircled not by a moat of water but by impenetrable poverty and violence.

A courthouse should project the business of the courts as dignified. There are eight triumphant sculptures symbolizing law, justice, truth, might, love, wisdom, liberty, and peace that stand guard before this building. First appearances may be deceptive. In addition to these symbols of justice, another structure stands as a foreboding presence. Attached to the courthouse structure by walkways and tunnels that act like the arteries and veins of an organism is the Cook County Jail—linking the structures of due process with the physical adjacency of punishment.

Cook County Jail is notorious; it sprawls across ninety-six acres on Chicago's southwest side, the equivalent of nearly seventy-two football fields of concentrated punishment and pretrial detainment. This makes the Cook County Jail the largest single-site jail in the nation. At its worst, it houses nearly ten thousand inmates and has been under federal supervision for overcrowding. The vast majority, 67.3 percent, of those admitted to the jail are young African American males between the ages of twenty-one and thirty from Chicago's South Side and West Side—creating a perversely convenient arrangement whereby the jail is closest to its target population. Another 19 percent of the population comprises Latinos or "other" nonwhite individuals—a further convenience of having a jail and court in a predominantly Mexican neighborhood.[5] While the jail systems in Los Angeles and New York have more inmates—14,193 and 12,283, respectively (as of June 30, 2011)—they disperse the inmate population across multiple sites.[6] In contrast, the Cook County Jail sits as an imposing cage of pretrial and post-conviction punishment—a behemoth site linked, physically and culturally, to a court system. In the criminal courts of Cook County–Chicago, the lines between due process and punishment become so entangled that they are indistinguishable both to those who "consume" the justice and to those who dole it out, be they prosecutors, defense attorneys, judges, or the support staff of clerks and sheriffs.

When Justice Means Punishment

Scholars of law and punishment, including criminologists and sociologists, impose distinct divisions between criminal courts and jails—distinctions that are not shared by the people who find themselves inside these institutions and, in many cases, by the people who work there. When lawyers say they are going to the courthouse, they do not say "the court." They say that they are going to "26th and Cal" (26th Street and California Avenue). It is spoken about as a general place where one practices criminal law and seamlessly navigates from the jailhouse to the courthouse and back.

On the surface, this blurred boundary between due process and punishment may seem like ignorance on the part of the community. For the lawyers, perhaps, it sounds like nothing more than local lingo. Yet community narratives elaborate the blurred lines between the court and the law and jail and punishment. The local narratives are based on the community's lived experience, where the lines between due process and punishment do not exist; they also act as a rebuttal to scholars who have artificially manufactured distinctions between institutions for parsimony, symbolism, or the veil of procedural justice.

One can imagine that such a regal white structure of a courthouse linked with a jail the size of seventy-two football fields, placed in the middle of urban desolation and relentless violence, creates a mockery of sorts for the people who live near the criminal justice complex and those who are forced to visit as consumers of justice—be it as a defendant, a victim, a witness, or a supportive family member. Urban sociologists argue that space becomes place through the meanings and collective narratives that people attach. Community nicknames for the court and adjacent jail abound, providing insightful commentary about the complex meanings that the criminal justice complex holds for the consumers of justice or those who live in its shadow.

Crook County and the White Castle

One of the puns associated with Chicago's criminal justice system is to call it "Crook County"—a term that dismantles the lines of punishment between the court and the jail. Outsiders may think that the "crooks" refer to the pretrial detainees who are charged (and not convicted of their crimes) but too poor to post their bond. However, in this narrative, the "crooks" in the county are actually the professionals—the guards, prosecutors, judges, and even the defense attorneys who are sometimes laughed at as public "pretenders"—the true hustlers who rigged the system.

In the 1970s, Jonathan Casper conducted a series of studies that captured the "consumer" perspective of justice, which appraised the criminal justice system from the vantage point of the system's consumers. This was an important intervention at a time when the "Due Process Revolution" was extending myriad new rights and protections to the criminally accused.[7] He noted that defendants viewed the system as having the same lack of integrity as trying to survive on the streets—a system where the law and the lawless converged in a courthouse where attorneys played the same immoral "games" as a common street hustler.[8] These perceptions of illegitimacy live on in these cultural quips about the "crooks of Cook County," where the boundaries of punishment and due process are not the only things broken down; the boundaries of criminality and civility, the law and the lawless, the moral and the immoral are all blurred as part of the social features of the "Crook County" criminal justice system.

Some of the locals call the court the "White Castle." This term critiques the speed of delivering justice and the mechanisms for achieving it. White Castle is a fast-food chain that is often a fixture of many impoverished neighborhoods. They serve up slider hamburgers, named not just for their size but also for the urban legend that they make you sick, sliding out the next day. This nickname designated the court as a place of drive-thru justice that is not about truth, wisdom, peace, and other symbolic pillars associated with the statues outside the building but instead connotes an assembly line of plea bargains. Beyond the sheer speed of justice, the quality is more like a Hobbesian vision, "poor, nasty, brutish, and short."[9]

Welcome to the Hotel California

Locals also call the jail the "Hotel California." On the surface, it is a play on the Eagles' 1976 hit and a euphemism for a jail located on California Avenue. The lyrics provide a powerful social commentary on the jail and the larger criminal justice system that was reappropriated by the accused and their families. Inmates mock the conditions of "living it up" in one of the most notorious jails in the nation and the legal need to bring your "alibis."[10] Those few who can post bond can metaphorically "check out any time" they want, but they "can never leave."[11]

Inmates released into rival gang territory around the jail, without even a bus pass to return to their own turf, find themselves running for their lives. "Hotel California" poetically describes the experience of justice at a central gateway of mass incarceration. In short, we hear from the community what it is like to experience mass incarceration, justice, and punishment in a court and jail complex encircled like Alcatraz Island—communities whose backyards are shadowed by jailhouse walls, with their sons and daughters held inside, just out of their reach.

Ordinary Dysfunction

While criminal courts vary from jurisdiction to jurisdiction, there are some similarities in all criminal court processes.[12] All courtroom workgroups are tasked with "doing justice" while disposing of cases—two goals that are often conflicting and difficult to balance.[13] All workgroups also have a common composition: judge, prosecutors, and defense attorneys who are familiar with one another's specialized roles but who retain their own unique tasks and vantage points in the system.

In the case of jails, most jails in large urban localities are subject to overcrowding. Bond court judges face the task of assessing risk of the accused with little information on defendants, little time to consider it, and little concern regardless of the level of resources. As such, Cook County may be ordinary in its dysfunction—facing the same struggles and burdens that mass incarceration has created for frontline practitioners throughout the nation. There are generalizable features that make Cook County–Chicago an excellent case to understand the experience of justice and the ideological vantage points of those who make justice run in our criminal courts, especially in an era of mass incarceration and the scarcity of resources it has produced in local state courts and jails.[14]

However, the nickname "Hotel California" raises questions about segregation and isolation of this court complex and what it has done to make Chicago an elegant case for examining the racialized effects of criminal justice in urban spaces—where those who are held accountable to the courts tend to be impoverished people of color and those who manage the courts are white, educated, and from places outside of the communities they hold accountable. When a criminal courthouse and a jail are placed in a segregated space, and the space is surrounded by impoverishment and violence, when, if ever, does imprisonment end and freedom begin? When is the supposed deliberative nature of due process distinct from the punitive nature of punishment? And, if surveillance in these neighborhoods is omnipresent, then the sheer proximity of the court and jail to the community disciplines everyone—even the children who have to walk by the court and jail en route to school, church, and other daily fixtures of life.

Us versus Them

An elderly black woman sat silent and still in a courtroom. She hypnotically gazed at the courtroom proceedings through bulletproof glass as white professionals shuffled papers, walked between attorney tables, and casually navigated the daily exchanges that defined the court call: plea bargains, probation violation cases, bond forfeitures, and status updates that defined the mundane features of the business of the courtroom workgroup. The microphone was off, so you couldn't hear, but you could see the professionals laugh and smile as if they were in a casual workplace. The interaction was like watching a silent movie and the audience of mostly black and brown people who sat watching the bulletproof glass—and the professionals beyond it—were like obedient churchgoers at a solemn funeral.

A white court watcher, dressed in jeans and a hoodie, sat among the public, discreetly writing notes with a pen on a form that was a bit crinkled from being in his pocket. The ominous and awkward silence in the court gallery was thick—the type of silence where you are conscious of your own breath. As the court watcher jotted notes, the elderly woman glanced over, taking quick peeks at what he was writing. At court recess, she asked boldly, "What are *you* doing here?" He was one of the few white observers of the court, and despite his hoodie and jeans, his race made it difficult for him to blend in. What was unclear was whether she was asking him why he was writing notes, or a more direct question: What is a white boy like *you* doing in the public gallery with everyone like *me*?

He revealed that he was "court watching" for a study. She revealed that she was related to a victim and a defendant. She asked him specifically to "remember" what he saw "here." As he was trained to do, the court watcher asked a follow-up question: "What do you want me to remember and I will write it down." She turned to the bulletproof glass and responded, "What do *you* see is wrong with this picture?" There was a long pause. "They're [attorneys] *all* white."

Like the outside perimeter of the court with its breadlines and parking shantytowns, the inside of the courthouse and the courtrooms themselves are demarcated and divided along racial lines. People of color stood in separate and longer lines; they were treated as criminals, searched, scrutinized, and mocked. In this space, race is a basic division—delineating the professionals from the public, the "insiders" from the "outsiders," and the power to act informally versus formally.

The concept of "boundaries" is assuming an important role in scholarship that extends across many social science fields. It is associated with empirical works on social and collective identity, racial and ethnic memberships, and cultural capital, to name a few.[15] Even one of the founding fathers of sociology, Émile Durkheim, contrasted the realm of the sacred with that of the profane as essential dichotomies that exist side by side, like the yin-yang visual.[16]

Distinctions need to be made about social boundaries—what they are, how they are maintained, and how they operate—to understand the segregated social arrangements that define the courthouse. Boundaries may be "symbolic" where social actors make conceptual distinctions between people or practices. These symbolic boundaries help separate people into groups, generate feelings and ideologies about those groups, and may impact status and, therefore, access to resources and privileges. Once symbolic boundaries become entrenched, rigid and socially agreed upon, they congeal in an institutional form of "social boundaries," where social differences lead to unequal access and opportunity.[17]

Social differences in the color-defined breadline of the security gate, for instance, are visible and objectified forms of patterned, racial segregation, but symbolic forms of segregation and inequality are equally powerful. In the context of law, access to "resources," "privileges," and other terms that describe the consequences of boundaries (whether symbolic, social, or both) are, alarmingly, principles of due process rights, constitutional guarantees, and the appearance and integrity of justice—fundamental issues essential to American citizenship and human rights, more broadly.

Scholars who study boundaries often use conceptual handles to understand group difference or differentiation. They describe boundaries as an "us" versus "them" dynamic. Such scholarship was unknown to the 130 court watchers who entered the court to observe the everyday nature of the courthouse. Yet overwhelmingly, the most common language used by the anonymous court watchers to describe the court was that it was a social space defined by an "us" versus "them" dynamic—where the "us" was the white professionals and the "them" were the people of color that defined the everyday citizens.

When I worked as a court clerk, I passed on the side of privilege, the "us" in the prosecuting power of the courts. I arrived at the courthouse in a sedan driven by a prosecutor. I knew to park in the garage because my membership as a law clerk afforded me access. Walking with case files, while in a suit, signaled that I was one of the insiders. Being an insider not only gave you privileges, but offered protection from the abuse, humiliation, and harassment associated with being one of "them."

While numerous examples of these arrangements were outside the courts as well, crossing the main security entrance marks the cultural threshold where the social boundaries between "us" and "them" are policed through the threats, hostility, aggressiveness, and abuse by armed sheriff's officers. As one white court watcher noted:

> Upon entering the courthouse, deputies quickly began yelling at the general public to get in the appropriate line by gender, to take off their belts, and to empty their pockets. . . . it appeared regardless of how fast one complied, the deputies would continue to yell at people and even say covert threats such as "if you can't get that belt off, I'll get your butt out of the courthouse as fast as I can."

Another observer noted a sense of paternalism about the abuse, with visitors scolded like inferiors or children for what should be minor infractions.

> I did not realize exactly how rude people could be until I spent time in 26th and Cal. The first time I passed through security, I was yelled at so many times that I

began feeling like a child. This yelling included being told to "get dressed some-where else" when I tried to put my belongings back in my pocket.

In interviews, defense attorneys were aware of and critical of the disparity in treatment between the general public and the professionals, and noted the unjust appearance inherent in these racial divides that welcomed the public to the courts. One defense attorney provided such a critique:

> If you walked in that building every day, as I do . . . and you see people standing out in the freezing cold, or being rained upon going in to have their experi-ence with the criminal justice system, that's a bad thing. We're talking jurors, witnesses, defendants, victims, family members of victims standing out in the freezing cold just to get in and then when you get in, you get yelled at.

While officers yelled orders to all outsiders, security enforcement unapologet-ically highlighted racial disparity. White researchers were often asked why they were in the building, as though they were out of place. In many instances, these white observers were asked whether they were students or lawyers even when they were not wearing business attire. If they could provide a student ID, they received a host of quality-of-life privileges; they could bring in drinks and snacks and could violate other small security measures. As one court watcher observed:

> Passing through security was very easy—there was barely a line at all and the se-curity personnel let us through with no problems. However, I did notice that the personnel were not as "carefree" with certain other people (primarily African Americans) who they made empty out their entire purses/bags.

In contrast to the privileges extended to white researchers, blacks and Latinos—including researchers from this study—were mistaken for defendants and treated like criminals. One student of color was shocked when a sheriff asked if he needed help finding where his case was. While he noted that the sheriff acted in a professional manner, he also observed that his racial identity "marked" him as a criminal in the building.

Beyond this assumption of criminality, people of color were overtly treated in separate and unequal ways. After setting off the metal detector, a white re-searcher noted that she was checked, matter-of-factly, with a detecting wand and promptly allowed to proceed. Behind her, a Latino man set off the same alarm and was instead asked, "Do you have a knife?" by a sheriff. A separate incident involved a black man. He emptied his pockets for security but subse-quently forgot to collect his money. Upon remembering, he asked the deputy to retrieve it. As he left, another deputy asked his co-worker, "Were you trying to steal that guy's change?" "No," replied the first deputy. He then continued, "But he'd earn it back on the street corner tonight anyway." These abusive remarks were made within earshot of the target.

For a defense attorney insider, this dynamic was the norm and not the exception—part of the daily practices that defined the courthouse. This white attorney noted that bringing a black law student to the courthouse threatened his "insider" privileges and opened him up to more scrutiny and delays. In a sense, the defense attorney was pulled out of the VIP fast lane because of the race of his new law clerk.

> You get a sense of knowing what's going right and what's going wrong just by be-ing there every day . . . as I do every day with students. We had an arrangement with the Sheriff's Office that they [students] can go through the employee line and not have to be shook down every day as long as their names were on the list. When I walk in with my white students, and we walk right in . . . and, then first day I show up with a male black student, he gets pulled out of line and [they] say, "Who are you? What are you doing here?" Now, he looks just like the rest of us . . . he's dressed in a suit and tie, he's got a little ID card but his skin is black.

The hallmarks of modern racism are its subtlety, especially in contrast to the overt abuses of the Jim Crow era. Yet at the threshold of this courthouse, racialized comments or singling out people of color was an unabashed part of the social arrangements of the space and immediately positioned the armed sheriff's officers as "the police" of this boundary work. The racialized mock-ing and differential treatment occurred within earshot of other people of color and researchers—demonstrating a distinct culture so brazenly hostile that the niceties of modern racism break down.

In this culture, people of color were treated as second-class citizens as soon as they entered this space, and white court watchers consistently noted an awareness of white privilege despite formally being a courtroom outsider. As one court watcher wrote:

> I'm white, and I'm one of the few whites who isn't a judge or an attorney . . . Although I'm trying to dress the part and blend in with the other participants, in my heart of hearts, I know I don't want to be confused for someone who's here to participate, or at least not for someone who's here to participate as a defendant or family member. Defendants and their family members are the bot-tom of the social heap at 26th and California. For the most part they are poor,

uneducated minorities. They are not dressed in the suits and ties that judges and attorneys wear; they wear t-shirts, jeans, and shorts. Sometimes their clothes are old and soiled . . . At 26th and California, defendants and their families essentially become second class when they enter the courthouse door.

For outsiders visiting this space, this racial "shorthand" assaults the senses, as it is so different from the racially sanitized niceties normalized in the larger American culture. Initially, in my first field notes, I began recording the demographic of the racial divides that define the court. On the first day of my ethnography, when I was nineteen years old, I reflected:

> I kept a tally of the racial composition of the defendants that were brought into the courtroom for a status or hearing. Of the defendants that went through the court, only 4 of them were white. The rest were African American or Latino. Of the four that were white, two of them needed a translator . . . All the people working in the court including the attorneys, the public defenders, the judge, the officers, and the transcribers were white . . . the courtroom seemed completely racially biased. It seemed to lose legitimacy when I saw minority defendants come up before a courtroom run by the majority. The power lines were racially divided . . . and the institution of the court worked to reinforce this allocation of social power.

Likewise, in attorney interviews, defense attorneys reflected on their first impressions working in the system. These impressions included remembering how shocked they were to "see" how racial disparity defined the criminal courts, how the disparity desensitized them but how outsiders (their clerks or students), were a constant reminder of that initial shock of coming to the courthouse complex for the first time. As a defense attorney explained:

> [What] really shocked the hell out of me when I started was, I'd go back in lockup and everybody's black. Now, that doesn't shock me anymore but that still shocks my students . . . then, I was just shocked by the way people were treated. By "people," I mean victims, defendants, defendants' families.

Beyond the disparity in the defendant pool, first-time visitors saw a disparity of conditions that were separate and unequal. Such conditions led to little privacy and, therefore, little dignity for defendants, victims, and their families. While professionals have their own offices and private spaces, public spaces, occupied by blacks and Latinos, in and around the court complex are dilapidated. Floors are sticky; paper towels and toilet paper are available unpredictably.

Water fountains are often broken or pathetically dripping water from a rusted spigot. Courthouse bathrooms are filthy—with flooding and clogged toilets, stalls without doors, and graffiti etched into the walls. With feces smeared on the wall, the bathrooms are reminiscent of the oppressive conditions of the adjacent Cook County Jail, blurring the symbolic and physical delineations between court and jail conditions.[18]

While white professionals must also walk through these areas, they have private spaces of respite. Offices to eat lunch. Separate and clean bathrooms. Televisions and personal items in their offices. Pictures on the wall. Details that personalize and make the space human. For the public, no such respite is offered, not even to victims.

Drinks and food are not allowed in the building. What is left is a small cafeteria that sells Snickers bars, sodas, chips, and other junk food. This cafeteria has the monopoly on food and drink options, but none of these items can be brought into the courts. Researchers described fasting for the entire day as a necessary condition of the security rules and the necessity of being in court. A diabetic researcher admitted that she could no longer endure the physical consequences of going back to the courthouse for more than one visit, which led me to wonder how diabetic defendants, families, and victims were able to handle such conditions required of them. This is especially problematic because diabetes disproportionately affects poor communities of color.

On the wall near the bond court, families, defendants, and victims wander to find their cases and courtrooms. What they find is an enormous dot-matrix printout with incessant lines of data. Families are required to scan and decipher a dizzying stream of charges, abbreviations, ID numbers, and defendants' names to find their courtroom. Throughout the building, there are no benches in the hallways where one could confer with an attorney—a structural setup that de facto limits and absolves attorneys from talking to their clients or to victims. By the nature of the racial divides that distinguish the offender and victim population from the professional population, these courthouse conditions are inherently the way blacks and Latinos are further segregated from interacting.

The Currency of Time

In the Cook County Courts, timing is everything. If you are part of the public, a defendant, or a victim, you are either wasting time or fearing time. There is the waiting in long security lines, racing to the courtrooms to get to the gallery by 9:00 a.m., feeling sick over the possibility of being the first case on the judge's docket or being the very last. Most days, you just hurry up to wait in the courtroom with no sense or warning of when your case will be heard.

For defendants, victims, and families, there were high stakes to where your case fell on the daily docket. To be first meant that you had to hustle to the courtroom (before the judge made it to the bench) in order to avoid missing a hearing or forfeiting a bond—a mistake that could land you in jail. This was no easy task, given the security lines and the difficulty in finding courtrooms. To be last on the docket meant waiting in the public gallery for what could be hours. This meant missing more work, paying for more day care or parking, or risking an entire day off where you were forced to tell your employer that you were charged (if not convicted) of a crime.[19] Beyond the stigma of admitting a criminal charge, missing work for the court hearing could lead to being fired—especially from a low-wage or unskilled job. Regardless of where a case could be on the docket, defendants were required to wait without information, or little (if any) estimate of when their case would be called. As a private attorney described,

> Judge Colvin, perfect example. Circuit court rules always said "court starts at 9 a.m." They've said that for 35/40 years. At 26th Street, most people start at 10 . . . 10:45 a.m. . . . Judge Russo used to start at 11 a.m. except when he got cranky and then he would come in at 9:00 a.m. and if you weren't there, he'd find everyone in contempt. Judge Colvin always started at 9:00 a.m. There was never any foolishness in Judge Colvin's courtroom . . . just never happened. You go to a different floor in the building . . . completely different situation.

In my early research at the court, I would often run to court, only to find the bench empty and the gallery full. One time, during a court recess, I went into the judge's chambers, where they had just finished a series of plea bargains. I found the judge putting on lipstick, brushing her hair, and complaining about her new gray hairs to the female prosecutors; the male prosecutors and a few defense attorneys were throwing M&M's from the palms of their hands into their mouths like they were in a frat house. All the while, the public would wait . . . just wait, and the sheriffs would alternate between watching the public and joking among themselves.

I soon realized that the endless waiting without notice was part of my research findings. It was unpredictable, and therefore seemed like a cruel game. In some courtrooms, the public would wait obediently and would get there as early as 8:30 a.m. for a judge who would not be on the bench until 10 a.m. or even 10:30 a.m. In other courtrooms, court call started promptly at 9 a.m. Some courtrooms gave preference to private attorneys and allowed their clients to go first in the court call. This privilege signaled that having a private attorney allowed you to "jump the line" and reduce your wait time, and also communicated that being indigent and having a public defender meant that you were at a disadvantage. Beyond signaling the uncertainty of whether you had a competent attorney with courtroom clout, it clearly revealed that you were low in priority—waiting at the end of the line and, perhaps, wasting your whole day in court at the discretion of the judge and with no advocate to influence that discretion.

In other courts, private attorneys would politely ask and advocate for their client's case to be heard early in the court call based on issues like a medical condition that made it difficult for the client to wait, or the loss of work or the threat of losing a job. Sometimes private attorneys merely needed to be in another courtroom or courthouse for another client. In some courts, such requests were respected. In other courts, they were met with punishment from the judge. The audacity of asking for preference meant that the defendant (and his attorney) would be purposely bumped to the end of the docket. These polarized reactions seemed arbitrary to outsiders and subject to the discretion of each judge.

The court often used "recesses" for both business and breaks for lunch. A recess could be as short as ten minutes for a series of quick plea bargains or it could mean an hour-long lunch break. Regardless of the duration, the public was often left guessing whether they could leave for a bathroom break, or for a snack or drink of water (since such items were banned from the court). As one judge called a lunch recess during a trial, a female defendant in the gallery who was waiting only for a new status date on her case (due to her defense attorney's absence), walked out of the gallery venting her frustration to another woman in the same situation. The lunch recess helped the professionals, but given the lack of food in the café and around the courthouse, it meant little to the defendants and families doing the waiting. As she complained,

> This happened last time. They think we have nothing better to do than sit in court all day on those hard benches. I don't want to wait through trials and eat their dog-ass food.

The key finding across all courtrooms was that schedule and order of the court call were arbitrary and unpredictable to outsiders, but part of the insider knowledge that was withheld from the public. Some judges gave preference to plea bargains versus trials, private versus indigent defenders, the schedule of a witness or police officer and their testimony. Some public defenders and private attorneys tried to communicate where a defendant's case was in the queue, but some did not. As a result, for the people of color in the gallery, waiting was an exercise in subservience and power and there was little respite from the tedious nature of sitting obediently.

The unpredictability itself was excruciating. To leave to go to the bathroom, call your employer in the hallway, or quickly eat outside could result in the unfortunate possibility that your case could be called at the most inopportune time—the one moment when you let your guard down, they could call your case. If that was the situation, you could get bumped to the end of the docket or after a lengthy motion or bench trial. Or, more frighteningly, the judge could issue a bond forfeiture warrant for not being present in court and you could be taken into jail—losing your freedom and the money posted to receive that freedom. Often the money posted was a portion of a family's meager life savings. For families, they could miss the chance to see their incarcerated loved ones, even if it was only for a quick moment during a hearing or status update in court.

Sociologists like Armando Lara-Millán (2014) and Javier Auyero (2012) examine the power associated with the "politics of waiting."[20] In this waiting, the marginalized "learn that they have to remain temporarily neglected, unattended to, or postponed . . . a daily lesson in political subordination."[21] But, as Lara-Millán contributes, there are two sides to waiting. There are those who "wait" and those who create the conditions of "waiting."

After years of fieldwork, I wrote the same note over and over in my field notes: *time is a currency*. But it was a currency wielded by professionals. In this case, the currency was exerted through "waiting" and spending the public's time in a seemingly endless game of guessing when a case would be heard. Yet time was not just a symbolic loss. This "game" had real consequences on the physical endurance of people avoiding the bathroom or fasting for long periods. Or it meant losing money by missing work, or even losing the job entirely. Because maintaining employment is often a necessary condition of probation, this was often a losing endgame that could also get you locked up.

Many defendants could not afford high-priced, "Johnny Cochran–style" attorneys; instead, there were many private attorneys who flipped cases for cash. Their business model thrived on taking as many cases as possible and closing them as quickly as they could. Profits were in quantity of disposals, not quality of representation. These were attorneys paid in wads of cash like drug deals in the hallways, and often they barely conferred with their clients, let alone gave them updates on when cases would be heard. During a long recess, I heard a private attorney joking with a prosecutor in the court about how little effort he gave his clients:

> I have a guy that's been in the system for so long that when I'm late I just tell him what to tell the judge—ask for a motion for discovery, enter a formal plea, and tell the judge I'll do a 402 [plea bargain] when I get there. Guy just says "ok" and I barely do anything.

Defendants with public defenders were at a particular disadvantage; as courtroom insiders in the workgroup, public defenders had to be present in court for the full day, and so their clients often were fitted into the court docket whenever it was convenient for the professionals. This left public defenders with varying levels of information that could help predict when cases would be heard. As a result, they would just warn their clients of the consequences of leaving.

Street Cred

Many defense attorneys (in particular) reflected on the emotional toll of coping with the a priori racism that they encountered: the conditions, the segregation, the waiting, the violence, the desperation of the clients and their families. They described developing a thick armor to cope with the racial divides that they navigated. Often, it was the equivalent of putting on colorblind lenses to ignore racial disparity that once assaulted their senses. For example, one attorney reflected on the emotional toll of initially comprehending the racial disparity that was omnipresent in the building. After desensitizing himself to this environment, he was sobered by the emotional reactions of his students' seeing such disparities during a first-time trip to the courthouse and adjacent jail. As he described it,

> I had a guy walk out of Division 11 [jail] with me, a male student; he started to cry as we were walking out . . . I said: "Dude I don't know what's happening but, you know, we got to get past the guard shack before you lose it completely, otherwise your street cred's gone."

> We get out all the way past the shack, I said: "What's up." He said: "These people are pretrial detainees. Do you know what it's like in there?" I said: "Yeah, I've been going there since they built the place." . . . That sort of re-recognition every 14 weeks . . . is really valuable.

Sympathetic white professionals who work under these racially demarcated arrangements quickly become schooled and develop what some attorneys call "street cred" or "street credibility" among other professionals. This emotional armor allows attorneys to practice law in a place riddled with racial division and poverty—glaring inequalities that create cultural dissonance in an era of colorblindness. Attorneys must comport themselves in a detached manner that earns legitimacy and membership in the space. They must ignore any racial disparities because to notice such divides and talk about them is to identify yourself as young, inexperienced, and idealistic—all the reputational markers that could get you roughed up in the courtroom and quickly mark you as an outsider among the inner circle of professionals.

"Street cred" was a gendered term that required no emotional expressions of sympathy. Such an expression meant that you were one of "them" and not one of "us." You were a sympathizer; much like the word "nigger-lover" was used to undermine sympathetic whites who fought for the equal rights of blacks, losing your street cred lost you membership, privilege, access, and could also thwart efforts on your client's behalf.[22] Because defense attorneys appropriate the language of street cred from their impressions of what it means on the "street," I asked a series of former defendants to define the term. Overwhelmingly, they described street cred as reputation, and legitimacy on the streets. As one defendant characterized it,

> Street cred is like any credibility. If I have street credibility, I'm not a snitch. I'm tough. I don't take no shit, [I] pay dudes I owe, back them up no matter what, am always there for them . . . I'm about the business . . . make fast easy money—am a hustler—and if I've developed street credibility—people respect me and fear me.

Another defendant described unwavering loyalty to a culture:

> On the street, you earn street cred by being arrested, keeping your mouth shut, having prison time . . . meeting people inside while incarcerated, vouching for someone . . . it does not have to be gang affiliation. . . . it means you are part of the elite, the one who has power . . . it means there is a culture, a currency, and you have it.

"Street cred on the street" and "street cred in the courts" are perverse bedfellows; like the "street" definition, street cred in the legal culture means acknowledging a culture of power and respect; paying dues; being about "the business" as the culture dictates, and not snitching on that culture while maintaining a tough exterior of the "elite." Professionals earn street cred by ignoring race, ignoring that most of the defendants in the jail and in the courtrooms are charged but not convicted. It means ignoring that many people of color in the galleries are not criminals, but victims or family members. As we will see in subsequent chapters, maintaining racially demarcated boundaries and practicing law within such a space means shedding the civility that is written into formal law, and instead practicing law under a strict code of conduct regulated by violence. The attorneys were practicing "street law" for "street people"—a phrase that denoted violence in the law rather than civility.

I would think on these blurred boundaries as I wrote my field notes. I asked: *Who is moral? Who is immoral? Who is violent? Who is lawless? The attorneys? The defendants?* These questions were only for my field notes because as I quickly learned, asking them out loud would cause me to lose *my* street cred. I tested these symbolic boundaries . . . once. Out of fear, I never mentioned the word "race," though I asked my supervisor about her views on the association between poverty and crime. She responded with anger and then silence for much of the morning. I never made the mistake again. Never.

Space and Race Divisions in the Courtrooms

The racial demarcation in the courthouse extends into the courtrooms where professionals practice law. On two floors, the courtrooms are nicknamed "fishbowls," because the public galleries are partitioned off from the courtroom professionals by bulletproof glass. The glass divides the courtroom into two parts, separating the minority consumers of justice from the white purveyors of justice. Even in courtrooms without a physical barrier, sheriffs exert a constant threat of violence that polices the professional space from the public gallery with symbolic boundaries as impenetrable as the bulletproof glass itself.

Sheriffs act as henchmen as they aggressively police this racial line by limiting the public access to the court proceedings. Visitors view the court proceedings from behind this soundproof barrier and rely on a microphone at the judge's bench to pipe sound to the gallery. Researchers noted that the sound was periodically turned off either by oversight of court personnel or for professionals to have sidebar discussions. There was no explanation to the public.

Given the limited access to the proceedings, defendants, victims, and their families had many questions for attorneys, clerks, and sheriffs. *Am I in the correct courtroom? Who is my public defender? Is my son on today's court call?* In these cases, a family member would try to ask questions during recess periods, by slowly approaching the partition door, or signaling for a defense attorney, clerk, or sheriff. In the best of circumstances, these signals were ignored. In other circumstances, the move to cross the barrier was matched with the hostility of a physical threat.

Such hostility was so intimidating that I observed an elderly Latina walk toward the professionals with her arms up in a surrender position like she might get shot. Viewing me as a court professional and clerk, she asked me, in Spanish, whether she was in the correct courtroom to see her son, who was a defendant. *"Mi hijo es Alejandro Villarreal. ¿Dónde queda su cita de corte? ¿Me puedes ayudar?"* As I began to answer her question, the sheriff barked for her to "sit down and step back" while aggressively walking toward her as though she had a weapon. I averted my eyes from the woman so that our further interaction would not escalate what was already a frightening response.

My actions weighed on my conscience. It was difficult to erase the memory of an elderly woman raising her hands like she was the criminal. There was also the trauma of the sheriff's violent reaction to the possibility of me helping her. The violence conditioned me to the culture of the courts while it made an example out of the woman to the entire public gallery—a public lesson that disciplined us all into maintaining the segregation of the court. I knew that averting my eyes not only saved the woman, but also saved me from losing the very street cred that allowed me to witness such abuse for my field notes. Complicity through silence maintained my research access, but it weighed heavily. I wrote my confessions in field notes: *What is the cost of this research? When is my silence abuse? Have I become one of the insiders?*

In another case, an elderly black woman came into a courtroom that did not have bulletproof glass. The judge was not on the bench, and only a few prosecutors had started to thumb through files to begin the day. The gallery was nearly empty. The elderly woman slowly, yet defiantly, walked across the boundary into the professional space and went to the prosecutor to inquire if her son's case would be heard in that courtroom. The prosecutor referred her to the clerk. Before she could redirect her question, the sheriff yelled for her to step back. He pointed to the symbolic division between the public and the professional space as though there was a line drawn on the floor as powerful as bulletproof glass.

With so few people in the court, it was confusing where he was pointing. The woman walked backward to the gallery and stood obediently behind the imaginary line. The sheriff scanned the names of the inmates in the courtroom's adjacent lockup and snapped at the woman, "He's not here." He set the papers down and turned his head, which emphasized that his veiled effort was over. In defeat, the woman left the court, but persistently asked one more prosecutor walking into the courtroom where to go next. Seeing this, the sheriff tore the woman up with insults.

> That lady felt compelled to ask everyone along the way . . . [he spoke to the prosecutor] Tell her: "Your son is executed."

In earshot of other members of the public, such cruel threats disciplined others from making the same mistake of crossing boundaries or asking questions.

Unable to speak with professionals, the public often tried to whisper questions to one another for support and clarification. If the public tried to whisper and talk in the gallery, this too was met with a threat of violence. In court, the gallery should be neither seen nor heard. For instance, a court watcher noted the following:

> One sheriff was particularly brusque. In response to some muffled chatter, she pointed rather menacingly at the "offenders" and mouthed "Stop talking!" while making a throat-slashing gesture with her hand. On another occasion, the same officer rudely directed a mother to step back from the partition, without providing an explanation as to why her moving was needed. Instead, the officer merely repeated, "Back up!"

Laughing Like No One's Watching

Beyond affecting access to justice, the courtroom boundaries corresponded to boundaries of behavior. They reinforced the "us" versus "them" divisions that defined the culture and the Jim Crow–like separation between white professionals and the public gallery of predominantly people of color. Professionals who were seasoned insiders could joke and act in casual ways that minimized the gravity of processing cases and people through the system, while racial minorities in the public gallery were policed into formal, obedient behavior. They were either criminalized for participating and asking questions or ignored to the point of invisibility.

Laughter, jokes, and mocking of defendants during court proceedings defined the professionals' informality and occurred with the microphones on. At other times, laughter was visible but the jokes were inaudible. One court watcher noted that the judge stopped the court record "to tell personal jokes to the sheriff, clerk, and prosecutor." In another courtroom, a court watcher described the sheriff as akin to the judge's "sidekick" (like Ed McMahon to Johnny Carson), rather than an officer of the law. In another courtroom, when the proceedings ended for the day, the courtroom deputy started playing a Michael Jackson song over computer speakers while other court personnel and the general public remained in the courtroom. And another court watcher recorded that "attorneys and court staff retreated to an adjacent room during a break. Through the open door, they appeared to be watching TV (based on their conversations, it may have been the U.S Open)."

Even judges contributed to this outlandish behavior, some by their joking and some by their indifference. One court watcher noted the following:

> The minute I walked in [the court] the judge was disparaging a defendant, and the judge, sheriff, and gallery were all laughing at defendant's expense. I noticed this a lot. It was like the judge did not take anyone seriously—defendants or attorneys . . . the judge took out Girl Scout cookies. He passed them out to the attorneys and even to one defendant . . . Often, he turned the microphone off when it was time to make a decision. This made it so that anyone in the gallery had no idea what was going on. Many people in the gallery made comments when the judge did this like, "There he goes again" or "He always does this."

In another courtroom, a court watcher noted that a judge turned his back during a hearing (a bench trial or motion). He appeared to be slumped over as he rested his head on his hand. The court watcher noted that he appeared to be sleeping during the trial. While they could not confirm whether he was actually asleep, they noted that the mere appearance of such left those in the public gallery to exchange worried glances and whisper about whether he was dozing off. This theme of indifference, neglect, and disregard for the seriousness of cases was a pervasive pattern and occurred with little regard for people in the public gallery who were watching it unfold.

As the observations from the 130 court watchers rolled in, I was not surprised by the Girl Scout cookies, the sleeping judge, nor the other joking and banter that were part of the court culture. In fact, I'd seen worse. In the early days of my research, when I was working as a clerk, I watched the sentencing hearing of a young man who was convicted of murdering three elderly African American women and one elderly African American man as they played cards around a table. The victims were all more than eighty years old, and as the prosecutor described the case, I imagined the victims' frail hands holding those cards in the last peaceful moments before they were murdered. One of the victims was the defendant's grandmother. The defendant was high on drugs and asked his grandmother for money. When she refused, the young defendant stabbed each person around the table with a butcher knife from his grandma's own kitchen—starting with the man and proceeding to each woman in turn. As the prosecutor argued for the death penalty, she suggested during the sentencing hearing that the male victim was targeted first because he may have posed the greatest defense to the drug-fueled rampage.

The family in the gallery cried for their lost grandmother and her friends. The tears were of grief and rage at their nephew and son who was the murderer. The family clutched one another in total despair. The defendant had pled guilty, and the sentencing hearing would determine whether he would spend his life in prison or be sentenced to death. As the sentencing hearing closed, the white judge somberly went to his chambers to deliberate. The defendant's public defender lowered his head to a wooden table in front of him during the deliberation as though his energy was spent. I was close enough to the defense's table to hear the thud.[23]

I wrote in my field notes that it was "Take Your Daughter to Work Day." As the door opened and shut during these sentencing deliberations, the people in the gallery could see the judge laughing with his daughter. She sat on his desk and played with his face as he made a decision between life in prison and, literally, death. As the door opened and shut, it was like the curtain being pulled back on the "wizard" in the *Wizard of Oz*—revealing the pretense of somber, serious justice that was exposed for all to see.

Another court watcher noted a similar incongruence between the seriousness of a case and the lack of reverence extended to the defendants, families, and victims. While a family was waiting for the verdict in a murder trial, they told the court watcher that they saw the judge as "playing" with the defendant's life rather than making an actual legal decision:

> Those awaiting the results of the murder trial (that were there for the defendant) did not think the judge cared. "It's not about his life, he just plays with it like a piece of paper, what does he care? Fucking asshole."

Professionals' jokes and informality demeaned what the public viewed as life-or-death decisions. The court watchers noted an indignity in the treatment of the normative notion of law. In these cases, the stakes could not be higher—guilt or innocence, life or death. However, even defendants convicted of nonviolent drug crimes worth anywhere from a one-year to a ten-year sentence were keenly aware that their lives were at stake, their livelihood, their access to their children, or their citizenship. Court watchers observed the sense of outrage on the part of the public at the lack of professionalism afforded to their cases. One court watcher noted:

> The PDs and prosecutors did a lot of laughing (loudly) and seemed very friendly with each other. I overheard a family behind me being extremely annoyed . . . they used profanity amongst themselves showing disbelief of how lightly the lawyers were taking the court proceedings. As the lawyers continued to joke, the family became more agitated.

Front-Stage, Backstage

Sociologists often talk about front-stage and backstage behavior and use the metaphor of social interaction as a type of performance or drama. Front-stage behavior is more formal in nature, where the social actors are conscious of the onlooking audience, and therefore act with the appropriate social norms and tact in the space. In contrast, backstage behavior is more informal in nature, where the social actors can let their guard down and stop performing the more formal roles.[24] For example, a waitress in a restaurant, when she crosses into the kitchen, can stop "performing" for her tips, and perhaps engage in some harmless mockery of her customers. She can stop performing the professionalism associated with the role. However, the racial divide between the "us" and the "them" in the criminal courts alters the traditional front-stage and backstage distinctions as sociologists often observe them playing out.

Working in concert, the racial demarcation of space, the violent policing of boundaries through intimidation and fear, and the informality of professional behavior render the public silent and obedient. In the forum of the criminal court, with an audience defined by people of color, professionals give little attention to the divisions of front-stage and backstage.[25] Gallows humor, mockery, and laughter occur at the main security entrance, within earshot of the gallery. Professionals stop "performing" the expected courtroom norms unless they need to do so for the court record—a mechanism that can and is often turned on and off at the judge's discretion, with a motion of her hand. For example, as a court watcher noted,

> one could argue that court proceedings are too accessible, as trial or hearing participants are allowed to walk through the courtroom at will. During proceed-

ings, attorneys and police officers loiter about and exit and enter through doors flanking the bench. Of course, some of this movement and seeming informality is necessary. Attorneys must be able to take care of scheduling and converse with opposing counsel, and officers must be able to respond to disturbances and escort prisoners to and from lockup. But there does appear to be an excess of this behavior. For example, in Judge Richardson's courtroom, a female prosecutor walked in, mid-proceedings, with a garment bag and duffel in hand. Once at the attorneys' table, she removed her suit jacket from the garment bag and put it on. Apparently she had neither the time nor the wherewithal to get fully dressed at home or in her office.

With such sweeping informal behavior, laughter, and mocking within earshot of the public gallery, the professionals had free rein to misbehave, act with little regard for the seriousness of cases and lives, and ignore the public unless the public tried to violate courtroom norms and make themselves visible through questions or basic participation, like moving closer to hear court proceedings. Because such behavior was met with threats of violence, the public sat obediently behind the bulletproof glass, just as blacks and Latinos may have sat during the Jim Crow era. As one white court watcher noted:

> I often saw people ignored when they went into courtrooms, as if they were plague victims whose simple questions were too much of a problem to answer. In reality, I think the courtroom staff has just gotten to the point where they do not believe that anyone in any of these courtrooms could possibly be their equal.

Another researcher reflected on his alienation from the court proceedings by what appeared to be a separate professional "class" of attorneys—a dynamic cultural feature shared by all courtrooms.

> For those of us on the outside, it is alienating to feel as though you're not able to truly be a part of what is going on in front of you. It was as though the courtroom personnel and attorneys thought themselves to be in a class all their own, incapable of truly intermingling with the observers in the gallery. The positioning of the glass partition in the "fishbowl" courtrooms paints an accurate picture: the inside is separate and distinct from the outside. The cultures of the courtrooms I visited exhibited little to no differences from each other. They were all as I described above: friendly and collegial on the inside yet cold to the outside world.

While these accounts are convincing observations, some of the most compelling evidence of the racial disparity in the courts came from testing how the white researchers in this study were treated as they intermixed in what was thought of as a public gallery for people of color. While white researchers were undoubtedly collecting observations about how people of color were treated, some found that their presence in the courts was breaking unspoken boundaries of a racially demarcated space. Some would have to assume the surrender position and relinquish their pencils.

Privilege and Suspicion:
Being White in the "Black and Brown" Gallery

While undeniably the gallery was defined by a population that was overwhelmingly people of color and the professional space was mostly dominated by educated whites, some critics may contend that these "us versus them" distinctions are merely "insider versus outsider" dynamics. If this were the case, the "us versus them" dynamics could characterize other types of social membership. In fact, the notion of "boundary work" reinforces differences between many types of memberships, be it professional terrain, gender, or even political affiliations (to name a few). The comparative data collected by the 130 court watchers are particularly useful, allowing for comparison of how white researchers were treated versus how researchers of color were treated.

Overall, the experiences of the many white court researchers reveal how privilege manifests in the courts, the assumptions implicit in racial categories, and how white privilege could breed suspicion, hostility, and intimidation in an insular culture like the courts. Researchers of color were often assumed to be defendants and were ignored as part of the invisible masses in hoodies, jeans, and other casual clothes. Without visible signs of their elite educations or their affiliation as summer associates at some of the nation's most prestigious law firms, these court watchers of color blended into the general public to the point of being mistaken for a defendant or being unnoticed as they discreetly took notes among the crowd in the gallery. This reinforces the assumption that to be black and brown in this space is to be associated with being a defendant or to be socially "invisible." From a research standpoint, their "invisibility" allowed them to easily note the abuse, hostility, and threats that policed the boundaries of the court without being noticed.

In being debriefed after the court-watching experience, researchers of color felt an emotional toll—a sense of fear in such a racialized culture and a sense of helplessness in remaining silent. I, too, experienced those familiar emotions, but my sense of guilt came not only from my silence but also from my complicity in the culture and the privilege that I received because of it. I realized it was at the expense of those sitting on the other side of the bulletproof glass (the people who looked like my family, friends, and neighbors) that I maintained my insider status.

In contrast to researchers of color, whites experienced privilege—as noted at the main entrance—but they also confronted difficulties doing court observations. In their two-hour training sessions, I told researchers to go "unnoticed." I instructed them to exchange their suits, ties, and everyday business attire for jeans, sweatshirts, and hoodies. I said, "Blend into the crowd like wallpaper." I taught them how to take field notes and the importance of intermingling but not interfering with the field site. They were to observe but not to change the subjects or experiences they viewed. Therefore, going unnoticed was crucial to their data collection.

With such rigid racial demarcation, white researchers noted that observing the courts was not as simple or accessible as one would assume from the National Center for State Courts Trial Court Performance Standards (see Methods Appendix). First, when they walked into any number of fishbowl courtrooms, many white researchers noted that they were uncertain whether there was a "private" event or hearing. With so many African Americans in the public gallery, they sometimes mistakenly assumed that there was about to be a trial where everyone in the audience represented family, friends, or relatives of a deceased victim or a defendant on trial. Many expressed the social discomfort in first walking into the court as though they were accidentally walking in on the wrong funeral. They described a collision between what they viewed as private tragedies being paraded in public spaces. Their reverence was in stark contrast to the disregard, disrespect, and informality often noted in the piles of court-watching observations. It also denoted the rigidity of racial boundaries where merely walking into a space assaulted the senses like a force field.

In the best cases, white researchers entering the courthouse were made visible (unlike researchers of color) and met by a polite sheriff who asked them to account for their presence. "Why are you here?" was a common question. Just as police officers often advise whites (for their own safety) to clear out of "bad" neighborhoods, defined as those where people of color live, sheriffs approached whites as they entered the court space that was demarcated as native to people of color. For the sheriffs who assumed the policing role in the courthouse, the presence of a white visitor in the gallery implied that the visitor was lost, perhaps a student but certainly not part of the public gallery of black and brown defendants, victims, and families that defined the consumers of criminal justice.

When white researchers were approached by sheriffs, they felt compelled to give vague answers to keep their "cover." They often said they were students or just wanted to observe. When they confessed to doing court observations, the sheriffs invited them to stay or commented that "there wasn't much to see" despite a busy docket of cases scheduled for 402 conferences (plea bargains) or small motions—a comment that showed the little regard officers possessed for the mainstays of the court call.

While people of color were abused or ignored into invisibility, white researchers were often treated like tourists, with sheriffs acting as guides for a show. The centerpiece of this show was the public grief and humiliation of black and brown defendants and victims. Sheriffs often scanned the courthouse dockets for the best cases of the day. These cases were particularly gruesome or offered a spectacle or a freak show of sorts. It was quite common for sheriffs to intercept white researchers as they entered the court and then try to escort or guide them to the most sensationalized trial.

For instance, *pro se* defendants representing themselves offered ample entertainment for professionals and perhaps for visitors.[26] Without litigating skills, a law degree, and the cultural know-how to navigate their own trial, the defendants were often laughed at like bumbling idiots. This type of perverse entertainment was racialized because many of the defendants spoke Ebonics or Black English[27] in a white space, transforming the mocking of an amateur into a racial spectacle that was hauntingly reminiscent of a minstrel show of blackface comedy: the defendant was merely an actor dramatizing racialized stereotypes; he was not a man with rights, but a racial caricature of a coon or an inarticulate buffoon.[28] Attorneys from other courtrooms would often visit on their breaks to see the show. They giggled at the use of Ebonics or the attempts of the defendant to cross-examine the same police officer who had arrested him.

Given the sheriffs' social radar for gruesome spectacle, they often shooed these white researchers away from courts doing court call and plea bargains to other courts to see a "cool" murder trial rather than the everyday court call and its docket of nonviolent drug offenses. As one court watcher described:

> After explaining to the sheriff in that courtroom that I was a law student . . . he told me that I should go sit in some other courtroom where there was a "cool murder trial" where "a guy killed a whole house of people."

Such actions illuminated the racial disparity in treatment between whites and people of color and showed the little regard for black lives and tragic deaths.

Punished by Privilege

In the worst case, the privilege of whiteness in the gallery was met by suspicion and hostility that differed from the threats exerted on people of color. Historically, the idea of "court watching" was introduced into Cook County numerous times. The objective of such programs was to exert outside accountability upon the courts and the professionals who maintained them. Yet the programs were defined by failure. Often a court watcher was an elderly volunteer who literally wore a blue badge that read "court watcher" and had the effectiveness of a junior high hallway monitor. In some instances, these court watchers were seated as VIPs in the jury box, offered cookies, or treated like a visiting "grandmother."

During my clerkship in the prosecutor's office, an elderly white woman was immediately identified as a court watcher from a legal advocacy group. The prosecutor leaned over and whispered to me to be on my "best behavior" and to pretend I was taking copious notes in the set book (the case calendar). The prosecutors and judges began to "perform" the normative professionalism that one would associate with their roles. They talked formally to the record with detail and clarity. The prosecutors were formal with their defense attorney friends. Sheriffs escorted defendants to the podium with professionalism, authority, and respect. I ostensibly played along with the improvised scene, furiously jotting what appeared to be legal notes on cases but what were actually my field notes on these theatrics.

Once the court watcher left, the full-time attorneys burst into laughter. They had pulled off a *Law and Order* decorum that was convincing enough to get the court watcher to leave without incident. Once the court watcher left, the workgroup went back to business as usual: the jokes, the banter, the yelling, the berating, and the informality that were native to that courtroom domain.

One can imagine that the presence of unidentified white observers with notepads and pencils in a sea of black and brown faces assaulted the senses of the courtroom insiders, who were unaccustomed to white outsiders and certainly not accustomed to outside accountability in an isolated courthouse. The court community is like a small town where everyone knows everyone else. As with any outsider in a small town, a white researcher, even dressed in plain clothes to blend in with the general public, could be met with a not-so-subtle expression of "You're not from around here, are you?" The presence of white researchers writing notes on "their" courtroom symbolized outside accountability. These white court watchers were met with suspicion, intimidation, and hostility, as though they were muckraking journalists. In these instances, the judges called upon sheriffs to act as go-betweens to find out why they were there. One court watcher noted that the sheriff announced in the gallery, "Would the people with the notepads please stand up and present themselves?" As one court watcher explained in his notes, the question required only the "white people in the gallery to account for their presence" in the court. The sheriff told the researchers that "writing was prohibited" and that the judge "would want to talk to you." Intimidated, the researchers revealed themselves as law students and the judge invited them to the other side of the partition. As one court watcher noted,

> Once we were on the inside, he [the judge] was friendly and talkative. Asking what law schools we went to.

This exchange uncomfortably highlighted the racial divide between the treatment of people of color and whites in the gallery.

On the Margins for the Margins: Isolation, Segregation, and Bottom of the Legal Bar

Two structural features define the courthouse in Chicago and the social boundaries within it. First, like Alcatraz, it is isolated from the rest of the city. However, another type of segregation is at work as well. The criminal justice practitioners are segregated, socially, from the rest of the legal bar.

Sociologist John P. Heinz and his colleagues argue that the legal profession is divided into two sections or hemispheres of attorneys.[29] One sphere is prestigious and is defined by its corporate clients. The other section is less prestigious and defined by its representation of individual clients. As their research predicts, if you represent individual clients (as in criminal law), you are likely in the lower, less-prestigious sphere of the legal profession. And, with that being true, it is likely the case that you went to a less-prestigious law school and possess a host of other attributes that mark you as less "elite" than your attorney peers in the upper echelon of the profession.[30]

Cook County fits this pattern. Almost 80 percent of attorneys in both the Office of the State's Attorney and the Office of the Public Defender hail from regional law schools rather than those categorized as elite.[31] As for judges, who are perceived by the public to be in a position of prestige, the vast majority of

Criminal Division judges attended regional law schools as well: 30 percent received law degrees from John Marshall, 25 percent from DePaul University, 14 percent from Chicago-Kent, and 11 percent from Loyola University–Chicago. Only 7 percent received degrees from Northwestern University, and 14 percent received degrees from schools outside of Chicago.

One attorney who attended an elite law school but was practicing in the criminal justice system explained these professional divides between the criminal bar and the rest of the legal profession:

> There certainly was a difference between the lawyers practicing criminal law and the lawyers I knew . . . at law school; none of them were criminal defense lawyers. They were all corporate lawyers, trust and estates lawyers, tax lawyers dealing with primarily wealthy clients. The lawyers I met who were doing criminal defense work were not of that group. It was a different group entirely. And I suppose the difference would be . . . the nature of the clientele. There was also just the day-to-day knock-down, drag-out courtroom experiences they had . . . I won't say it's a hand-to-mouth existence, but certainly the fee practice in criminal defense was a lot different than charging an hourly rate at a law firm, sending out a bill and getting a check. And, there was the added . . . aura in the criminal defense practice of corruption back then . . . like having to pay off the clerk to get your case called.[32]

Among the judicial leadership of this court community, being an "insider" is central to jockeying for a position of power. Only one judge had not worked in either the State's Attorney's Office or the Public Defender's Office. Three-quarters had been prosecutors, and one-quarter had served as public defenders. As a result, judges are an "autonomous set"[33] and come from the community within—accountable to the norms and practices of their longtime colleagues and friends. A private attorney described this insular culture as a good-ol'-boys club where judges are not only accountable to their former peers but have a desire to be in the prosecutors' inner circle.

> Some of the judges that are younger, like the SAs [state's attorneys] that just get made judge and get put right back in the building. They don't want to buck the system. They still want to be a good ol' boy.[34]

Beyond these structural features of segregation and isolation, there were other variables that degrade courtroom "elites." Despite being publicly venerated in pop culture and the media, criminal law is dirty work.[35] Sociologist

Andrew Abbott argues that roles that are "publicly venerated" are often "least respected by the professionals themselves." Less professionally respected roles involve front-line professionals who are closest to the public and deal in tasks where "human complexities are not or cannot be removed."[36]

Criminal justice professionals are not just front-line professionals for the general public; they are the front-line professionals dealing with the "human complexities" (addiction, mental illness, and the like) of the most impoverished people in the country. This further withers their status on the professional "food chain" of lawyers and locates criminal justice not just on the margins of the city, but also on the margins of the legal profession.[37]

Similar to the visible inequalities in the courthouse setting, when observing criminal attorneys practicing law, one can see the problem with professional prestige that attorneys confront. I often wondered, *where is the dignity?*[38] For instance, prosecutors use pushcarts loaded with the daily caseload for their respective courtrooms. Like street vendors in suits, they haul these carts back and forth, a kind of mobile office that acts as a file cabinet and a desk on wheels. As for open court, sheriffs and judges demand decorum at all times, but the complexities of dealing with defendants with mental illness or addiction complicate this expectation. For instance, once a mentally ill defendant came to the podium and yelled at the prosecutor, embarrassing her in front of colleagues and a full gallery of people.

> Defendant: I don't know you tramp. I can't stand you, tramp. I said, "I don't know you tramp" I said it to her . . . fat ass tramp [to SA].

As the defendant walked back to lockup, she looked back at the prosecutor:

> Defendant: Big Ass, Scum Tramp.

The door shut and the laughter erupted from the professionals.

Such outbursts were common and uncomfortable for attorneys, but they were a fixture of their work due to the prevalence of mental illness among the defendant population. Rather than just focusing on the legal case, these outbursts of visible mental illness were an inextricable feature of practicing criminal law, diverting attention from a focus on the legal case itself.

In the trenches, you get your hands dirty. One prosecutor described her time in Felony Review when she was required to be on call, go to crime scenes with police officers, and elicit confessions from defendants after their arrest. She described walking into a room and the defendant peeing on her shoes. She also admitted to using a type of insidious intimacy to extract confessions.[39] She would build trust with the defendant by flirting. In a case where the defendant had sexually assaulted a child, she would assume his "psyche" and fake empathy in order to lure him into incrimination. *I saw what she was wearing. She's been flirting with the police officers. She liked it, right?* These questions often led defendants to admit the crime. Game over.

When I found myself in a new courtroom, I asked one public defender whether she was a defense attorney, and she clarified: "No, I am a foe . . . a fraud . . . a public defender." This stigmatized characterization mimicked the conditions of their work. Public defenders often consulted with clients in holding cells. These cells doubled as a bathroom, conference room, and eating spaces for defendants waiting for their hearing. As the public defender provided his legal advice, a chorus of defendants would gather around the "kid" like a craps game and advise the young defendant as to whether he was getting a good deal. In this scenario, the public defender found himself held accountable to a "public" of defendant "peers" in a holding cell with feces on the wall. As one defense attorney described,

> You're in there with the toilet and about 16–20 defendants and they're all putting their two cents in while you're trying to talk to your defendant.

Beyond the actual legal work, the office space for both the Office of the State's Attorney and Office of the Public Defender was described as oppressive even though the common public spaces provided for people of color were much worse. There was insufficient meeting space, and plumbing and ventilation were unreliable. As a prosecutor described, there was a sense of shame in these conditions:

> It's embarrassing when you bring in expert witnesses . . . [or] show family where I work. I've been here 14 years and I share an office with four other people, including the law clerks.

Public defenders described similar inconveniences of space and privacy but even worse conditions than their prosecuting counterparts. Public defenders complained of desks Scotch-taped together and periodic infestations. On my first day in the Public Defender's Office, I shadowed a public defender ("Carl"), who, along with his supervisor ("Carol"), took me on a tour of his new office. To my surprise, the office was a storage closet; he used a card table that he had brought from his home and underneath it was a brown box that doubled as a file cabinet. Carl had recently transferred from another courthouse in the county, and after three weeks he still did not have a desk.

I set my bag on a nearby bookshelf that I thought was communal space, and then I realized that it was not; another PD was using it as her desk. I decided that it was safest to use the floor as my desk space. I swallowed my pride, sat on the floor in my suit, and updated my field notes:

> Carol looked at the card table that Carl had set up . . . then apologetically re-membered that he would have to move his desk . . . Electricians were scheduled to work on this "office" . . . It was one final kick in the pants.

What are we to make of these status distinctions in this insular court community? Most often, it is assumed that all lawyers share the same goals and ideologies. However, in the criminal courts, a separate segment of lawyers practices in a domain isolated from the rest of the legal community. They are defined by similar educational backgrounds, and the more successful among them, if they play by the rules of this segregated court community, move up the ranks to become a judge. These social circles are not just structural divides that self-sort a homogeneous group of white attorneys into the ranks of the criminal courthouse; they produce an ideological orientation that defines the "appropriate" practice of law.

While professionals may be marginalized in their profession, in this courthouse, far from oversight of the bar and accountable only to a marginalized public, professionals wield a significant amount of power to govern the space. A court watcher described it best:

> Attorneys and judges are top dogs at the courthouse; I could always see it in the confident way they carried themselves and the aloof way they scanned the gallery when they entered a courtroom. They know they are on the top of the heap here at 26th and California—they are insiders, repeat players; they are educated; they are paid, but most importantly, they are neither accused nor convicted of a crime.

Such structural arrangements, coupled with a lack of accountability, influence a type of racialized, legal habitus—a complex cultural engine for the proverbial assembly line of criminal justice. Like an isolated island, new generations of attorneys, judges, sheriffs, and clerks inherit a social arrangement with a life history that is larger than any one individual actor. What we will see is that the criminal courts are degraded into a type of "street law" for "street people."

2

OF MONSTERS AND MOPES

Racial and Criminal "Immorality"

AN ELDERLY BLACK DEFENDANT in her seventies shuffled into open court in jail-issued slippers. Rather than a cane or walker, she clung to the metal pole of an oxygen tank for balance. Gripping it with two hands and bowing her head as she walked, she cringed as though she was either intensely praying or feared being beaten. Charged with murder, she appeared in court for sentencing.

In a court docket of mostly young men of color and a stream of nonviolent offenses, it was a rarity to see an older woman, especially one who was charged with a violent crime. The defendant was frail, as if she had stepped out of a nursing home rather than a jail. Her coarse hair was knotted, uncombed, and stretching upward—a telltale sign of neglect from a lengthy stay in the Cook County Jail. Her eyes were swollen and red.

When she entered the court, a hush fell upon the professionals, and for a moment they were as quiet as the obedient public gallery. I leaned over to my supervising prosecutor and whispered, "What could she possibly have done?" She crassly responded, "She shot her husband in the ass, and the prick died on her." She shoved the file at me to read for myself.

The judge asked the defendant if she wanted to address the court before he imposed sentence. The defendant began sobbing while she spoke so that she was ultimately gasping for air between words. There was a tonal dissonance of hearing Black English spoken in what was a white, professional domain. The defendant said that she had been abused her whole life and she could not take the abuse any longer. She meant to hurt her husband, not to kill him. She was sorry and she pleaded not to die in prison.

This was the first time that I heard a person plead for his or her life; it was not my last. With a voyeuristic circle of stoic white onlookers and the dark shadows of the public gallery behind bulletproof glass, the ornate courtroom's dark oak detailing and the crest of the state seemed neither honorific nor dignified; it assumed an aura of medieval ceremony.

As the woman spoke, she clung to that oxygen tank as though the metal pole could provide her human comfort. The white judge paused and asked: "Are you done?" with a terseness and inflection that implied, "Are you done wasting the court's time?" The defendant replied affirmatively.

I expected the judge to merely give the sentence in a somber tone. Surely the hush in the court invited such a response. I privately hoped for leniency. I tried not to tear up and lose my street cred because when I saw this defendant, I saw a woman who walked with the same cadence as my grandmother.

The judge stood, rested his palms on the desk, leaned over the bench, and looked down upon the defendant. He tilted his head by letting his chin lead, like he was ready for a fight. He said slowly: "You're a *bad . . . bad* woman," and then he began to yell in a rant that degraded her character and denied her identity as a victim. He emphasized her complicity in her own abuse and stopped just short of swearing. His comments focused on her as a person, not on her actions as criminal. The judge berated her in a manner so harsh it appeared to reenact the domestic abuse that I read in the case file; this time the judge was the public abuser and, incidentally, the judicial arbiter.[1]

A few prosecutors turned their backs and laughed. Some were wide-eyed in disbelief, shooting glances at one another but unable to speak. The obedient gallery sat in silence as they watched, through the bulletproof glass, the public skewering of a black, elderly woman by a white man. Throughout the tirade, the defendant clutched that oxygen pole. I noted all of this in my field notes and then vigorously underlined one short, summarizing sentence: "The defendant wept."

Racial Degradation Ceremonies

In 1956, Harold Garfinkel published a classic sociological article titled "Conditions of Successful Degradation Ceremonies," placing such ceremonies within the scope of what he called the sociology of moral indignation, where the "ritual destruction of a person being denounced . . . is intended literally."[2] This ceremony transforms a social actor, like this elderly woman, and withers her social status until she is marginalized and separated from the social body. It involves a denunciation in which we "publicly deliver the curse: 'I call upon all men to bear witness that he [in this case, she] is not as he appears but is otherwise and in essence of a lower species.'"[3] In the context of a degradation ceremony, the defendant is not a victim; she is not frail; she is not to be sympathized with nor indulged with respect and decency. Instead, she should be seen and called out publicly as the "lower species" that she is revealed to be.[4]

In a racially segregated court with rigid lines that demarcate "us" (as white professionals) from "them" (as poor people of color), such racial degradation ceremonies illustrate a collision of moral dialogues: (1) the moral indignation of deviance and criminality and (2) the moral indignation associated with modern racism. In the case of this elderly woman, the judge denounces her as a "bad, bad woman." His rant negates her humanity, and instead places her very essence, as a person, in the realm of the profane.[5]

Paradoxically, when you ask the professionals about race and the criminal justice system, they claim they do not see race; they see only a case. How do such sincere fictions sustain themselves in the racially demarcated courts? This chapter explains how these sincere fictions are created while showing how racism operates as more than just rhetoric but actual cultural practices that are fundamental to the business of justice.

Colorblind racism is more than just a "doing" of rhetoric; it is a type of complicated habitus that informs institutional practices and cultural memberships, and even aids in the organizational efficiency of the criminal courts.[6] The criminal courts offer an elegant case to understand how professionals can "do racism" while "doing justice." "Morality and criminality" and "morality and racism" mix like a poisonous cocktail in criminal courts—where one's moral status is conferred by both legal categories and racial categories. The "immorality" of defendants, like the elderly woman who shot her husband, is both a criminal distinction and a racial one. With the authority of the law, a host of racialized abuses and violations of rights not only are allowable in court but are seen as deserved and justified, even with regard to the frailest, most vulnerable defendants (who happen to sometimes be victims).

Professionals engage in such racial degradation ceremonies in segregated courtrooms, all the while defending the courts as race-blind locations of justice. Race is everywhere but nowhere: in the structural arrangements, in the policing of racial boundaries, in the recoding of rhetoric, and in the delineation of defendants as "deserving" or "undeserving." By wielding morality as a currency, professionals create "sincere fictions" that rationalize the "doing to justice" and the "doing of racism."[7]

How to Play "Niggers by the Pound" without Being "Racist"

Many of the judges currently on the bench in Cook County started their careers in the prosecutor's office in the 1980s and 1990s. That generation of prosecutors played a game that had two titles: one that masked the game's racism and another that flaunted it. The game was "The Two-Ton Contest," or "Niggers by the Pound" and was described in Steve Bogira's *Courtroom 302.*[8] Here is how you play: Look at the weight of the defendant in the case file. Convict the defendant, and then tally the weight as a conquest to earn yourself points for pounds. One strategic tip: Convictions of the heaviest defendants are worth big points in this game, so you must offer them good plea deals, regardless of their crime, to incentivize the conviction of the fattest defendants. Be the first prosecutor to convict four thousand pounds of niggers and you win!

One judge nostalgically jested in Steve Bogira's book,

> A lot of fat guys . . . were getting great deals . . . Let's say a prosecutor's got a guy who's 350 pounds. Where the guy normally would have gotten ten years, the prosecutor might offer him a year . . . Skinny guys wouldn't get offered anything.[9]

Bogira questioned whether the game was racist. While the judge acknowledged the title as offensive, he called the game harmless "gallows" humor. What was left unasked was whether this was an appropriate practice of criminal law or a regard for public safety. Defendants potentially "deserving" of longer sentences received short ones. Conversely, other defendants received harsher sentences not on the basis of their crime or the evidence against them, but according to their weight. No regard was given to actual guilt or innocence. No consideration was given to the problematic practice of law inherent in this game. And, certainly, no heed was given to due process; it was dismissed by the judge as a charade to be played by this white boys' club representing the force of the state. The hallmarks of post-racial denial were at the heart of bastardizing the law into a game.

For this book, 104 interviews were conducted with nearly equal numbers of judges, prosecutors, public defenders (PDs), and private attorneys (PAs). To ensure candidness in this colorblind era, young white interviewers asked these attorneys: *Do you believe that defendants are treated fairly within the court regardless of their race or class background?* By including the word "class" to defuse the word "race," I hoped the phrasing would allow for an open discussion about race and criminal justice.[10]

The interviewers noted that among judges and prosecutors, the question was often met with awkward silence, and even hostility. The question itself was accusatorial. In the best of cases, professionals described the courts as racially blind and felt that there was no discrimination against poor defendants of color. Of course, no one could deny that defendants were disproportionately black and Latino, but for judges and prosecutors, the ubiquity of racial divisions was minimized and ignored; many asserted that these issues failed to register in anyone's thought processes, and others refused to discuss the matter entirely because they said they could not remember any such issues. As one prosecutor said, "I don't even notice if a defendant is white or black." The three African American judges in the sample conservatively suggested "hypothetical" ways that the defendants' race or class *could* affect defendants' treatment by prosecutors, but they stopped short of suggesting that discrimination existed. They used silence and uncertainty in their explanations to evade the questions and any specifics that would provide a clear answer. Even the African American judges spoke in the rhetorical maze identified by Eduardo Bonilla-Silva as characteristic of the expression of colorblind racism.[11]

Interestingly, there was a contrast between judges' and prosecutors' race-blind accounts and defense attorneys' view of the system. Like the court watchers who visited the courthouse and my ethnographic observations, defense attorneys perceived another picture—a court culture of indifference, disrespect, and hostility. Chapter 3 addresses these differences in greater detail, but virtually all public defenders and many private defense attorneys responded that discrimination occurred during court proceedings. Their concerns were not about case outcome. Instead, they criticized what they described as the cruel character of justice.

Defense attorneys questioned the level of decency extended to their clients—describing prosecutors and judges as "desensitized" to the humanity of defendants from minority communities. Their colleagues assumed the criminal justice system was part of the natural life course of people of color. As one defense attorney explained:

> They're [defendants] not seen with a future. They are de-futurized. They [prosecutors and judges] are just . . . "this is you, this is your destiny, you're going to be a convicted felon by the time you're 19."

Former prosecutors who left the office to be defense attorneys were more candid in addressing how race and racism worked within the office politics.[12] For instance, they were asked: "What other criteria, beyond the formal criteria, were required for promotion in the prosecutor's office?" Some attorneys described bias (based on both race and gender) in promotion. One prosecutor mentioned the high-profile gang unit as emblematic of an exclusive culture monopolized by white men:

> It has always been a very big boys club, full of white males. You would get put in assignments that would ensure that you didn't get the number of jury trials needed to be promoted. There used to be guys with porno and beer dispensers in their office in the gangs unit. [That kind of thing was] one of the reasons I left.

I asked my supervising prosecutor how promotion worked in the office. She said abruptly that to get promoted, you have to "suck the most dick." Her deadpan expression was serious, as though she was trying to slap a sense of reality into a naive twenty-year-old-girl who had asked a dumb question. Eventually, she smirked and said she would have to settle for being a second chair for life.[13]

Beyond the sexual harassment, the prosecutor defined the office as a "white" and male domain. This was a theme inherent in the notion of maintaining street cred, which requires emotional stoicism associated with masculinity. Ultimately, this prosecutor left the office because of these issues. A former prosecutor described race, particularly being black, as a liability in the State's Attorney's Office—almost guaranteeing that an attorney would get passed by for a promotion, or perhaps would leave, as a result of the racialized culture:

> Race. It's a case where race matters, particularly for black males. If you're black you don't have a chance. [There's discrimination and it's been that way for 30 years.] There are 80 felony courtrooms and there are no black first chairs. You can count on your fingers how many black first chairs there have been in the last 30 years.

Sexism and racism acted as companions in power. Through the notion of street cred, the court culture exerted male dominance on the workforce of attorneys while requiring professionals to suppress all emotion toward defendants or their cases, thus guaranteeing that they were dehumanized. Beyond reproducing court culture, sexism and racism maintained a powerful boys' network in the prosecutor's office. This power structure affected the pool of judges. Nineteen of the twenty-three judges interviewed served as prosecutors. Likewise, nineteen judges were male and only four judges were female. Many judges were former prosecutors, and thus were preselected to the bench as members of the white boys' club. The white females who could perform or "do gender" in masculine ways that maintained a stable, racialized, and violent culture of power also benefited from this system.

People of color could rise through the ranks, if they were willing to develop the street cred to fit into the culture. During the time of my research, all the major leadership roles were filled by attorneys of color. The Cook County state's attorney, Anita Alvarez, was a Latina. She worked three years in the same gang unit that sexually harassed women and placed mug shots of defendants of color—young men of her own race and likely from her old neighborhood—on the wall as conquests. The chief public defender was an African American attorney named Ed Burnette, and the respected chief judge, Timothy C. Evans, was African American.

As the election of Barack Obama provided the optimism of post-racialism, the diverse leadership in Cook County provided a false sense of security, that the days of "Niggers by the Pound" were part of a dark past rather than a visible present. Despite the presence of people of color in leadership roles, the case of the Cook County Courts demonstrates how racism festers in culture, social processes, and institutional norms that are larger than the symbolic roles of individual actors or leaders.[14] One could argue that it was on their watch that the cultural persistence of racism, abuse, and racial degradation ceremonies thrived as the boundaries between due process and racial punishment became blurred. Focusing on the racially symbolic leadership ignores the historical seeds of segregation of the courts, the racially disproportionate mechanisms of mass incarceration, and the structural arrangements and cultural persistence that defined the courthouse. While many of the attorneys stopped using the word "nigger," the games were played by the same rules. The culture of the court invented new lingo that could code such beliefs into toxic practices and make it all seem justified, and even noble.

The Moral Violations of "Mopes"

In the vernacular of court culture, defendants are identified by vulgarities: "scum," "piece of shit," "bad guys"—even "banana suits" (which refers to the jail jumper that defendants in custody must wear in court). One term predominates among these epithets. That term is "mopes," used mostly to refer to defendants but sometimes used to describe professionals as well. The meaning inscribed in this term is central to the moral rubric applied to defendants by courtroom professionals.

Work ethic, competency, and motivation are central elements of court culture. Efficiency and speed of disposition provide daily evidence of the court professional's work ethic. Not surprisingly, plea bargains rather than trials define this proverbial machine of efficient justice, and judges and prosecutors pride themselves on efficiency. Adjacent courts compete to achieve the most "dispose" (dispositions), or completed, cases in a day. The sheriff's officers act as go-betweens to update judges and courtroom workgroups on which court is "winning." One court watcher noted a judge screaming, "Let's go! Do something!" at his colleagues when there was a brief pause in a stream of plea bargains. Achieving a "dispose," or a completed case, is the chief indicator of this work ethic, with little regard to the people who represent the "disposed" cases in the system. Prosecutors specifically, when surveyed about the qualities and values inspiring "disrespect" in the Office of the State's Attorney, overwhelmingly reported "laziness" in a fellow prosecutor as the worst quality—even worse than "incompetence."

"Mope" is shorthand for a person who violates these values. Professionals find it difficult to regard a defendant as anything but a mope. By the professionals' logic, if someone was motivated, hardworking, and competent, he or she would not be charged with a crime—especially one like dealing drugs, stealing, or other common nonviolent felony infractions that define the court docket. Thus these criminal charges signal not a type of criminal act but a type of racialized being.

In daily courtroom interaction, "mope" is most often used for defendants, but during interviews with attorneys and staff, some also used the term to refer to professionals. As one attorney explained:

> I've always understood mope to be something of a catch-all term for someone that you have a low opinion of for one reason or another. Within the 26th Street vernacular, pretty much anyone can be a mope—a defendant, a witness, a lawyer, a deputy, even a judge. I think I hear it used most frequently when the speaker is trying to communicate that he/she thinks someone else isn't very bright, [is] undermotivated, or [is] a ne'er-do-well.

On the surface, "mope" is wielded on an equal-opportunity, race-blind basis. Anyone, even a judge, could be a mope for his or her incompetence or lack of motivation. For instance, exercising basic due process rights like conducting motions or calling witnesses could warrant the "mope" label for slowing the pace of the court call.[15]

Yet, with defendants, additional racialized narratives accompany the term—narratives often associated with readily available racist ideology about the cultural failings and negative stereotypes of blacks and, to a lesser extent, Latinos.[16] Consider the following side exchange with a probation officer and private attorney during a violation of probation (VOP) hearing captured in my field notes:

> Mope is a term I've heard thrown around. According to the officer, mopes have the "mentality of a child." He went on and mocked a defendant who was walking away from the podium.
>
> Probation Officer mocked the defendant (in Ebonics): See this guy . . . he's like "oh man dat ain't right . . . dis shit ain't right. Why da judge be like dat, man?" . . . If all I had to do was just show up every day and report to probation, pay $25 fines, and do some community service, just to stay out of lockup, I would. Is there a choice?
>
> The officer went on to describe the alternative, which was going to jail:
>
> Probation Officer: When you roll around in shit, you start to become shit . . . [reference to being locked up] they bring your lunch in a garbage bag; it's bologna between stale, hard bread. They throw it at you like you're an animal. You eat your lunch looking at shit on the wall. In the morning, they give you runny, powder eggs that look like snot.
> Private Attorney: Man, you are like a jaded soldier from 'Nam. You are like at war. You got shell-shock.
> Probation Officer: Listen, putting some of these guys on probation is like throwing trash in the ocean . . . it just comes back to you. This guy's a piece of shit . . . just watch; he'll be back [reference to current defendant].

Rather than discuss the crime, the probation officer mocks in Ebonics the defendant's lifestyle choice as the criminal act itself. According to court professionals, being a mope is a conscious choice. Given the bleak conditions of the jail, if a defendant is convicted for violating probation, he made the incompetent "choice" to live like an "animal," to "roll around in shit," and be "trash." Defendants who fall into this category, regardless of their personal circumstances, are thus dehumanized and are seen as deserving their plight.

Coding racial divisions with a moral rather than a racial rubric allows professionals to ignore the ubiquity of race and racism. As their colorblind logic goes, disdain for defendants is based not upon the color of their skin but upon the moral violations they embody. Given this rationale, crass, racialized humor outside the scope of colorblind racism is acceptable and not based on "race." Professionals use a bastardized performance of Ebonics to verbalize the "voice" of defendants in order to mock them. For instance, before court call, as we waited for the judge to appear on the bench, the sheriff alerted the clerk that the defendants were arriving at the lockup. The sheriff referred to the defendants as "children"—not unlike calling a black man "boy" in the Deep South during segregation.

Sheriff: Looks like we got kids.

The court clerk answered in Ebonics and corrected him:

Clerk: Chitlans, Chitlans.

The sheriff used the word "kids" to demean the defendants, but the clerk actually corrected the sheriff to speak in a more racially blatant manner. It was unclear whether the clerk meant "Chitlans" as the Ebonics word for "children" or whether she was literally calling the defendant "Chitlans" as in "fried pig intestines." Regardless, such language worked to objectify defendants as a racialized underclass.

Professionals undermined or mocked what they viewed as "black" names. For instance, I entered a plea bargain conference in the judge's chambers. Professionals discussed the case of an African American defendant named Loveric. "Loveric" was a name that was a hybrid of two words. The word "love," which presumably described the tender emotions felt toward the child by the parent, and the given name "Eric." The statement of the defendant's name elicited laughs from the attorneys in the room. All the attorneys were white.

At the conference, I sat on a couch in the corner of the judge's chambers, taking field notes. When the judge noticed that I was not laughing, she proceeded to let me in on an inside joke between her and the courtroom workgroup of attorneys; she found the joke so funny that she had let her daughters in on it so they could laugh together on an ongoing basis. In her days as a prosecutor and judge, she encountered a few defendants named "Female" as their first name (pronounced *fuh-mah-lee*). As the judge explained to me, "these" mothers just named their baby whatever it said on the hospital wristband. As the judge recounted, she and her daughters would often laugh at the name "Female Jones." At the heart of these jokes was an inability to see defendants as people with relationships and humanity. The judge used the phrase "these mothers" to place the defendants in a separate and distinct category. Although the judge was a mother herself, she made it clear that the mothers and women she processed in her court were distinct and different from her and her children. With the coding of immorality as a criminal distinction, such racialized mocking was seen as nonracial, and even worth teaching to another generation of white children.

To maintain my street cred, I gave a laugh that was sickening to my ears. I shook my head as though the joke was too funny, but really I felt ill in my role as a clerk and a researcher. Professionals do not use the word "nigger" within earshot of open court or their offices. Instead, "mope" and the associated narratives, which wielded the same social bite, were used in an equivalently stigmatizing manner. "Mope" was often spit out with the same disdain as "nigger"—with disgust distilled into an all-encompassing word. I had just laughed at a "mope" to sustain my membership in this courthouse community and my relationship with the judge. I was complicit. This introspection poured into my field notes as deep reflections, or perhaps confessions.

Burdens on Their Backs

For professionals a mope represents someone who is uneducated, incompetent, degenerate, and lazy. Poverty is seen as a natural consequence of those choices. Akin to the historic "white man's burden" to socialize a racialized underclass that is "half-devil and half-child," professionals similarly view their role in the criminal courts as one of sorting and managing a population with these features.[17]

The child-like mope is seen as a burden whose failings, incompetence, and laziness are placed on the shoulders of the professionals. What results is a paternalistic righteousness and resentment about working in a sector of the legal profession that places many of society's burdens on their backs. When I overtly asked a prosecutor about her views of the role of poverty and crime, she responded in anger:

> I'm just sick and tired of them living off my back. The way I see it is as long as there is a McDonald's "Help Wanted" sign in the window, there's a job for them.

Here, the prosecutor leverages a common welfare trope that positions poverty as a symptom of moral failings rather than a reflection of larger social and economic inequalities. In the view of the prosecutor, the defendants that she processes are parasitic—living off of her "back" because of their lack of work ethic.

In similar logic, when a judge was asked about the least satisfying aspect of his job, he described to a white interviewer that the defendants and their families were his biggest burden. He reflected that he had to "fight" to understand "them":

> You're dealing with the underworld, the underbelly of society. Every day you have to fight to understand people. You can barely understand them. A defendant and his girlfriend were scuffling in the back of the courtroom—ignorant, uneducated, rude, and crude people. You get exhausted trying to get people . . . trying to get witnesses into court.

This judge also uses pronouns like "them" or "these people" to refer to defendants as a second and lesser class of people, and as a burden he must bear. In these courts, such rhetoric, commonly associated with old-fashioned racism, is brazenly wielded by sharp tongues.

Order in the Court:
Obedience, Authority, and "Lessons" That Discipline

Defendants are constructed as blameworthy for their moral failings, and therefore a host of paternalistic lessons, humiliations, and violent threats is regarded as justifiable. Paternalism and social control extend to "teaching" people of color (regardless of whether they were actually defendants) how to dress and behave, especially when they violate courthouse norms of segregation. These practices transmit a powerful public service announcement to defendants and the public: submit to authority, be obedient, remain invisible, languish in silence, and agree that your failings are your fault.

Professionals punish defendants through informal culture and processes just outside of formal law, off the court record but within the boundaries of legality. This behavior is an informal kangaroo court of sorts where professionals play judge, jury, and executioner to any mope that they view as breaking the rules of courthouse culture.

Criminal defendants labeled as mopes are viewed by professionals as unworthy of basic due process rights. Accordingly, trying to participate in court proceedings, exercising due process rights, asking questions of professionals, or rendering themselves "visible" to the court professionals in general are all punishable offenses.

During my ethnography, one sheriff bragged with other professionals about the following "practical joke" during a jury trial. The moral violation committed by this defendant was exercising his right to a jury trial, thereby interfering with the workgroup's production ethic. The sheriff wrapped an extension cord around the defendant's chair and plugged it into the wall. The sheriff said: "OK, you're all plugged in and ready to go"—as though the defendant would be brought to an actual electric chair. What was unclear from his story was whether the sheriff committed this stunt with the jury present, during a recess with a gallery present, or whether it was a threat unleashed at the defendant and his attorney more privately. What was clear was that my co-workers heard the story, laughed, and never questioned the legal ethics of such a practical joke. I scrawled in my legal pad a twist on Malcolm Feeley's title *The Process Is the Punishment*: due process is racial punishment.

Because people of color are viewed as or mistaken for defendants, they could be the target of these "lessons" and "punishments" regardless of whether they were actually defendants or just people of color in the public viewing area. Families were punished in cruel ways for trying to participate and locate their defendant family members. This was the case even when the person did not step over a gallery boundary and into the professional space. A sheriff, "Debbie," joked with the courtroom prosecutor that when families call the courtroom to check on a defendant, she answers, "County Morgue." When they ask whether their loved one will be present in court on a particular day, she says, "Oh, they're dead," and then hangs up.

While a court watcher waited for court call to resume, he noted the following incident in his field notes:

> Judge Harrison noticed an African American male teenager wearing a tight sleeveless white undershirt, large baggy shorts, and sneakers. The teenager had entered the gallery, looked around and was on his way out when the judge shouted at him to stop and come up to the bench. When the teenager entered the courtroom and approached the bench, Judge Harrison proceeded to embarrass and lecture the young man on his attire. This happened between hearings, but it seemed extremely inappropriate when the young man was just looking for a friend and when the judge had other matters to attend to.

What was unclear to the court watcher was whether this young man was actually a defendant, a victim, or a family member. What did seem clear, though, was that being African American in the courthouse meant that you could be brought before the bench on the judge's demand, even if you were not charged with a crime. The judge could paternalistically tell you how to dress and behave, regardless of your criminal status. In fact, your racial identity implied your criminal status, as illustrated when court watchers of color were mistaken for defendants. If professionals viewed you as embodying the child-like ignorance of a mope and you wore it on your skin, your demeanor, and your clothes, it was the professionals' burden to school you into civility.

While one might assume that being black, adult, and male might amplify the chances of being taught a paternalistic lesson, black and brown women and their children were vulnerable to such lessons as well. Clearly, as demonstrated in the example of the judge mocking black motherhood and the names of black children, the notion of being a black or Latino mother earned you neither reverence nor respect in the court.

Mothers of color were viewed as incapable, incompetent, and complicit in the moral failings of their children and partners. As Dorothy Roberts explains, mothers of color, particularly black women, are constructed as the vessel of the "pathological, black, urban poor family from which all ills flow; a monster creating crack dealers, addicts, muggers, and rapists."[18] It is through her body that social ills transform into criminal elements, and for that, mothers and grandmothers could be punished and certainly not trusted in the courtroom as capable, moral figures.

Several researchers witnessed an incident of abuse initiated by one prosecutor in the courtroom. Like Babe Ruth calling his shot, the prosecutor pointed to a black teenage girl through the bulletproof glass and like a ripple effect, a sheriff stormed into the gallery to do the prosecutor's dirty work. He took the girl into custody without warning, and despite her mother being present. The child's offense? This girl was silently playing with a cell phone in the gallery—a fixture of modern teenage life. For that, the teen was taken into the court's holding cell while the judge was off the bench.[19]

Multiple court watchers saw this event and described prosecutors as "laughing and joking about the incident while the mother was crying in the courtroom." In this instance, even a young black girl, who was there as an observer, witness, or victim, was the subject of a racial degradation ceremony. She was "made visible" and ritually "revealed" as a criminal rather than a child.[20] Therefore, she was deserving of punishment. The mother was ritually revealed as well. She was too incompetent to parent her own child. Both a black mother and child were ritually denounced as "in essence of a lower species."[21]

In addition to the lessons taught to families and the public, a defendant could be taught a "lesson" during court proceedings with a gallery full of spectators. A black defendant charged with possession of a controlled substance was escorted by two officers after his hearing. In their formalized way, one officer walked in front of the defendant while the other walked behind him. The officer in front of the defendant told him to stop because there was trouble with another inmate in the lockup. The officers behind him barked orders to move faster. At first, the officers did not realize they were yelling opposite commands, but then the officer in front realized the error.

Officer: I said stay, he said go. Now, who you gonna listen to? What ya gonna do?

She was up in his face, tilting her head like she was posturing just before a street fight. Once again, I noted: *Who is the criminal? Is this street law or a court of law?* There was a silent pause for the defendant's reaction. He averted his eyes in submission. The sheriff snapped a smile to the other officer and they got the go-ahead to bring the defendant into lockup. "Move!" commanded the officer in the back. The defendant obeyed and kept his head down. The gallery watched these ongoing, open-court lessons and sat with the same obedience that the defendant embodied in his submissive eyes. They followed the cultural rules of the court: submission, obedience, invisibility, silence, and the tacit acceptance of blame.

The White Privileged Pipeline

While people of color were disciplined by this rigid moral rubric, and any person of color could be seen as a criminal deserving of punishment, whiteness was a veil of privilege that not only protected one from abuse but also changed the very meaning of criminal charges and the sanctions they warranted. For instance, if a mope was caught in possession of a controlled substance, he was often assumed to be dealing even if the criminal charge did not include the "intent to sell." Often, in plea bargain negotiations, prosecutors would accuse defendants (through their attorneys) that "straight possession" was just a dealer who did not get caught. The defense attorney would have to clarify the formal charge to fight for a rehabilitative option like drug treatment.

In contrast, white defendants were, by default, outside the mope construct of degenerate, lazy, and undeserving. They were innocent until proven guilty of being a mope. Yet, whiteness did not automatically gain one favor. They had to "prove" their whiteness by exhibiting an upper-middle-class demeanor that shared common ground with the professionals who governed the courts. This upper-class white privilege changed the very meaning of criminal charges. Whiteness allowed a defendant to be seen as "ill" rather than criminal. As a result, criminal charges like possession of a controlled substance, driving under the influence, or retail theft were symptoms of "illnesses." These white defendants were hitting their "rock bottom" moments, at which their addiction or mental illness cast them into the prison system along with common criminals. Rather than being viewed as a pattern of criminality, their experience was seen as the seminal turning point in their recovery—a passing episode that would scare them straight. In these cases, judges and prosecutors were complicit, disciplining white defendants into recovery, much like an intervention. They made efforts to protect "college kids'" futures and carefully considered the consequences of charging and sentencing for employment prospects, expungement, or professional reputation.

By providing special considerations, professionals created a segregated, privileged pipeline to channel wealthy white defendants into rehabilitation options or less-punitive alternatives like probation. This protected the white defendants' futures, which the professionals viewed as valuable.

A gray-haired white woman sat in court for much of the day's court call. She was sitting on the front bench—away from the people of color in the gallery. She wore a large diamond wedding ring, her hair was perfectly coiffed, and her nails were manicured and pristine. At one point, she crossed the barrier between the professionals and the gallery to talk to the court clerk. She was able to finish her question, was answered respectfully, and then the sheriff kindly told her to sit down—acting more like an usher than the abuser who had been barking at the public all afternoon.

Initially, in my field notes, I assumed that the woman was a professional because she was able to cross into the professionals' domain. I was shocked when I realized the woman had a daughter in lockup. The daughter was about eighteen years old and came into the court in pigtails and a prison jumper. Her demeanor was bubbly and childlike. In the context of the court, she seemed high as she smiled at the judge. But the judge smiled back—the first smile I had seen from the judge. In fact, earlier in the court call, the judge had berated several defendants with ferocity.

This young white defendant was in a special program called the "Women's Justice Program." Such programs were small and selective. For instance, the core program offered 160 beds, while another program designed for mothers had only 24 spots available. This program allowed for inpatient treatment "in a modified therapeutic community setting within the Cook County Jail."[22] Again, a segregated pipeline of protection for a select group of offenders. The judge looked carefully at the defendant's file and violated the efficiency norm of the court by praising the defendant for good work. He even acknowledged the defendant's mother in the courtroom as though he, the mother, and the defendant were working together. This was in stark contrast to the mistreatment of the mothers of color, who often were degraded, abused, or ignored.

The judge gave a pep talk to the defendant:

> Judge: You're young. You can kick this.
> Defendant: Yes, I can, judge. I will.

The judge was vested in the white defendant. He engaged the mother (in the audience) while rooting for the defendant to succeed. For this judge, the mother was an important part in the defendant's journey to reform—not her criminality, but her illness and addiction.

While whiteness gave defendants the benefit of the doubt, it was not a guarantee that one could avoid being subsumed into the mope categorization. Whiteness had to be performed convincingly by exhibiting middle-class capital, dialects, degrees, or other signifiers that could verify class membership.

Consider the case of Chris Bennett. Mr. Bennett was a white defendant who was held in custody. He was in the standard prison jumper—the "banana suit." He appeared tired and confused. As the prosecutor's law clerk, I looked into his file and read that he was only nineteen years old, despite looking sick, withdrawn, and prematurely aged. Sporadically, he looked at the ceiling or around the room while the judge was talking. As Mr. Bennett came out of the court lockup, a man wearing a beautiful, impeccably pressed suit came forward to represent him. This was a departure from the norm. Most defendants from the lockup were too poor to make bond, let alone hire a private attorney. In this case, Bennett presented as poor, potentially mentally ill or a former addict, but he was represented by a private attorney who appeared to be polished and professional.

> Attorney: We request a 402 [plea bargain] conference on my client's behalf, your honor.
> Bennett: Judge Taylor, Judge Taylor, Can I just say . . . ?
> Judge: Mr. Bennett, let your attorney represent you. Okay?
> Attorney (whispering to defendant): Chris, I'll handle it.

As the plea bargain conference proceeded in the judge's chambers, she described her contempt for the defendant. Instead of using Ebonics, she mocked the defendant's voice using the tonal cadence of a Southern "redneck":

> Judge: I was going to max that guy. Miss Taylor. Miss Taylor . . . That's my mother-in-law. I'd rather he call me Holder-Taylor. Miss Taylor. Miss Taylor.[23]

As she made fun of the defendant, the "hick" or "redneck" accent mocked his intelligence and racialized him in a particular manner. The historical notion of "redneck" assumes meaning by proximity to blackness. Historically, rednecks were known for their skin being burnt in the sun as they toiled adjacent to poor blacks and their poverty was paraded as ignorance and incompetence.[24] As comedian Jeff Foxworthy described, a redneck is "the glorious absence of sophistication."

Unlike the rigid categorization of people of color, white privilege was performative and exclusive. While this defendant was white, his performance of underclass whiteness earned him no favor. Instead, his language and demeanor diminished him into a white mope. The defendant was categorized as within the mope construct but mocked with a caricature that was tailored to fit.

By encoding racial divisions with symbolic meaning about violating the shared moral values of hard work, competence, and motivation, obvious racial divisions (even Jim Crow–style divides between white professionals and minority defendants) are applied in a way that is all but invisible to professionals. The codes become shorthand categories to quickly sort and categorize the worthy from the unworthy and the moral from the immoral. Professionals develop a collective identity (the "us" in the "us versus them" cultural divide) in opposition to defendants—one that elevates the moral legitimacy of their own work while at the same time vilifying defendants as inherently deserving of their situation. By punishing defendants and their families, through teaching "lessons," professionals exclude people of color from participating in court proceedings. By performing degradation ceremonies to defendants and the general public, professionals can elevate their own status while degrading the status of blacks and Latinos to the point of abuse.

There are many consequences to this seemingly race-blind code. First, it allows racism to exist in the courthouse space without professionals being "racists."[25] This code provides a veil of impunity where racism is not only tolerated but morally justified. This is similar to the persistence of racism that exists in the rhetoric surrounding the deserving and undeserving poor. In this environment, *mope*s are the most "undeserving"—so poor, lazy, degenerate, and "child-like" that they are criminal. Once race is coded out of the picture, a host of abuses are allowable against defendants and their families. Because this is divided along racial lines in the courthouse, it is tantamount to whites abusing blacks with impunity.

Of Monsters and Mopes

Caseload is most often measured by the number of case dispositions in a year, a week, or the number of cases on the docket of each judge. However, the enormity of the criminal caseload in Cook County is visually captured each morning in the hallways of the courthouse. Prosecutors haul carts that are packed to the brim with case files. They are stacked two levels high and so tightly that the files stand upright on their own.

Courtroom officials know that the majority of these files are small and thin, with discovery materials and reports copied in such a cursory way that they are barely readable, and therefore are nearly in violation of Brady obligations of evidence disclosure.

In my role as law clerk, I spent much of my mornings creating these files, which were called FDOCs (First Day on Call). Most of these cases were simple drug possession or other nonviolent offenses that were easy "disposes."[26] "Dispose" is used by professionals as a noun for a completed case. It can also be used as a verb when professionals refer to wanting to "dispose" or throw away these cases as quickly as possible. This highlights the lack of concern these cases are afforded. Each of the small cases on the cart represents a mope to be managed and quickly pled off the docket and disposed, as the probation officer noted, "like trash in the ocean."

In contrast, a smaller portion of the cart has eye-catching "accordion files"; they stretch a foot wide with reports, evidence, pictures, and victim statements. These are files of offenders that are characterized as "monsters"—charged with murder, sexual assault, and the like.

Professionals simplify the court docket into two racialized categories; defendants are either monsters or mopes. As Kipling conceived, the white man's burden is managing a racialized underclass that is "half-devil and half-child."[27] If mopes are the archetype of the "half-child," then this rarer offender represents the "half-devil" or as prosecutors call them, "monsters." One would expect these offenders to be marked with the worst stigma among the entire pool of offenders, but instead, they represent the "real" cases that prosecutors feel require their time, effort, and litigating skills. In their logic, if there were not so many mopes or "social threats" overwhelming the system, they would have time to focus on the monsters that are the real "criminal threats." It is through these dichotomous characterizations that professionals, prosecutors, and judges in particular construct their professional identity and their moral righteousness in practicing law in the courts. Also, in simplifying the court docket, racial categories aid in the efficiency of the system.[28]

When God's Work Becomes Dirty Work

No prosecutor wants to shuffle papers in an assembly line of justice. Nor do prosecutors begin their careers with a commitment to social "injustice." They are not motivated to incarcerate the poor or to subject people of color to abuse. Instead, prosecutors have an idealized notion of their work that is oriented toward victims' rights, protecting society, and doing trial work. Some of the artifacts of this value system are posted proudly on a bulletin board that greets visitors, police, and victims. It also models the organizational currency of the Office of the State's Attorney, where prosecutors are promoted according to the quantity of trials they win. The first win is particularly momentous for a young prosecutor. As I wrote in my field notes:

> When an attorney wins their first jury trial, it's tradition to cut off a piece of their clothing and hang it on display on a bulletin board. The piece of clothing is attached to the court file with the name of the defendant on the folder and the date the decision was made.

The "prize" of winning your first trial was measured by the severity of the felony charge, how close the sentence was to the maximum allowable by law, and how fast they could win the case (an efficiency paradigm that extends from plea bargains to trials). Prosecutors commemorated this passage like macho frat boys losing their virginity—another example of the boys' club culture.

While the focus of the bulletin board was trial "wins," its centerpiece was suffering. While this board is an ever-changing artifact, at the time of my clerkship, a single file was in the middle of the bulletin board with the rest arranged around it. "The People vs. Garcia . . . Alan's First Jury Win." Alan's tie was pinned to the file along with a mug shot of the defendant taken after the verdict. The picture showed a young Latina crying so hard that her mouth was wide open, frozen in grief and time. Underneath the picture, the attorney wrote: "D not very happy with verdict." The defendant's suffering was displayed like a decapitated head. Her identity was minimized to a single letter, "D," and her narrative to a single punch line. Much like the gang unit's mural of mug shots, this bulletin board was not just about a "win"; it placed the defendant as the ultimate showpiece, especially if the showpiece was a defendant considered a "monster."[29]

For prosecutors, the *real* work of prosecution rests in serving a "higher duty."[30] Prosecutors see themselves as the "good guys"—doing what is morally "right" in society. When they describe the most satisfying aspects of their job, they most frequently emphasize how the real work of prosecutors allows them to be on the right side of justice. Often their language is reminiscent of the simple didactic frameworks that divide mopes from professionals. Morality is like picking teams. You are either a good guy or a bad guy. There is nothing left in between. As one prosecutor observed,

> It's the one place you can be a lawyer and do what's right. If you can't prove a case you can dismiss it, and if you really think they're guilty, you can fight . . . [We are] held to a standard of doing what's right and that's where I want to be.

Prosecutors characterized their work in relation to putting away "monsters" rather than mopes, even distinguishing their work as the "one place" where a lawyer can do what is "right." One prosecutor described the satisfaction of putting "the really bad guys" in prison—the ones "who hurt kids . . . a wild dog, murdering people—the really violent guys." Another prosecutor described the satisfaction of vindicating heinous crimes as

> making sure that in particularly heinous cases that the defendant will never be able to harm a victim again . . . sometimes helping get closure for victims' families.

In another instance, a prosecutor described putting the bad guys away to protect society. He described the defendant being "put away" with other monsters—a true lifetime of punishment:

> Putting the bad guy away; not just locking them up, but making sure they don't hurt others again, or if they do, it will be other inmates, because they don't stop.

As a result, prosecutors are fighting the "good fight" for victims and surviving family members. Paradoxically, many of the victims and surviving family members are the same people they are abusing in the gallery. Yet there is no recognition that people of color and victims are often one and the same. In fact, the worst part of my time in the prosecutor's office was having attorneys describe and perversely show me images from case files with pictures of dead, starved babies, shriveled in heinous neglect, or other gore that I could not "un-see" from my mind. The flashbacks that resulted transformed my brain, temporarily, into a horror film that I could not turn off. The images were magnified by the callousness with which the attorneys paraded the photos or the one-upmanship that defined how they traded these stories about victims of color.

Despite the gruesomeness with which they manhandled these cases, prosecutors viewed their work and their professional identity as being on a higher moral plane. One prosecutor described this moral calling as "God's work on Earth." When discussing the most satisfying aspect of his work, he responded,

> Giving victims or surviving family members [the] most possible closure they can get. We do God's work on Earth. You can't undo it when someone's murdered . . . do as close as you can.

This higher purpose requires hard work, which is something you must perform for victims in order to reveal your moral commitment. As another prosecutor described,

> Just the feeling that we're doing the right thing; helping the victim, the family of the victim of violent crime; showing them that you're working hard, they see that; and it's also satisfying knowing that this person [isn't going to harm society].

In their ideal, prosecutors emphasized trial work as crucial to performing work ethic. Fighting through a trial is the "true" work of litigators:

> I knew since I was 19 that I wanted to be a prosecutor. I love being a litigator, and real litigators are in the courtroom every day; you could be pushing paper in private practice. I strongly believe that the people I prosecute need to be prosecuted. The biggest factor is that I so strongly believe in what I do.

However, the work of prosecutors is far different from their imagined glory; the majority of their day is not trying "monsters" but processing mopes, with the attendant "paper pushing," as described above. Cases bombard the system; the average felony prosecutor in Cook County has three hundred or more open cases at any one time;[31] nearly 95 percent of the cases are resolved through plea bargains rather than trials, and most crimes are victimless. These are inherent contradictions for attorneys who ideally define their work as doing trials, working with victims, and protecting society.

Given the disjuncture between the myth and the reality of the trenches of justice, mopes' bombarding the system is perceived as the real problem, getting in the way of real cases, real danger, and undermining the heart of what it is to be a prosecutor. Not only are mopes undeserving based on both their racial and their criminally immoral stature, but their presence in the system literally obstructs "real justice." By this logic, as a matter of moral imperative and even public safety, mopes should be handled as expeditiously as possible. Work ethic is reinterpreted as dutifully "disposing" of these cases. The faster prosecutors can dispose of mopes, the better they exhibit the work ethic that so strongly underlies their identity. This imperative comes at a cost; it requires viewing due process not as a right but as a privilege. And, certainly, by definition, mopes are deemed unworthy of such privileges.

Professionals must reinterpret "due process" for this undeserving set of defendants. The "mope" construct is useful in that respect. It justifies the defendant as unworthy of his or her due process rights, rights that (if exercised) take up time and importance on the court docket. This allows professionals to practice what I call "due process for the undeserving." These practices require: (1) the streamlining of scripted due process requirements, (2) the curtailing of due process through informal sanctions that are often not part of the court record, and (3) the absolute exclusion of mopes from participation in the legal process—even in cursory ways mandated by law.[32] As we will see, racialized justice is efficient justice, and therefore it has an organizational utility.[33]

Ceremonial Charade: Due Process for the Undeserving

Given the categorization of defendants as mopes, court proceedings are constructed as a "ceremonial charade," in which due process is reduced to ceremony without substance for those deemed to be undeserving.[34] For instance, when I interviewed a prosecutor about whether defendants understood their rights when pleading guilty, he did not elaborate on principles of any legal ethics that he recalled from law school; instead, he mocked the defendants as inherently unable to understand their legal rights, which made due process a "waste." This was explained using Ebonics, which emphasized the racialized nature of the defendants' perceived ignorance:

> They probably don't understand . . . they only listen to what matters: "what you can get . . . and what I be gettin'." Somewhere along the line they were trying to protect their rights but yea, most of it's a waste.

Given this view, as well as the view that the paper pushing of plea bargaining was not "real" legal work, fundamental due process protections are regarded as mere formalities, at best a type of ceremony without substance. This allowed professionals to achieve a lowest common denominator of due process.

Socialization was central to the institutional continuity of this belief system and practice. Experienced prosecutors and even judges taught new attorneys how to streamline processes to the bare minimum of legality, or laughed at attorneys who were so wet behind the ears that they cited case law. For instance, two senior first- and second-chair prosecutors in one courtroom coached their third-chair novice how to avoid doing plea bargains the "long way." The third chair would naively read a detailed account of the facts of the case that the defendant was pleading guilty to when asked to do so by the judge. The attorneys told her that this detail was a complete "waste of time." The first chair explained to the third chair that she should put fewer facts on the record.

> First Chair: All I say is "on such and such date," he was found stealing. So, stipulated? OK. Let's move on.
> Third Chair: They [formal management] said I wasn't putting enough facts.
> Second Chair: Mary, you can never put too little.

From a practical standpoint, detailing too many facts of the case posed a problem. If defendants heard what they viewed as inaccuracies in the police report or details that were in conflict with their experience, a plea bargain could fall apart in open court; what was worse, this could happen after a defendant had already waived his right to a bench or jury trial. To professionals, this was a significant "investment" in time and negotiation. In these instances, the professionals, including defense attorneys, would instruct and even tacitly coerce the defendant to accept the stipulated facts of the case.

Maintaining the defendants' ignorance was bureaucratically helpful to the production ethic of the courts.[35] For instance, one defendant misunderstood the plea process. He agreed to waive his right to a trial, and was moving on to plead guilty. The judge asked for the factual basis of the case, which cued the prosecutor to read into the record all the pertinent facts that warranted a conviction. The prosecutor read the police report and detailed the facts of the case.

> Judge: Are those the correct facts?
> Defendant: That's what the police say. (His private attorney leaned toward him.)
> Private Attorney (whispers to defendant): Yes!
> Defendant: Yes, Judge.

Despite the defendant's resistance, the judge's threatening glare and the defense attorney's coaching led the defendant to plead guilty to a crime that he believed was fabricated. The informal sanction was not on the court record; it was only in my field notes.[36]

In other instances, where defendants persisted with their resistance by asking questions, they would be whisked away by sheriffs, yelled at by the judge, and ignored by their attorneys—only to go back to the jail and wait until their next court appearance. Given the oppressive conditions of the jail, sending a defendant back to the Cook County Jail to sit and wait a month for another hearing was a not-so-subtle way of extracting a plea and teaching a mope a lesson. In what amounted to a punishment on top of a punishment, the judge would write notes on the file that would remind her of the defendant's behavior so she would be sure not to offer him a good deal.

Some mopes were denied public defenders and indigency hearings—a practice that streamlined case flow, tacitly induced an incentive to plead guilty, and acted as punishment to mopes. Because mopes are thought to be unemployed, when they post bond to secure pretrial freedom, judges assume that the bond money was acquired illicitly, even if it was their grandmother's life savings. As a result, judges find these defendants unworthy of both indigency hearings and, by extension, unworthy of the services of public defenders—a clear violation of Illinois statute and federal constitutional law. When defendants protest judges' decisions, they are admonished for talking and slowing down the court process.[37]

Although defense attorneys were sympathetic to defendants, they were often complicit in subversions of due process. For instance, a Latino defendant was FDOC (first day on call). His lawyer was also Latino. As a matter of formality, the judge checked to see if the defendant needed a translator:

Judge: Sir, do you speak English?
Defendant: Little bit (with a thick Mexican accent)
Private Attorney: Judge, he speaks enough to be arraigned . . . I talk with him
    in English . . . I think we can do it without the interpreter.

The defendant was honest with the judge about the limitations of his English. However, speaking conversational English did not mean that he possessed the English skills to comprehend criminal proceedings. In this case, a bilingual attorney made the discretionary call about how much English was "enough" to participate. In fact, the defense attorney admitted that he spoke only English to his client, but this admission said nothing about whether the client actually understood his attorney's legal advice. To determine whether a defendant understood "enough" English to understand the legal proceedings, the defendant had only to say "yes" or "no" when cued. In the view of the private attorney, there was no need for any further understanding because, frankly, defendants are not expected to participate. By complying with the norms of the ceremonial charade, the defense attorney exhibited a sign of good favor to his courtroom colleagues and signaled that he was an "insider" despite being an attorney of color.

In another instance, a public defender ("Sara") was able to build favor with the courtroom workgroup by ignoring her clients entirely. She rarely visited clients in the lockup. Instead, she would confer with clients only during the defendant's quick hearing in open court. This amounted to talking over them with legal jargon that was incomprehensible to a layperson. In general, Sara talked "to the record" but not to her clients. In response, defendants often attempted to ask questions of the judge—trying in vain to get the judge to referee the situation. To get the defendants to be quiet, professionals used their legal rights against them, admonishing them "not to speak" about their case (to avoid incrimination), even though their questions often pertained to basic concerns about sitting in jail, confusion about the hearings, or wanting a new attorney.

This was Sara's mode of "efficient" representation—a technique that put her in good favor with her prosecuting colleagues as well as the judge, while the other public defenders were socially isolated in the same courtroom. In one instance, when the legal dialogue was speeding past a young black defendant, he decided to speak out and was able to sneak in a few words of dialogue:

Defendant: I'd like a new attorney, Judge. (Reference to Sara)
Judge: Where is your attorney? You have a public defender. It takes money to
    get an attorney.

This was all the defendant was able to ask. The judge assumed the defendant was ignorant and did not understand that his public defender was an attorney. Her answer confused the situation by cruelly reinforcing that it takes "money" to get an attorney, thereby implying that public defenders were not "real attorneys." The judge never allowed the defendant to express his concern with his public defender's competency or commitment.

The legal proceedings continued (about discovery, motions, and set dates). The defendant gingerly raised his hand like an elementary student in a last effort to be heard. He kept it up, and the judge swiftly motioned to him to put it down. It was how a teacher would silently reprimand a student or child. Again, these actions were off the court record and included only in my field notes.

The defendant was then taken to lockup immediately. Sara even laughed at the defendant to the judge because he was so mouthy. She sat down on a bench and instead of following up with her client in lockup, she clicked away on her smartphone. I peered over Sara's shoulder and saw that she was playing solitaire. With time a valuable currency, I set the timer on my phone. Sara's game went on for nearly thirty minutes while her client was sent back to the Cook County Jail to linger for weeks as a pretrial detainee with no interaction with a lawyer and with a judge who supported, if not protected, the denial of representation.

Watching an outsider practice law within these norms illuminated the cultural practices that defined local justice in Cook County. This outsider, "Patty," was a stark contrast to Sara, who earned good favor with the judge and prosecutors but denied her clients access to representation and participation. Patty was brought in to represent one defendant in a case with multiple defendants. She was an attorney from the public defender's Multiple Defendant Division.[38] Patty was a highly regarded outsider but experienced in practicing law in Cook County. She was known in the Public Defender's Office but was not accountable to one particular court, as most public defenders were. The public defender regulars in the courtroom held her in high regard. For instance, "Mark" whispered to me as Patty walked into the court, "She is a great attorney . . . bright, conscientious. They want to promote her to supervisor but she loves what she does."

In this case, she was pursuing a motion for her client—a move that could have been read as running counter to the production ethic of the court culture. She introduced herself for the record.

> Patty: For the record, Patty Marco, Public Defender, Multiple Defenders Unit. Judge, we are making a motion to quash arrest and suppress evidence. We are ready to go today on this motion.
> Judge: State?
> SA: We are not ready to do the motion today. The police officers are not in court. We did give an offer on this case already.

The prosecution did not normally go through files in a rigorous way, unless the defense required them to do so by pursuing a motion or trial. Because mopes were expected to plead guilty, there was little need for engagement in their cases. As in this case, the prosecutors did not prepare the case in reference to actual "legal work," but in the currency of the culture, they got something "done." Their "rebuttal" was providing a plea bargained offer. Interestingly, the prosecutor did not even consider the actual legal grounds of the motion. He had done his share on the case by "giving a good offer," so he told the judge about that. In a sense, the prosecutor was tattling on the public defender for making the motion despite the offer.

> Patty: Judge, there was an identification that took place at the police station but it was not by the arresting officer. We want to proceed with the motion.

Patty was significantly more aggressive than the other PDs who were assigned permanently to particular courtrooms. Because this was a case with multiple defendants, "Mark," a courtroom regular, was representing the other defendant. He merely listened to this exchange and the judge asked if he would like to make the same motion. He said "yes," passively, and jumped on Patty's defensive move. This was a rare moment of hearing an attorney actually give a factual basis for a motion.[39] Prosecutors had to be "provoked" to engage this deeply in a case file. It took a public defender from the outside to initiate a motion, which in turn allowed the regular public defender, Mark, to jump on the coattails. Rather than rebutting the motion with a legal argument, the prosecutor merely snitched on the public defender by saying to the judge that she already provided an offer. The subtext was that this offer was not enough to make her go away.

For attorneys, there was a considerable amount of socialization that institutionalized these cultural practices. One defense attorney talked about his indoctrination into this culture. As a new attorney, he spent a considerable amount of effort crafting legal arguments to support his motions in case he was questioned by a judge, only to receive violent responses from the judge rather than any good favor.

> One of my first introductions to the system was in front of Judge D'Angelo. I'm arguing back in chambers and the judge says, "What's this motion about?" and I said, It's based on People v. Jones," and Judge D' says, "Fuck People v. Jones." I was a young lawyer then [looking in disbelief]. It just struck me as a system that was not doing what it was supposed to do and that every participant in it was complicit in its failures.

Another attorney reflected on a similar incident that shows the persistent nature of this culture, a culture of practicing law that dated decades into the past.

> I can remember going into [judge's] chambers after filing a motion to quash arrest on a case and having a judge say to me, "Counselor, I need some reasons for granting this motion," and as a young, fresh-faced lawyer, I started listing all the constitutional precedent, the statutory violations and everything else. He goes, "No no, I need some reasons." . . . I keep giving him the law. Finally, he looks at the deputy and says, "Tell him, I need some reasons." And the deputy goes, "He needs some reasons" (motioning with his hand like he had money). I said, "I'm sorry . . . I don't have any of those reasons."
> NVC (Nicole Van Cleve): What year do you think it was?
> Defense Attorney: That would be 1984. And that was in the wake of Greylord . . . that was still going on.
> NVC: And that's the culture that you were talking about.
> Defense Attorney: That's exactly right.

This defense attorney went on to describe these culture practices as persistent and entrenched. As he explained, there is little internal resistance or "motivation" to change, even in the face of one of the largest federal investigation scandals in the nation's history, Operation Greylord.

> You didn't have an internal motivation to change; you had external motivations to change in the form of indictments. That's not really a cultural change . . . that's "oh my god, I got caught." . . . So, that didn't really affect that much culturally. That was like the difference between general and specific deterrence. There is certainly some specific deterrence: guys [attorneys and judges] were going to the joint. But, generally speaking, the culture persisted in a less obvious way. The culture continued to be an "us and them" culture with defendants. The defendants are outside of us.

The boundaries between the criminally charged and those attorneys responsible for managing the courts are blurred. This attorney even imports criminological theory, specifically deterrence theory, to understand his attorney colleagues. Even the federal indictment of nearly 100 judges, prosecutors, police, and court personnel did not make a dent in the cultural armor of the place and how they practiced law, skirted due process, and understood the defendants as a racialized "other." The culture could manifest in less-subtle ways outside the radar of federal oversight.

After speaking with this seasoned defense attorney for more than an hour, I asked whether these practices are just a case of bad lawyers or "bad apples spoiling the bunch."

> No, I think you're talking about the collective . . . the collective conscience of the system . . . the collective culture . . . I mean I keep coming back to that word. It really is a culture. Because, you know, if it's not accepted in one courtroom, everybody, back then when things were so crazy, would change their perspective and do what they're supposed to do . . . If they don't tolerate deputies speaking to people poorly, it's not going to happen. If they don't tolerate people making fun of defendants then, that won't happen. And, so that creates things.

As for the court watchers who were law students, many were shocked at decisions made in open court with little or no information about the legal basis for the judges' rulings. This streamlined an efficient way of disposing cases that to outsiders and new attorneys seemed to be just short of crossing the ethical boundaries of professional responsibility. However, because mopes were viewed in racialized terms, they were undeserving of due process and therefore there was little moral ambiguity about these subversions of law from within the court community.

Minimizing Mopes Out of the Process

Similar to the abuses that enforced racial segregation in the court, defendants were policed out of the legal process through open-court humiliation. Like children, defendants were to be seen and not heard, and defense attorneys were expected to "control" their clients—another paternalistic term that referred to the child-like nature that underpinned the meaning of "mope." "Controlling a client" meant that defense attorneys were not there to defend a client's rights in the system but to prevent the client from interfering or exercising those rights, or participating in proceedings even in the cursory ways required by law. Even the word "control" alluded to the defendant as a type of unruly being, an animal who needed a leash or a misbehaving child in need of discipline.

In many cases, a defendant's hearing began before the defendant was at the podium, with a sheriff barking orders at him. All the while, the court record would continue as though the defendant was able to actively listen to the status of his case. Some defendants would attempt to ask the judge about the case, only to be hustled off by sheriffs, with the judge yelling, "Motion defendant, sir"—a legal term that meant little to the defendant and did not address his question. Because defendants often sat in jail awaiting trial for months, these "valuable" hearings amounted to a cruel charade for the defendant.

In the case of plea bargaining, which defined the quick rhythm of the court call, a deal was agreed upon with the expectation that the plea should be quick, painless, and without disruption from the defendant. In cases where there was an interruption from the defendant, the defendant or his attorney would pay the price. For plea bargains, judges would recite a script to defendants—detailing all the rights and privileges they were giving up by pleading guilty to their charge. These scripted recitations were repetitive, monotonous, and so rapidly delivered that court watchers noted the recitation to be incomprehensible.

As one prosecutor jested, while a defendant listened to his rights, "Sit back, relax, enjoy your flight"—a biting observation, since the defendant was "flying" to jail for ten years. Judges would pause in a cursory way and allow defendants to address the court, for the record, before imposing a sentence. Although this was a formal invitation for the defendant to talk, the informal norms shunned such participation. If a defendant attempted to participate, the defense attorney would be told to "control your client." Given this dynamic, most defendants would not address the court. Many submissively hung their head. On occasion, a few defendants mistook the judge's question about participation as an authentic invitation to express remorse. If the defendant spoke, he or she was *asking* to be verbally berated in open court, with the tirades focusing on the personal moral failings of the defendant. One would assume that in admitting moral failings, a defendant could earn favor with the judge. But slowing down the case disposition for a mope was a gross violation of the workgroup's production ethic and misuse of the currency of time.

The following examples show the violent sanctions (in the form of racial degradation ceremonies) imposed on defendants. These cases both sanctioned the individual defendants who violated the courtroom norms and deterred other defendants from making such errors. Defense attorneys often considered this potential "punishment" by the court culture when they advised their clients. In fact, they were often complicit in it while maintaining their status as courtroom "insiders."

For instance, a defendant was reprimanded as a mope because of errors made by his defense attorney. The Latino defendant was scheduled to report to boot camp.[40] The judge called him to the stand even though his attorney was not present and there was not a language translator. The attorney's absence slowed the court process and violated the courtroom's production ethic.

> Judge: Where's your attorney? Do you know his phone number? Why aren't you talking?
> Defendant (speaking softly): Me no speak English.
> Judge: If you are PRETENDING you can't speak English, you will be held in contempt!

After screaming in open court, the judge called the translator, who took ten minutes to arrive.

> Judge (to interpreter): Seems the defendant has forgotten how to speak English ... me no speakie English.[41]

Through the translator:

> Judge: Where is your attorney?
> Defendant: He's not here.
> Judge (screaming): THANK YOU. Where is he?!? How do you get in touch with him?
> Defendant: My wife does for me.
> Judge (off the record to courtroom professionals): It is for a plea today. How much you want to bet that someone just got high before he got here? No wonder why someone forgot how to speak his English. No wonder his wife is hiding in the hallway ... Looks like he was just walking like he had his toenails extracted.

Latinos who struggled in English were particularly vulnerable. They were met with a racial degradation ceremony tailored to amplify their contested citizenship in the United States and the parasitic trope that accompanies such contestations. The mope construct assumes blacks as the reference group, a category of people who are seen to be lazy, degenerate, and leaching off society and the criminal justice system; the notion of Latinos as "illegals" is also compatible with this construct. They are mopes for overloading the system and for their perceived parasitic drain on the country's resources. Being brown inscribes criminality on the body with the implication that "Latino" and "illegal" are one and the same. In fact, the notion of "illegal" implies criminal guilt. For that, abusing Latinos, anyone with brown skin, and especially those with language difficulties becomes an acceptable sport of the culture.

Mope Lovers, Racial Contamination, and Paying the Price for Defending

Defense attorneys who could not or would not control their clients paid high reputational costs for their cultural disobedience. During my fieldwork, prosecutors categorized a defense attorney as "good" or "bad" by whether he or she could "control" the client into a guilty plea—a categorization based solely on their complicity in a racialized culture of the courts.

There were dire consequences for fighting too hard, pursuing "too many" motions and trials, or pushing due process necessities beyond the absolute minimum. These defense attorneys were labeled "clueless," "difficult," "incompetent," or worse: "mopes." Because the term "mope" could be used against white attorneys, these practices reinforced the illusion of race neutrality. In reality, the shared stigmas demonstrated that a defense attorney could be racially contaminated and therefore professionally subsumed with the racialized attributes of his or her clients.

Many of the racialized meanings that were encompassed by the term "mope" were imposed on the defense attorneys as well, which meant that they too should be punished as one of "them." Nonverbal cues like rolling their eyes, shaking their heads, or exchanging glares with other courtroom players punctuated the court proceedings—enabling these racialized norms to be expressed without being reflected in the court record. Defense attorneys who were constructed as mopes could be expected to be humiliated like them.

For instance, an overweight attorney finished a plea bargain with a prosecutor. The exchange was intense because the defense attorney asked for treatment for his addicted client rather than just prison time. The prosecutor was visibly disgusted by the request and stood firm. It was prison time, nothing less.

Because the defense attorney had asked too much in the negotiation, the prosecutor made his punishment personal. Knowing that the defense attorney had another case in an adjacent courtroom, the prosecutor snidely instructed him to cross to the other courtroom via the lockup so he could be with the "bad guys" or mopes. Such directions were equivalent to being told to "go to hell," as close as you could come to being called a mope to your face—a piece of information that was more often transmitted as rumor, mocking, and whispers when you left the room.

Prosecutor: You can always go through the bad guys' room.
Defense Attorney: I will go through the conference room.

Once the defense attorney left, the sheriff punctuated the social punishment by personally and publicly degrading the attorney's weight in open court.

> Sheriff: I'm not sure he could fit through the bad guy room. (Sheriff pretended to talk into his walkie-talkie and improvised the static of the device.) "We need back up in Court 402 . . . please bring plenty of butter and margarine."

Much like the mocking of mopes, marginalizing defense attorneys through subtle and not so subtle abuse and humor ensured that defense attorneys complied with the culture of the courtroom. This behavior drew distinct boundaries between outsiders and insiders in a space where membership offered privilege—both professional and reputational.

Beyond the reputational consequences, defense attorneys were "punished" like mopes by some judges and/or prosecutors with harsher consequences for their clients. For instance, this defense attorney described a culture that was retaliatory and could inflict retribution on attorneys, defendants, and even entire families.

> PD: Yes, the prosecution filed a motion to revoke my client's bond because they got mad when they found out that I had submitted a motion to suppress evidence . . . When you take cases to trial, they might withdraw offers or give worse offers to other clients. There was one judge I worked with who liked to plead out cases . . . If you went to trial he would slam the guy if you lost. He did give fair warning about it; he was honest that this is what would happen. I was just talking to my friend yesterday about having this interview, and she told me that she had two clients who were witnesses in a case. One of her clients had been shot; his family had been threatened; he kept telling everyone that he didn't remember what happened . . . The prosecutor threatened to put him in lockup and said he would personally prosecute the client and make sure that he went to jail . . . In one case, the client had called the prosecutor and told him that he couldn't make it to court that day . . . He came in to court the next week and the prosecutor wouldn't tell the judge that he had called him. He (prosecutor) said that it would be easier for him if the client was in lockup because he wouldn't have to track him down. The same stuff happens over and over.

In this case, the mope construct is the justification for the infliction of punishment and even lying to judges and defense attorneys. Unwieldy mopes are better off in jail where they can be controlled, with little regard to the value of their freedom, the bond they may have posted, or the consequences of pre-trial incarceration on family and employment. As Justice Robert Jackson once noted, "The Prosecutor has more control over life, liberty and reputation than any other person in America." While this statement usually refers to the prosecutor's broad discretion to prosecute until in "his judgment the ends of justice are satisfied,"[42] here we see prosecutors using retaliation and retribution against livelihoods and reputations to enforce a *way* of doing justice—one informed by racialized tropes about the unworthiness of due process for mopes.

A public defender named "Sue" was always on the losing end of the reputational game. She was one of the courtroom regulars who was stigmatized in the courtroom workgroup. According to the prosecutors, she pursued too many motions and trials and wasted the court's time on mopes. She paid the price among her professional peers and was considered a "mope lover," a characterization that shared many of the meanings associated with the phrase "nigger lover." Her sympathy for mopes labeled her as incompetent. Prosecutors would often turn their backs on her while she spoke on the court record—rolling their eyes to other prosecutors, probation officers, or the sheriffs. She was socially isolated and treated as an outsider despite being a courtroom regular.

While shadowing her as she consulted with her client in the jail lockup, I witnessed sheriffs playing cruel jokes on her like they would on the defendants. They would periodically lock her in with her defendants. They would sometimes make excuses about having to attend to tasks in other courts, but often she would be knocking on the soundproof lockup window while the sheriffs either did not respond or did so with visible disdain and certainly no urgency. I was with her during one of these stunts and sat in total fear, waiting, at the mercy of the sheriff; rather than being fearful of the defendant, I noted, I was terrified of the sheriff. The three of us—Sue, the defendant, and I—sat in unity in a closet-size consultation room as we endured a "lesson" that lasted for ten minutes. While sitting with this defendant who languished in the Cook County Jail, I noted that no type of small talk could make the silence palpable. Languishing in the jail, surviving the conditions there while removed from family and the daily rhythm of life, left the defendant hollowed out. As we sat imprisoned together, I noted that the defendant barely looked us in the eye. Shame and pain were evident on his face as he averted his eyes from the people sent to protect him. Perhaps he realized that, like him, even his attorney was abused by the system. As I wrote in my notes, *What hope is left when your attorney becomes punished alongside you?*

Defendant Willie Johnson was unknowingly represented by this mope lover. Mr. Johnson was a two-time offender who was currently charged with possession of a controlled substance. He wanted to express his remorse and ask for a longer sentence of intensive probation with a drug program. Alternatively, he could have taken one year in the state penitentiary, but he was appealing to the judge for treatment.

> Defendant: You are most gracious and honorable judge. I truly want to be a productive member in society. I want to change my behavior and put structure in my life. Your Honor, I am speaking from the kindness of my heart. I need to change and be there for my six children. I want this longer sentence for the drug program. I need the structure in my life.

The content of this appeal spoke to the important ethical frames that defined the courtroom workgroup's notion of "morality." This defendant was "asking" to be a productive member of society, a responsible father, and he was willing to work for his recovery by taking a longer sentence; certainly he was not looking for an easy way out. It was as though the defendant was trying to prove that he was not a mope; instead, he was trying to be revealed as a father with humanity and "kindness" in his "heart."

However, the defendant was already guilty of being a mope. By speaking in court, the defendant violated the production ethic of disposition that all but required that defendants be submissive, silent, and invisible. As he left court, escorted by the sheriffs into the lockup, Sue began accounting for her client's violation.

> PD: What can I say? I guess he's a talker.

There was a tone of mockery and embarrassment in her voice as she nervously laughed and shook her head. She tried to mitigate his mistake while protecting the little reputation that she had remaining. Despite a plea bargain conference on Johnson's behalf, his request was later denied. As he heard the judge deny his request in open court, Johnson begged.

> Defendant: You are a most gracious judge. Please, Your Honor.

Johnson pled guilty, regardless. Yet, rather than neatly agreeing to all that was stipulated with a plea of guilty, he repeatedly expressed confusion, even saying the prosecutor's facts were wrong as they were read into the court record. As I wrote in my field notes: *Johnson caused a commotion to the machine-*

like flow of casework. The judge was annoyed as she raised her voice and slowed down her recitation of the legal "script" read into the record during a plea. She spoke into the record and at Johnson as though he was hearing-impaired rather than a person who had concerns about relinquishing his rights.

Again, in this situation, comments, sighs, and rolling of the eyes were prominent reactions but were not noted in the official record. Clearly Sue not only pursued too many motions but also could not control her clients. Sue and Willie Johnson were both found guilty. For this offense, she would continue to be punished alongside her clients, perhaps in the lockup or perhaps in open court. In the moral currency of the courts, mope lovers got what mope lovers deserved. To maintain my street cred in the court and the access that I needed to collect data, I quietly distanced myself from Sue and started shadowing other defense attorneys in the Public Defender's Office. By shifting my alliance, I was never stuck in a lockup again.

I Don't See Race; I See a Case:
Blind Faith in Bureaucracy and the Facade of Fairness

Professionals have "faith" in bureaucracy. As much as they loathe the tediousness, the forms, and the hassle of it, bureaucracy—and more broadly, procedure—are symbolically powerful. They represent the equality and fairness of justice. Each defendant is read the same admonishments; each defendant's case is read into the record at the same speed; each defendant is "disposed" with the same forms and court fees. Procedure and bureaucratic formality allow professionals to take comfort in a type of "procedural" justice that treats all similarly situated individuals in similar ways.[43]

Of course, procedural justice is often thought of as the many rights that all defendants may exercise regardless of their race, creed, color, or other extralegal features. All defendants technically have the right to a jury trial or the right to pursue a motion that challenges their arrest, for instance. But defendants do not exercise these rights en masse. After the due process revolution, Malcolm Feeley used this observation as a starting point for his book *The Process Is the Punishment.*[44] At a time when there was an explosion of new legal protections being offered to defendants, no defendants opted for a jury trial, for instance, and many were without an attorney.

For professionals in Cook County, procedural justice has been reduced to a ceremonial charade that *universally* mistreats all mopes. Beyond diminishing due process to a ceremony without substance, the performance of procedural rights and the bureaucratic tools (like the court record) create a facade of fairness that protects the professionals rather than the defendants. In addition, bureaucratic rationality and comparison provide an additional companion to the wielding of racism in the courts. The treatment of all mopes as "cases" rather than people allows the illusion of both procedural justice and race-blind justice. According to the professionals, minimizing defendants, homogenizing them, and excluding them from proceedings are in their interest because those actions promote "fairness" and legitimize the system. As one prosecutor summarized in an interview, "I do not even notice if a defendant is black or white." While this is a common post-racial statement of colorblindness, it also speaks to the professional notion of procedural justice: *I don't see race; I see a case.*

Given such a framework, prosecutors have a distinct way of "seeing" the defendants they "deal" with—a view that is strikingly different from the view held by public defenders. State's attorneys view defendants in homogeneous terms—not as defendants or human beings with rights, but as cases that can be processed uniformly and judiciously. Homogenizing defendants is rooted in the overarching principle that there is equal treatment under the law—a standard that prosecutors uphold as their mission. If the system is legitimate, and laws are applied uniformly, the caliber of justice is unquestionable regardless of the informal norms that reign in the court.

Symbols of this uniformity are even embodied in how the defendants are walked from lockup into the court. Defendants are dressed in homogeneous beige jumpers—their "D-O-Cs" (for "Department of Corrections"). Some jumpers are color-coded—yellow, orange, or beige—which denotes the jail or penitentiary location. Sometimes these colors allow professionals to identify a defendant without using a name. For instance, one private attorney mocked his own client to appease the sheriffs who often served as obstacles to attorneys seeing their clients in lockup. The private attorney asked if he could talk to his client. The sheriff responded, "Which one?"

> Attorney: Just look for the guy dressed like a banana.

In this case, even his attorney did not need a name to refer to the offender. His prison jumper color-coded him like a branded object. In addition to this color code, an identification number is imprinted on the back of the defendants jumper and like livestock or slaves, this number is imprinted on the body with permanent marker, a label on the forearm that must be relentlessly scrubbed after release to reclaim your identity. This system creates a clear appearance that all defendants (at least the ones in custody) are treated the same—as one homogeneous class of offenders subject to the uniform application of the law—faceless, nameless, and branded in number, not name.

Beyond these visual cues, how do these beliefs operate in practice? Defendants are minimized, viewed as objects without human complexity. They are a case without a face. Such a bureaucratic rubric justifies and hides the racial underpinnings of dehumanization. For instance, on case files, created by prosecutors, the largest "name" is the abbreviation of the client's charge, along with an identification number. This allows for the defendant to effectively *become* a charge and that charge then is associated with the monster or mope trope.

As a sheriff explained in more detail, all defendants are assigned a number that serves as the Department of Corrections' tracking system. According to the sheriff, the Department of Corrections does not need the defendant's real name or even a Social Security number. When the defendant is arrested, fingerprints are taken and the identification number is assigned. As a result, the defendant's name and actual identity are lost. He is forever that number and the fingerprints associated with it. During this research, the Department of Corrections began using DNA as well. As a sheriff explained, laughing,

> Your actual name means nothing . . . sometimes when the police are booking and there is some long, Polish name, the police will write down a few letters and that's the guy's name.

To the sheriff, this anecdote was a funny insider trick known among officers. In fact, it showed how poor ethnic whites could also be racialized and punished for racial difference. Literally, entering the system means losing your name and identity and allowing the criminal justice system to define you by your fingerprints, an inventory number, and a charge.

With their names rendered inconsequential, defendants, in the best of circumstances, could be referred to by one letter, "D," as shorthand. In one instance, a public defender requested that her client's name be corrected on the record:

> PD: His last name is actually Fredricks. Can we correct this spelling?
> Judge: Good luck with that.

The judge wrote it down but acknowledged that the bureaucratic memory was long and unforgiving. Despite his pen updating the file, the judge's tone and a roll of the eyes undermined the request. These bureaucratic practices transformed the complexity of individuals into manageable entities—docile, racialized bodies that could be processed in the system.

Beyond the bureaucracy itself, rhetoric and language played a role in transforming defendants into objects. If a defendant was out on bond and gave a judge a reason to think he should be in custody (showing up high or drunk, for example), the judge would use the term "scooped"—a verb that sounded as though the defendant was a piece of excrement that needed to be removed. In contrast to informal language, some language was part of the formal processes of the courts. The word "shipment" was used to refer to the process of transferring defendants from the Cook County Jail to IDOC (Illinois Department of Corrections or the penitentiary). "Shipment" is another term that objectifies defendants; it is used for inanimate objects, and historically for slaves. These terms were part of the insider language that, by default, referred to the inventory-style movement and management of people of color.

By reducing defendants to numbers, professionals remove all biographical features from them so they are transformed into their criminal charges and identification numbers. Because a criminal charge denotes only your moral status as a mope or a monster, your name, marital status, employment status, familial ties, illness, addiction, and the other biographical features that humanize a person as a *person* are erased—leaving the racial tropes as the simplistic, didactic categories by which defendants are defined. One can understand that these simplistic racial tropes become efficient decision-making handles in one of the busiest felony courts in America.

Racialized rubrics and bureaucratic rubrics are reinforcing of each other. Minimizing defendants is bureaucratically efficient, appears procedurally just, and also reinforces the racialized scripts that define mopes. In moments when defendants are constructed with biographical features, as having relationships and sympathetic aspects to their personas, professionals violently resist these expressions. A group of four co-defendants was escorted single file into court to be arraigned. None was older than twenty-one. The largest defendant, with a shaved head and tattoos, cried as he walked out. He was cuffed and could not wipe the tears from his eyes. He contorted his head, to wipe his tears on the shoulder of his jail jumper.

As he entered the court, he looked at the courtroom door in the back of the gallery. A young Latina pressed against the glass of the courtroom door, holding a newborn. She held the baby up as though the glass of the courtroom door was the window of a maternity ward nursery. She and the defendant made eye contact, and the defendant wiped his eyes against his shoulder again.

The four defendants turned toward the judge for their cases to be arraigned. Discovery material passed back and forth and dates were set for hearings. On the way out of court, the same defendant turned back to the door and moved his fingers to acknowledge her in a small symbol of love. Once her partner was out of sight and in the lockup, the woman wrapped the baby, put the infant back in the carrier, and used the baby blanket to wipe her own tears. She walked to the exit shushing the baby, who was not crying; perhaps she was comforting herself instead.

Professionals saw these exchanges differently. These emotional exchanges amplified the biographical features of defendants who *should* be cases. As a result, they were met with hostile responses. While the courthouse did not allow children in courtrooms (especially during trials), individual judges had discretion as to how stringently to enforce this rule. On a different day, when a few babies were in another court, one judge jested that it was "Baby Daddy Day" and that it "disgusted her." This term highlighted a "Maury Povich" image of the broken family of color—an unwed couple connected only through their illegitimate offspring. The judge characterized these mothers as being strategic and pulling a "manipulative ploy" to play on her emotions, and she proceeded to kick the families out of the court, ceremoniously and violently. According to the rubric of uniformity, the presence of these mothers changed defendants from cases to be disposed of, or mopes to be punished, into "fathers" who had humanity. This was a type of contempt of the court.

Fairness as a Dangerous Delusion

Like blind faith in colorblindness, blind faith in bureaucracy is a dangerous delusion. The coercive tactics required of the ceremonial charade were undetectable to bureaucratic instruments like the court record. It did not take long for me to realize that the court record, the emblematic symbol of bureaucratic fairness, was a tool for manipulation—shifting power away from the defendant and to the professionals with a mere wave of a hand. The judge could quickly motion and actually stop the record, thus exerting influence on the "official" story inscribed in her courtroom and making that story the only narrative of justice—a narrative that indemnified professionals from any misconduct and fictionalized decorum above reproach.

Most obviously, I noted that menacing or intimidating looks from a judge could not be captured by a stenographer. Laughter and mocking were off limits. And despite being in the court as a clerk, I saw the record not as a source of protection that accurately documented court proceedings but as a tool of censorship that protected the mainstays of court culture and its brand of racial abuse. Such practices were ubiquitous during court call, but a public defender described how such practices extended to jury trials as well:

> Have I had a judge storm off the bench? Yes, there have been times when the judge was bullying me . . . I didn't call a witness because the judge yelled at me, and I thought, "If the judge yells at me, then the jury will see it and it will work to my advantage." And he didn't actually yell; he leaned over the bench and glared at me, so [as] not to go on the record. It was a grand jury hearing, and I don't think the case would have changed if I had called the witness, but I made a mistake not to call the witness . . . I also have a law license, and I shouldn't have backed down, but neither should I have been in that situation.

Such censorship transforms what should be a device that protects defendants into a device that actually violates their rights. Professionals literally have the power to abuse defendants and then rewrite history.

The gravity of this hit me hard. While I was conducting this research in the late 1990s, I had a friend who was a staff attorney in the Illinois Appellate Court and worked reviewing civil and criminal cases and their court transcripts. I told him tales from the trenches. The ceremonial charades. The covert coercions. The daily abuse and the street cred that I needed to maintain. I realized that he knew nothing of these norms. He only received scrawled letters written by convicted defendants trying to challenge their cases. He would go back to the transcript and find no evidence of their claims. Really, he could do nothing for them. It was at that moment that I realized my field notes were the only evidence of such abuses of due process. My ethnography assumed new meaning. As I chillingly wrote in my field notes,

I am the court record.

3

RACE IN EVERYDAY LEGAL PRACTICES

AFTER CREATING HUNDREDS OF PAGES OF FIELD NOTES documenting the culture of Cook County, I realized that defense attorneys were omnipresent in those notes. As I aligned on the side of the prosecution team and watched passively as my bosses degraded the defendants paraded through the courts, I wrote, *Where is the criminal defense?* Beyond rhetorical questions, sometimes in frustration, I mocked defense attorneys in my field notes: *Is that really the best you can do?* It gave me a bit of psychological respite.

Despite the shared blame that I could lodge against all the workgroup members, some of my greatest contempt for the culture of the courts was directed at the defense attorneys. Public defenders were fixtures in the courtroom workgroup. Some private attorneys often acted as though they would rather be on the side of the prosecution. They cowered during plea bargains. They sold out their clients with the same slurs and stereotypes that prosecutors used to denigrate mopes. Often they mocked their client's poverty and laughed at the racist jokes in the room. In my quest to find a target for my anger, I directed it to the defense attorneys because it was on their watch that these norms thrived without resistance. It was on their watch that they mocked Gideon's promise,[1] standing as ineffectual puppets that emboldened this court culture and the racism that fueled it.

When I started my ethnography as an undergraduate student, I was assigned Abraham Blumberg's classic 1967 article, "The Practice of Law as a Confidence Game," which characterized the criminal defense attorney as a co-opted courtroom player who ultimately acted as a double agent for expeditious prosecution.[2] Reading the literature only fueled my anger and justified my conclusions. What I was witnessing was worse. Defense attorneys were co-opted players for *racialized* justice, facilitating the ceremonial charade that mocked due process and degraded entire racial categories of people.

Admittedly, these were convenient conclusions, the conclusions that I came to while watching defense attorneys from the distance of the prosecutor's office and the judges' chambers. I sat side by side with many of these defense attorneys, but to maintain street cred with the prosecution and the judges, I barely said more than a polite "hello." When my bosses laughed at a public defender who could not control his or her client, I'd roll my eyes to fit in. I exchanged glances with my supervisor to show her that I had learned and understood the rules that earned me my street cred. But I admit that mocking the defense attorneys was a small act of agency. From my vantage point, these defense attorneys *deserved* it.

During one court recess, I had a contemplative moment to watch a public defender in action. I saw the public defender wait like a child outside the courtroom lockup door; he was waiting to talk to his client after the defendant's court appearance. The sheriff on duty said that the attorney could not go into the lockup because security was "tight"; there were not enough sheriffs to secure the defendants in the lockup and walk them into court as well.

It was a lie; I had just seen two sheriffs in judges' chambers eating out of the candy bowl with little urgency to get back to work. In frustration, the public defender walked away shaking his head and said he'd be back. He went to the gallery to talk with another client, who was out on bond. After ten minutes had passed, the public defender tried the lockup again, and the sheriff said that the defendant was being transported back to the Cook County Jail—a process that could not be stopped. The public defender's protests fell on deaf ears.

At that moment, seeing the public defender argue with an armed, abusive sheriff made me wonder, *What would that public defender think of my impression of defense attorneys?* If my ethnography were to (hypothetically) stand trial against a jury of defense attorneys, would they feel that I had painted their image in the service of *my* theory or their reality? The solution was to create an "inconvenience sample."[3] If I wanted to understand the role of defense attorneys in this racialized culture, I needed to do due diligence to examine their voice and suspend the assumption that their voice was interchangeable with those of prosecutors and judges. I could not depend on hearing their narrative through the filter and the oversight of other courtroom actors.

Therefore, I did the most inconvenient thing. I changed alliances and clerked for the Public Defender's Office. There, I could incorporate their counter-narratives about the field site and see, perhaps with fresh eyes, how the Cook County Courts looked from the other side of the criminal bar. It was there that I found out how you defend the "damned."[4] Not the "monsters" who mythically define the prosecutors' conception of the work of defense attorneys, but the mopes who constitute the majority of their clientele—the addicted, the poor, the mentally ill, the racialized.

Defending the "De-futurized"

Traditional accounts of defense attorneys tend to define them by their front-stage, courtroom behavior. At best, they are brokers for expeditious prosecution or "beleaguered dealers" in want of resource and training.[5] Admittedly, in earlier stories in this book, and in my early field notes, the defense attorneys appeared to be indistinguishable from their workgroup colleagues. In their open-court behavior, defense attorneys seemed to be entrenched players actively working to reproduce racialized justice in representation. Attorneys who tried to overtly advocate for their clients were often labeled as mope lovers, and some were actually called mopes—a move that created the facade of racial neutrality. These attorneys were ostracized from the workgroup, marginalized into ineffectiveness, and abused alongside the clients they were tasked with saving.

However, defense attorneys deploy a separate ideology when outside the purview of their courtroom colleagues. On my first day in the Office of the Public Defender in Cook County–Chicago, I received an orientation packet. After clerking at the prosecutor's office, I found this packet a welcome contrast to my first indoctrination into the Gang Crimes Unit of the State's Attorney's Office. In the packet was a note introducing the Public Defender's Credo— the mission that "motivates and inspires public defenders." Written by a Cook County public defender, James J. Doherty, the credo reads:

I am a Public Defender.

I am the guardian of the presumption of innocence, due process, and fair trial.

To me is entrusted the preservation of those sacred principles . . .

With every fiber of my being I will fight for my clients.

My clients are the indigent accused.

They are the lonely, the friendless . . .

My voice will be raised in their defense . . .

This will be my credo . . .

And if upon my death

There are a few lonely people who have benefited,

My efforts will not have been in vain.

Written more like a prayer than a professional mission statement, this credo articulates the moral call to be a zealous advocate for the criminally accused. The moral currency of legitimizing one's role in the criminal justice system was omnipresent. While prosecutors saw themselves as doing "God's work" on Earth, this credo conceives of defense attorneys as angel-like guardians for the isolated, voiceless, powerless, and "the lonely, the friendless."[6] It equates the role of defense attorneys to being champions of both the sacred principles of law and their clients.[7] Again, their side is identified as the sacred, while the state likely represents the profane. Would these attorneys tell the tales of racialized justice in their interviews? While they seemed at ease stating their mission, would they be candid about the racialized culture that they were fighting against?

Though their mission statement clearly articulates the principles that motivate defense attorneys, my interviews with public defenders and private attorneys showed that while they had a clear vision of the criminal justice system as abusive to their clients, they often spoke with the slippery rhetoric of colorblind racism. Among defense attorneys who viewed the system as biased or unfair, colorblind ideology left them hesitant to describe the racialized mechanisms that perpetuate it. Some respondents were reluctant to identify how individuals and courtroom colleagues reproduce racialized justice.

To ensure that the mostly white attorneys in the sample could talk candidly about race, interviews were completed by white women who had never practiced or participated in the criminal justice system in Cook County–Chicago. They were young researchers, which helped with additional candor. There was no shortage of attorneys who wanted to explain their version of justice in the court system to a young female clerk.

Likewise, gender and youth worked in interviewers' favor with attorneys speaking in a candid way about the criminal justice system—a privilege that I was starting to lose as I entered the field site older, wiser, and in my thirties. In fact, during my time in the Public Defender's Office, defense attorneys were accusatory and suspicious. They accused me of being a part of the Public Defender's Office "management,"[8] a journalist, a spy from the prosecutor's office, and a scholar who would just write another uninformed journal article that accused them of being incompetent or co-opted. Yet, even with such methodological precautions, it was with great hesitancy, caution, and maybe fear that defense attorneys revealed the racialized courts as they saw them. And, like the hallmarks of colorblind racism, there was no monolithic consensus about the role of racism and the courts.

In interviews, defense attorneys were asked, *Do you believe that defendants are treated fairly within the court regardless of their race or class background?*[9] Public defenders were nearly universal in their agreement that bias existed in the courts. They discussed obvious racial disparities and divisions in the ways prosecutors and judges treated their indigent clients. While they did not focus on outcomes and sentences, they acknowledged that in their view, race and poverty were liabilities.

Private attorneys were asked the same questions, but their answers revealed central features about colorblind racism and participants' willingness and apprehension to acknowledge racial bias. Private attorneys were mixed in their

TABLE 1. Public Defenders: Do you believe that defendants are treated fairly within the court regardless of their race or class?

		Frequency	Percent	Valid Percent	Cumulative Percent
Valid	Yes	3	11.5	12.0	12.0
	No	21	80.8	84.0	96.0
	Didn't Directly Respond	1	3.8	4.0	100.0
	Total	25	96.2	100.0	
Missing	Wasn't Asked	1	3.8		
Total		26	100.0		

TABLE 2. Private Attorneys: Do you believe that defendants are treated fairly within the court regardless of their race or class?

		Frequency	Percent	Valid Percent	Cumulative Percent
Valid	Yes	11	44.0	47.8	47.8
	No	11	44.0	47.8	95.7
	Didn't Directly Respond	1	4.0	4.3	100.0
	Total	23	92.0	100.0	
Missing	Wasn't Asked	1	4.0		
	Don't Know	1	4.0		
	Total	2	8.0		
Total		25	100.0		

answers. About half of the private defense attorneys answered that bias did exist, while about half responded that it did not.

One could look at these binary, closed-ended answers as the complete picture of defense attorneys' views on bias and racism in the court system. However, Eduardo Bonilla-Silva cautions us about the tendency to miss the ambivalence, nonracialism, and slipperiness of the rhetoric that characterizes colorblind racism. Even the public defenders' near consensus on bias does not reveal the complexity of views on the criminal justice system and the subtle nuances of racism.[10]

Because the cultural climate of what can be said about race and racism has changed in the post–civil rights era, I had to "excavate the rhetorical maze of confusing, apparently ambivalent answers to straight questions."[11] Understanding the answers of defense attorneys required weeding through the semantic moves or rhetorical strategies that reflect the cultural climate of an era of colorblindness. Their answers were sometimes contradictory, evasive, and riddled with disclaimers like—"I don't know" or "Yes . . . but." This makes some open responses unintelligible and requires a particularly careful read. From a methodological standpoint, these findings show that measuring views about race with binary choices that force respondents to "pick a side"—on whether bias does or does not occur—is simplistic and perhaps deceiving.

For attorneys who responded "yes" to defendants' being treated fairly or "I don't know" if defendants are treated fairly, their open-ended explanations for their answers illustrated that bias is nuanced, complex, and perhaps difficult to admit especially because these attorneys work in that very system. One public defender cynically explained that there was no bias because everyone was equally vilified.

> PD: Judges have equal contempt for all defendants.

In contrast, a private defense attorney expressed ambivalence after answering that she "did not know" whether defendants were treated fairly. She clarified the lack of intentionality of bias, wavering back and forth about how judges "try" to be fair, even repeating the same point about "trying" three times. Finally, she qualified her statement that despite the "effort," they were not able to achieve standards of fairness.

> PA: I don't know—as a whole, yes, judges try to do the right thing, yes; they do try, with the exception of a judge or two . . . I don't know any judge who is not trying to be fair; whether they can be is another story.

Another private attorney also focused on the "effort" to be fair while using a host of qualifiers and clarifications that bias was "not prevalent" and then saying it "depended" on the judge. The attorney acknowledged his personal experience with bias only to undermine and waver back and forth as to whether it was a few judges, one judge who had left the bench, or a remaining 10 percent that did not "try" to be fair. While the respondent answered that "yes, defendants were treated fairly," her open-ended response included an uncomfortable circular confession about judges exerting bias, but also a reluctance to point the finger at judges, as a group, for perpetuating such practices. Bias was described as a fact of "being human." In this view, because defendants are black and poor, it is enough to try; however, there is little expressed regard for the dire impact on defendants.

> PA: For the most part; most of the judges try to be fair to everyone; there was one judge [who is no longer there], I was convinced that if you had the same facts with a white defendant and a black defendant, the white defendant would get a better deal; but that's not prevalent; it depends on the judge, and I'd say 90 percent plus try to be fair [no matter, race, class, religion]; some have particular weaknesses for particular charges [like some female judges may have a difficult time with rape cases] because they are human.

The language used by defense attorneys who responded "no" to defendants' being treated fairly in the system, was often as evasive and apologetic as that of the respondents who denied such bias, and it showed the avoidance and nervousness that accompanies the incursion into the uncomfortable terrain of race talk. Defense attorneys' definitive statements about race were juxtaposed with equivocations or qualifications that lessened the sting of the accusations they were making against their white courtroom colleagues. For example:

> PA: I don't think it's on a conscious level; when I see a black defendant [versus a white defendant], they're treated differently; there was a white kid caught with 10 tabs of LSD, [and I knew they wouldn't send him to prison, and they didn't]; if he'd been black, they'd have been, "screw him."

Even when defense attorneys admitted that bias existed, some were apologetic about it, making excuses or backing off from their statements entirely. For instance, another attorney was aggressive in his initial response, challenging the researcher to "see for themselves" in the courthouse and noting the obvious disparity of black clients coming out of the lockup, which implies their inability to pay bond for freedom. The attorney even goes so far as saying that black defendants become invisible—only to end his statement by undermining the pervasiveness of this dynamic.

> PA: Go out there someday and see what you think . . . black clients come out of the bull pens. I don't think the judges even see them after a while. That isn't universal.

Another attorney used a similar rhetorical dance, describing in great detail how defendants were racially mocked, much like the previous chapters have demonstrated. He was one of the few attorneys to reference white attorneys using the bastardization of Ebonics to mimic defendants' voices, only to qualify these definitive statements with two repetitions of "I don't know."

> PA: I've been in pretrial conferences when comments are made about race . . . Stereotypical references, you hear voices being mimicked . . . In terms of being treated less fairly, I don't know . . . I don't know if they are getting an unfair deal.

What are we to make of these responses? In an era of colorblind racism, it is difficult to disentangle racial views even when one asks what seems like a yes or no question. This becomes particularly challenging when studying a sample of linguistically savvy attorneys. As compared to the non-college-educated respondents, the college-and-law-school-educated respondents express subtle, rather than blatant, racism. These skills are even more well developed among educated professionals, who are adept at the rhetorical sleight of hand necessary to navigate the precarious terrain of identifying racism in the criminal courts, let alone identify their longtime colleagues and fellow attorneys who create it.[12]

Colorblindness is operative in the deferral of blame.[13] This allows defense attorneys to discuss bias but does not require them to identify the perpetrator. Consequently, this verbal strategy shrouds the criminal justice system with a veil of legitimacy.

Yet despite this cultural climate, a large portion of the attorneys expressed their contempt of the system. Many defense attorneys were straightforward about describing the courts as bastions of racial bias. One private attorney said quite unequivocally that blacks received worse treatment regardless of social class.

> PA: Black defendants are treated worse, no matter what their vocation is.

Another private attorney stated that judges "lose the ability to see [defendants] as human beings," while another described judges as rendering defendants completely invisible.

> PA: I don't think the judges even see them after a while.

Another public defender discussed how bias was both racially and economically based:

> PD: A white defendant gets more leniency; a defendant with a private defense attorney gets a better deal. [Probe: Is this the judge? The prosecutor?] Both of them.

Beyond referencing bias in terms of plea bargain "deals," most attorneys discussed the character of justice as the place where racial bias was most identifiable. This public defender described bias as the lack of decency afforded defendants as compared to white suburbanites. She also described systemic bias from arrest to sentencing like two separate and unequal criminal justice systems:

> PD: I see obvious racial disparities in terms of basic treatment . . . manners . . . who's prosecuted and who is stopped by police in the first place . . . what they are charged with, what sentences they receive . . . it is very apparent that defendants who are white and suburban get preferential treatment.

Another public defender described the system as being both racist and classist, with prejudice being systemic. This attorney referred to the defendants' "work ethic" and possession of a job as important qualities for distinguishing the defendants who are worthy of consideration:

> PD: There is systemic racism in the system, and also economic disparity; a client who is working gets different treatment . . . Certain assumptions get made given the defendant's race.

Finally, a public defender described the finite amount of "good deals" as being distributed along racial lines, with whites getting the lion's share of probation and everyone else—poor, people of color—being incarcerated.

> PD: White people get probation; that leaves the bad deals for everyone else; and who do public defenders represent? . . . A judge can't give out good deals to everyone; if you're white, you do better; but it's also economic.

Most importantly, defense attorneys described defendants as being "de-futurized" by prosecutors and judges. As mentioned in Chapter 2, a private attorney used this term to describe how his courtroom colleagues see his clients.

> They're not seen with a future. They are de-futurized. They're just . . . "this is you, this is your destiny, you're going to be a convicted felon by the time you're 19."

Here, being a felon is part of an inevitable destiny, where the boundaries of race and criminality are blurred into a single narrative about the defendants as an underclass. Most frighteningly, those who hold this view of defendants' "destiny" have the power to make that destiny come true.

Another private attorney expanded on this notion, even detailing how poor defendants of color being stripped of their futures affected fairness in sentencing. He detailed the practices as de facto racism (rather than colorblind racism) and described how the desensitization to black defendants renders them invisible—a common theme in defense attorneys' descriptions.

> PA (laughs): You can see the white skinny kid charged with a gun crime [he gets a lighter sentence than a black kid]; you have to be superhuman not to categorize people . . . It's de facto, it's not based on the classic racism—although there are racists in the system—but there are judges who start on the bench trying to do the right thing, and they get desensitized; [it's difficult saying,] this guy is different, he has hope, if we extinguish that hope, we'll have to pay [for keeping him in jail] for the rest of his life.

Although riddled with qualifiers and the concession that to judge bias-free is to be "superhuman," this attorney highlights a predetermined perception of defendants as without a future that reproduces and justifies racialized practices. Alarmingly, despite the keen insight, the "cost" is not seen in terms of the pain and suffering of defendants nor on the consequences on their lives. The burden of the consequences is measured only in the cost (or price) to the state that maintains their incarceration.

While many of these quotes detail compelling testimonials regarding the defense attorneys' views that defendants are stripped of a future, invisible, and subject to bias because of their race and poverty, identifying the causes or sources of racism is much more difficult. The "system" is identified as biased, but few attorneys place the blame on prosecutors or judges. Many attorneys talked about bias as a feature of being human. Or, they assert, one would have to be "superhuman" not to have some bias. Other comments highlighted the "effort" made by professionals to be fair. And still others talked about racism as unconscious and unintentional. This dynamic is representative of the rhetoric of colorblind racism. There is racism in the criminal justice system, without racists.

What are the consequences of this colorblindness? Because overt condemnation of the courtroom workgroup would tacitly implicate all the actors, including defense attorneys, such deferral of blame acts as a protective defense against being complicit in the practices of the courts. If anyone is to blame, then everyone is to blame—even the defense attorneys themselves.

While there is no doubt that we must contextualize these responses in today's supposedly post-racial climate, one must also consider them in the context of the Cook County Courts. If I had not worked inside those courts, I may have underestimated the role of violence as a tool of governance, even for the attorneys who work there. It is no small incident that defense attorneys confess to being bullied by the bench. Nor can we minimize the sheriffs as the henchmen in this culture, holding disobedient defense attorneys in lockup, humiliating them in front of their colleagues, preventing them from seeing their clients by lying or creating undue barriers.

In such scenarios of abuse, fear breeds paralysis and then perhaps shame. Shame for watching and not stopping the abuse. Shame for being complicit in order to maintain street cred. And shame for protecting your psyche and not internalizing the abuse that is happening to clients. Defense attorneys discuss mythical figures in the defense bar—those defense attorneys who let down their emotional and psychological armor and then lost their lives. One private attorney warned me about a seasoned public defender who committed suicide and became a cautionary tale. The devout Catholic filled his bathroom sink with holy water and slit his wrists because the burden of defending was too much to handle. Tragically, and poignantly, his family found a prayer card for Saint Jude, the patron saint of lost causes and cases, floating in the red water.

The private attorney described his own emotional armor as being akin to an old-fashioned rolltop desk in which he can compartmentalize what he sees and then close the cover at the end of the day.

> I live my life . . . intellectually . . . and emotionally like in a roll top desk. With all those little cubicles. This goes in there, this goes in there. And, when it's time to go home, I pull that puppy down.

Practicing law in the racialized culture of the Cook County Courts requires defense attorneys to act like that rolltop desk. While there is a deep contempt of the courts and their rules of practice, there is a proficiency in the rules because that is what's required for advocacy. Perhaps the ideological discomfort among defense attorneys is clear in their answers. To be a zealous advocate in these courts, you do it carefully and covertly. You do it with the strategic precision and healthy respect that you might use if you had to "dismantle an atomic bomb."[14] To fight this racialized culture, you have to work within it. You must be versed in its logic and rules, even if it means getting your hands dirty in the process. Defense attorneys can hate the game, but they have to be players.

Besieged and Beleaguered: Defense against (and Reproducing) Racialized Justice

Defense attorneys are not just fighting a case. They are fighting a culture— a culture that holds their clients accountable on many fronts. This accountability extends beyond the formal criminal charge and into the governance of morality. Criminal representation is more than just knowing the criminal code and applying that code to cases. It requires attorneys to be versed in the cultural rules that govern and punish their clients. Accordingly, they develop a sophisticated playbook. In an "us" versus "them" culture, one has to carefully advocate for "them" while still remaining part of the "us"—the insiders who control this legal habitus and any leniency that can be attained in it. How do defense attorneys create appeals on behalf of their clients while speaking to the racialized frames that define them? And how do defense attorneys carefully construct their clients as "worthy" among a defendant population seen as "unworthy," and therefore deserving of their plight?

Defending in this culture requires an "authentic" performance and requires integrating racialized frames into one's cultural toolkit.[15] This includes participating in the mocking of defendants, especially in circumstances where defendants violate the courtroom norms that, by law, are permissible. While defense attorneys do not actively subscribe to the mope framework, they are well versed in it and are able to leverage it in representation.[16] Although they may believe that their clients are not afforded respect and decency, their strategies of representation are nonetheless instrumental to the reproduction and governance of racialized justice.

Defending by Keeping Distance:
Moral Proxies, Apologies, and Avoiding Racial Contamination

Sometimes the best thing for your clients is to *seem* like you are doing nothing for them. Even better is to make it seem as if your clients are your burdens on your back, and be a mirror for the workgroup, reflecting the contempt and disgust through which they see your client. If you reflect that back to them, you are on the right side of justice even when tasked as being on the other side of the criminal bar.

Defending a racialized population poses risks. One risk is a type of racial contamination, in which you could be constructed not just as a mope lover or sympathizer, but you could actually have the word "mope" used to describe your professional identity. To avoid such racial contamination, defense attorneys must keep their distance—a task that is a precarious dance in a system of pleas that are resolved by informal interaction with prosecutors and judges.

In contrast to public defenders, who are randomly assigned clients, private attorneys can choose their clients. They therefore have to do a considerable amount of rhetorical and cultural maneuvering just to begin to plea bargain. They must account for why they are representing their clients. This means they must "sell" their clients by "selling them out" as common, incompetent mopes. Private attorneys usually make good "excuses" part of their informal opening statements in the judge's chambers. Often they explain that a more respectable or sympathetic figure (like a mother or wife of the defendant) has asked the attorney for a "favor" or "suckered" him or her into assuming the "burden" of defending the mope. This tactic has two benefits. First, defense attorneys could begin their bargaining by situating themselves on the same side in the "us" versus "them" arrangement that defines the courts. While they are on opposite sides of the negotiation table, they are on the same cultural side as their courtroom colleagues. Second, by incorporating a more morally respectable figure in their narrative, they could create a "moral proxy" and position this person as a more sympathetic recipient of any leniency afforded the defendant. For example, in the following case, while speaking in the cultural language of the courts, the private attorney uses this rhetorical strategy—describing a defendant's mother in sympathetic, moral terms and as the true beneficiary of any deal, while minimizing her son, the defendant, as "one of those street people":

> PA: Actually, his mother took care of my mother-in-law when she was in the
> nursing home. I'm doing this as a favor to her—help her with her renegade

son. She took care of my mother-in-law so well. What can you do? . . . [The defendant is] one of those street people . . . I can't just ask for probation; he deserves more time. Basically, he's crap but I'm just asking for the best possible scenario. I'm doing the lady a favor.

In this case, the mother is painted as the racialized image of the "mammy"—the caregiver of white people who cannot take care of her own son. The caricature of the mammy is the most obedient of the controlling images. She dutifully cares for whites, often forsaking the well-being and care of her own children. Here, another black mother is painted as being unable to care for her son, and it is the white attorney who must intervene like a savior. The attorney even asks, "What can you do?" as though he knows that other white attorneys have been in this place of dutiful, moral obligation—another form of expressing the white man's burden.

This technique was used by the defense attorney representing Chris Bennett—a white mope who was racialized for his inauthentic performance of whiteness. When we met him, in Chapter 2, Bennett exhibited signs of mental illness and was being mocked by the judge with a "redneck" accent. His defense attorney began the defense by accounting for his relationship with the client.

> PA: Judge, I've represented him since he was a juvenile as a favor to his father. He's got psychological problems . . . I was fed up years ago but his mom keeps asking . . . .
> Judge: Well, his record isn't exactly clean . . . I'm having trouble with a three-time offender getting a deal.
> PA: I'm not really asking for too much. I understand where you're coming from . . . He needs a structured life where he can't go out at night . . .
> Prosecutor: Or during the day![17]

The attorney quickly vilifies the defendant to preempt any perception of sympathy, and speaks to the expectations of the prosecution. In this case, he states that the defendant "deserved" more time and that the defendant has psychological problems. In both cases, the attorney creates a sympathetic "proxy" for the defendant. They establish a family member as a morally competent and respectable figure—one who is coping with a "renegade," "out of control," or mentally ill son. The benefits of a deal are not for the mope but actually for the moral proxy in the defendant's social network.

In the Bennett case, more problematic than the rhetoric required to defend a mope is the fact that the defendant is mentally ill. Rather than pursuing a mental fitness evaluation, the defense attorney uses the categorization of mental illness as a way of acknowledging to the rest of the workgroup that he shares his fellow professionals' disdain for his stigmatized client. He even says, "I'm not asking for much" and "I understand where you're coming from" to reference that he understands he is representing a mope who is undeserving.

The case of Chris Bennett proceeded to open court. During the proceedings Bennett's mother sat in the back of the courtroom. It looked as if she was hiding. She sat away from the minority families in the gallery. The private attorney whispered the outcome of the deal to her. As the attorney gave her the news, she stared down at the floor, her lips pressed together. When the attorney finished whispering, she looked up and stared expressionless toward the front of the court, as though she were shell-shocked. As Chris Bennett came out to the open court, he stood at attention waiting to plea. The scripted reading of rights by the judge began. *Do you waive your right to a bench trial? To hear witnesses on your behalf? To have a jury? . . .*

Bennett: What was that? I don't understand.

The judge spoke louder and slower, much like a person might insensitively (and fruitlessly) scream louder at a someone who does not speak his language. The judge frowned in frustration. There was still no acknowledgment of mental fitness.

Judge: Are you LISTENING, Mr. Bennett? You have to listen to understand.

She went back to the internalized script and continued reciting. The defense attorney helped Bennett plead guilty and shortly afterward, Bennett was taken into lockup. He looked back at his mother as he was taken away. After the lockup door closed, she exited out the back of the courtroom.

The defense attorney shaved one year off the defendant's sentence by speaking the cultural language of the workgroup. He used the defendant's mental illness as "proof" that he understood the client's stigmatized status as a mope. In addition to reproducing the mope framework, the consequence was a subversion of due process rights and hustling this mentally ill defendant quickly through the system by leading him to forfeit rights that he appeared not to understand. Such a ceremonial charade allowed for efficiency, which left the defense attorney in good standing as he bargained to reduce his client's sentence by a year. While all the attorneys were complicit in this project, the judge's greatest concern was the interruption of the open-court process. After court was over for the day, the judge laughed and reflected on the Bennett case to the prosecutor and me—as though she were an actor in a play.

> Judge: I hate when someone interrupts me during a plea. I completely lose
>   track and I feel like I have to start over from the beginning.

She then got up from the bench and left a pile of files for the clerk, each one representing a defendant who had been in that court call and was being shipped to jail or prison.

Winning One for the Workgroup

In some cases, defendants are constructed as so undeserving that defense attorneys must create appeals that ignore the humanity of the defendant entirely and manipulate the workgroup's concern for the production ethic of the court. Granting a "deal" for the defendant is not a victory for the mope, the family, or the attorney, but it is in the best overall interest of the workgroup. In this next case, a defense attorney asks the prosecutor to consider a bold request—reducing the defendant's charge. Yet, to earn favor with the prosecutor, the request is coupled with the defense attorney's mocking the defendant's state of poverty—a direct appeal to the dominant frames of the workgroup's moral disdain for the failings of the defendant and a move that establishes that the defense attorney is on the same side as the prosecutor. The following informal exchange between the prosecutor (SA) and the private attorney (PA) occurred in the hallway:

> SA: Jack, I'm not reducing it . . . he's a bad kid . . .
> PA: It's not his fault, it's poverty (laughing).
> SA: Well, poverty isn't my fault so I guess I can't do much for you.

The negotiation continued as a more formal conference in the judge's chambers.

> PA: I'll start by saying that he deserves to be put away. I want to string him.
>   There's certainly no more money in this for me . . . Let's just get this over
>   with. Last time, I waited in court all day . . . I worked on that deal . . .
>   then, he [defendant] skipped out.
> SA: The guy's a bum . . .
> PA: Listen, Bob (SA), I don't care if you hang the guy . . . do whatever you want.
> Judge: I'm going to give him one extra year IDOC . . .[18]
> SA: Jack, take it, and consider it a gift.

PA: Well, he's not going to take it, and I'm going to have to go to trial . . . Don't
    punish me and make me stay . . .
Judge: 18 months and that's the best I can do.[19]

The attorney positions himself as the true victim of the defendant's moral failings because he is subjected to the burden of defending the client. By taking the victim stance, the attorney assumes a position of solidarity with and submission to the workgroup—even totally relinquishing control to the prosecutor. The language itself is racialized—sounding like a modern-day lynching with phrases like "string him," and "hang the guy . . . do whatever you want." Even the "threat" to go to trial is couched as abuse of the defense attorney—subjecting him to the "misery" of representing such a client. Such tactics allow the defense attorney to team up with the workgroup to get the "burden" off the docket—a central mission of the workgroup's production ethic. As a result, any deal would be helping the attorney and the workgroup, rather than the defendant. In the end, this strategy earned the defendant eighteen rather than twenty-four months in jail.

The Court Jester:
Comic Relief, Triage, and Saving Mama's Money

Public defenders are accountable as regular workgroup members and must learn to carefully interject their defense amid the hostile banter about their clients—the indigent accused. These defendants are the worst of the mopes; they are too poor to secure private counsel and often do not have family deemed respectable enough by the courtroom workgroup to be moral proxies. The "best" public defenders were able to posture as aligned with the workgroup rather than the defendant. One particularly savvy PD played this role quite convincingly and often won small favors for his clients and even their families. In one instance, I walked into a 402 conference (plea bargain) where three prosecutors were sitting around the judge's conference table discussing a case without a defense attorney present. The system was literally proceeding without the defense—a not-so-subtle statement on the value that the judge and prosecutors placed on the defense attorney and the little regard they had for violating ex parte communication.[20] When the public defender, David, walked in, his 402 conference was already in progress. The judge recognized the mistake:

Judge: We had so many State's Attorneys, I didn't even realize the defense
    wasn't here . . . Well, I've done conferences without either party here. But,

I have to say, David does a good job for the State's Attorneys anyway. (smiles)

PD (David): I like to bring out all the bad stuff first, then tell my side of the story . . . (laughing)

This type of humble, self-deprecating humor offset any requests that could be read as aggressive or aligning with the client and allowed the public defender to defend while keeping his distance. In contrast to the mocking of defendants in open court, which policed "us" versus "them" status arrangements, mocking and humor in the context of public defending were central to attorneys' drawing clear boundaries between public defenders and their clients. This reinforced that their legal obligation to defending their clients was not read as actual sympathy for the defendant—sympathy that could undermine their effectiveness in receiving the best deals.

Another example of this tactic was a public defender representing a twenty-five-year-old African American woman charged with retail theft. The prosecutor detailed the facts of the case for the room. The defendant was caught stealing an expensive Tommy Hilfiger jacket from the downtown Chicago Bloomingdale's. This case was heard during a ruthless, record-breaking Chicago winter when the wind and cold burned your skin within seconds. There were week-long stretches when you could actually feel the moisture inside your nostrils painfully freeze as you breathed. I linked the cold weather to the crime committed. The woman did not want a coat; she likely *needed* it. In contrast to the stream of male defendants, many female defendants charged with shoplifting stole necessity items like coats and children's clothes.

Unlike my impression, the judge had a different reaction. When the judge heard that the coat was stolen from Bloomingdale's, the very store where she herself shopped, she shook her head and pursed her lips in disapproval. Unlike the cases that she heard that plagued iconic ghettos and "other" people's neighborhoods, this case had to do with a black woman coming into her favorite neighborhood store.[21]

Judge: I shop there all the time . . . And we wonder why the price of everything is going up.

The prosecutors detailed a long history of retail theft convictions. The list went on and on. A few of the items were children's coats and other cold weather necessities.

Similar to how sheriffs acted as the judges' and prosecutors' henchmen, public defenders acted as court jesters. The public defender did not respond with information about the defendant's poverty. He did not paint her as a poor mother trying to survive the Chicago winter. Instead, he mocked her criminal record—speaking in the language of the workgroup and reiterating his membership in it. In his best Rodney Dangerfield voice, he stated:

What? I don't see anything wrong with her record. I swear, she's reforming!

On the punch line, he raised his eyebrows and inflection, tilted his head, and froze his smile for emphasis. The judge acknowledged the joke with a look and a smile at the public defender.

Judge: Okay. What exactly did she steal, again?
Mary: She stole one Tommy Hilfiger jacket.
Judge: Well, she's got good taste.
PD: Well, mitigation will be . . . it's winter and it's damn cold.

The judge's joke initiated the "go ahead" to joke more on the case. This set the cultural boundaries for the defense attorney to craft his defense. All he had to do was dance within them. Authentic sympathy or even contextual factors about the defendant being a mother in poverty were not going to win favor. Instead, he explained the actual mitigating circumstance like a comedian. He said it was "winter and it's damn cold" and framed it as a joke.

Like any great performer, this public defender knew his audience. His client was not seen as a mother with children or as a woman in poverty during a brutal winter. His client was constructed as the classic mope—a person draining the system, stealing and raising the prices for society, and for the judge in particular. This characterization is not unlike the way mopes were viewed, as burdening the criminal justice system at large—as in the case of the prosecutor who complained that she was tired of defendants "living off her back." By mocking his client's poverty, masking sympathy, and couching it in the form of a joke, the "jester" managed to shave off one year from the prosecutor's recommended sentence, thereby winning the defendant one less year away from her children.

Public Defender Triage

Some clients can be saved; others are a lost cause. Some, unknowingly, must be sacrificed for the benefit of others, and defense attorneys must recognize the difference between the two. Previous research on criminal courts called this horse trading. The precariously linked fates of two unrelated defendants and a type of triage that public defenders must utilize are illustrated by the next case. They must consider the cost of fighting for one client as a consequence to the next. A public defender presented the first defendant, Santiago, as a man who was gravely ill. The defendant had full-blown AIDS, and he had contracted tuberculosis (TB) while in jail. His T-cell count was decreasing and his condition was worsening. Upon hearing the details of the medical condition, the professionals in the room snapped looks at one another. Not only was he a mope, but his degenerate state was literally contagious—a type of racial and biological contamination.

A few professionals asked if he was being "treated" for TB—anxious about his presence and their proximity to him in court. When a defendant had a communicable disease like TB or AIDS, and it was mentioned in court, the sheriffs would mouth "SON OF A BITCH" behind the defendant as though they were screaming at the prosecutors for help. The expressions on their faces communicated horror, disgust, and repulsion at the defendant's possible contamination of the courtroom and the professionals. Sometimes the sheriffs would step away from the defendant in unison to amplify the perverse humor of a defendant dying of a disease contracted in a jail that they were tasked with managing. The sheriffs stepped away from Santiago so he could easily see their contempt of him as an untouchable being. He hung his head and adopted a posture of deep grief.

Santiago wrote a four-page note to the judge about the gravity of his condition and his remorse for his behavior. This was a common act for many defendants. With what little resources they had in jail, they would put pen to paper and attempt to express remorse to the judge. Often, the pencil on paper and the lack of education transformed a heartfelt expression of remorse into a mockery or worse, a crinkled piece of garbage that was never read but was just buried at the bottom of the file folder.

Most public defenders did not present these notes to the judge or prosecutor. But in this case, in the judge's chambers, the public defender leveraged remorse as a type of achievement by the defendant. The defendant received leniency, not as a mope but by being constructed as a man who was nearly dead. In this case, the defendant with a lengthy criminal history was going to die, and the basic acknowledgment of remorse through the testimonial of the public defender became an achieved attribute that warranted special consideration. Because of the defendant's medical condition, the judge gave the letter more reverence—looking at it, shaking his head, and throwing it down in frustration at Santiago's impending death sentence for a drug crime.

> PD: Judge, he wrote out all these letters about his behavior. It's not good . . . I'll be the first to admit it, and he admits it too . . . He just doesn't want to die in custody. He won't be alive much longer. Can you give him five years?
>
> Judge: I feel bad . . . I do . . . If I give him five years, I'll never live this down. They are going to look at my record forever and wonder, what was I thinking?
>
> PD: Thank you, Judge.
>
> Judge: Now, your next guy is going to get it.

Regardless of Santiago's sentence, he would likely die in jail. The number of years was more symbolic than substantive. Although five years was a more lenient sentence, it did not necessarily grant mercy. The defendant would still die in custody. For a man with a low T-cell count and AIDS, a five-year reduction was a victory on paper but was the equivalent of the death penalty.

In this case, humanizing a dying defendant meant dehumanizing the next mope, for retaliatory punishment. Punishment had quotas and the judge needed to make his. As an act of emotional armor, I scribbled in my notes words from a sign in the prosecutors' office, *the beatings will continue until morale improves*. I braced myself for the next defendant.

For this public defender, Santiago's deal came with consequences. As a matter of bad luck, the next defendant, Devon Hayes, was going to "get it." I noted that using the phrase "get it" sounded like an old-fashioned threat made before a disobedient child got spanked. While the judge did infantilize the defendant, this punishment would be no spanking. It would be penitentiary time.

The prosecutor began by reviewing the facts of the case for the room and mentioned the arresting officer's name. As soon as the judge heard the officer's name, he was able to describe the facts of the case without the prosecutor's help. The officer was known for street justice; he would entrap boys that he and his fellow beat officers viewed as "troublemakers" in the neighborhood. Here was the officer's "shtick": Dressed as a drunken, homeless man, he walks up to the target, takes out three marked bills to pay for drugs, and when the defendant grabs the bills, the officer arrests him on the spot. The officer uses the same marked bills in each episode and even copies the arrest report word for word. This officer had been framing dealers with this "stunt" since the judge worked as a prosecutor. The judge had memorized the report and just for fun, he recited it to the room.

Always the teacher, this judge stopped the plea bargain and talked to me about cases where officers would reproduce the same police report detailing how drugs would "fall out" of defendants' pockets as they "fled on foot"—common verbiage used by police officers. The judge commented that a certain neighborhood had an epidemic of "holy" pockets. He laughed at the fabrication of police reports like it was a novelty rather than an abuse of power. Never once did the judge try to teach me about the Fourth Amendment and whether such police practices fell within the boundaries of lawful search and seizure. The lesson merely brought me in on their "inside jokes" with police.

In this case, the "fake homeless man" trap was the lure that landed Devon Hayes in jail. Numerous drug charges riddled his record. Regardless of the record, the judge had made a commitment to seeing that the "next guy" "got it," and Devon Hayes was that *next guy*. Thus Hayes was assured of spending a significant amount of time in prison. There was little defense that could be made for him. In fact, the judge skimmed the file and realized that cash was found in Hayes's pocket during arrest. Because mopes are constructed as lazy and unemployed, any money they possess is assumed to have been acquired illicitly.

> Judge: Not only is this guy getting time, but I am taking his money.
> PD: Judge, come on . . . it's Mama's money (using the rhythm and cadence associated with his interpretation of Black English Vernacular).
> Judge: It's drug money and I'm taking it for the State.
> PD: Let me find out whose money it is. I'll ask the mother and tell her that we need to know for paperwork. Then, after I find out who it belongs to, I'll come to you with a sad story from my PD book . . .

The public defender could not save the defendant, but he tried to save his money—money that might have been part of the family's savings or cash earned from day labor that was off the books. In the Hayes case, the defendant paid the price for concessions made for the previous defendant even though the arrest report alluded to the police creating a "cookie cutter" case that the judge knew all too well as a prosecutor. The public defender could only mitigate the damage by shifting his representation to the defendant's mother—a technique similar to the private attorneys' use of a moral proxy. The public defender used humor to position himself on the side of the system, even undermining the defendant's mother by racializing her as "Mama"—an appropriated reference to the endearing term for an African American mother, spoken in the cadence of his mocking of black speech patterns. This allowed the public defender to remain an "insider" on the same team as the judge and prosecutor, who laughed and shook their heads.

The public defender still pressed the judge to consider if the money belonged to the "moral" mother rather than the defendant. Because the judge had already determined that this defendant was going to "get it," the best "defense" was to construct the defendant's mother in sympathetic terms in order to protect her assets. The public defender undermined his own position in a self-deprecating manner to openly acknowledge the transparency of his action—joking about using a "sad story from [his] PD book." This statement reinforces that his sympathy is not genuine but merely a product of his position in the system. Like the cookie cutter police reports, this play "book" was a Rolodex of sad stories that were perceived as repetitive and fabricated sob stories rather than as true narratives of urban poverty and suffering.

Open Court Performances:
Resisting the Criminal Codification of Mopes

Defense attorneys often find themselves defending and distancing in open court in front of a gallery of people—a precarious performance for both their courtroom colleagues and the public. The next case provides an example of how a public defender navigated her defense while her client was mocked in open court.

In many instances, the type of criminal charge was an a priori indication that a defendant was a mope. Typical examples are possession of a controlled substance, possession of a stolen motor vehicle, or shoplifting. In the courts these charges imply social dysfunction rather than criminal risk. Violation of probation (VOP) was the most emblematic of these charges. "VOP" refers to defendants who violate their probation on a technicality or by committing another criminal offense. Technical violations are similar to welfare infractions: failure to pay court fees, sustain employment, remain sober, or comply with reporting procedures could all get you scooped up by the police and reported to your probation officer. The defendant would then have to return to court for a hearing on whether his probation was terminated unsatisfactorily or whether he would lose his freedom and be sent to the Cook County Jail. In the view of court professionals, "VOP mopes" drain twice the resources of the system—sentenced once and now returning as if they were in a revolving door of dependency for more hearings, supervision, and even jail time. In the words of the probation officer in Chapter 2, "putting some of these guys on probation is like throwing trash in the ocean . . . it just comes back to you."

In addition to his charge, the defendant, DeShawn Johnson, made the unknowing moral violation of working and intermingling within the boundaries of the prosecutor and judge's upscale white suburb. This was especially unacceptable in the Cook County Courts because DeShawn was a hefty, tall, dark-skinned black man. Despite his size, he performed obedience and docility. He folded his large hands behind his back as though he had invisible handcuffs on his wrists. He moved slowly and deliberately, as though he had internalized that his large size and dark skin disallowed any quick moves that could be perceived by whites as hostile or dangerous.

In instances of wealthy white defendants charged with crimes like driving under the influence (DUI) or felony drug possession, living or working in the wealthy North Shore of Chicago signaled that they should be "saved" from the system. They should be tracked into rehabilitation or released to the care of their respectable family for what was seen as a private matter of addiction and illness. In a double system of justice, however, there was another route for poor people of color. Like the case with the black mother shoplifting in the judge's favorite store, a black or Latino defendant in a white neighborhood (even for a job) was met with additional contempt. Such was this case with DeShawn Johnson, a VOP defendant with dark black skin, a large stature, and a job in a white community. Such a combination was a punishable social violation.

The judge asked the defendant why he did not report to his probation officer.

> Defendant: Your Honor, my report time is when I work. I work in Winnetka, and I can't git there on time.

When the word "Winnetka"[22] came out of the defendant's mouth in the tonal dissonance of Black English, Marie, the prosecutor (SA), shot panicked dagger eyes at another prosecutor, John, who was standing at the bench. Within earshot of the defendant, Marie demanded to find out where the defendant worked—not for the case but for her personal knowledge.

> Marie (SA): John, find out where he works![23]
> John (SA): What do I care? It's not Chicago. [where he lived]
> Marie (SA): Listen to me! I said find out where he works!

The proceedings stopped (as did the official court record) as John relayed the question to the judge. The judge asked the defendant where he worked in Winnetka, and the defendant explained that he had lost his job because of probation. The reporting requirements in Cook County interfered with his employment, and the defendant was in a no-win situation. To lose his job was to violate his probation; to report to probation meant losing his job, another route to violating probation. For DeShawn, all roads led to prison or at least the Cook County Jail.

Marie laughed in relief when she heard the defendant was fired: "It figures." Others in the workgroup laughed within earshot of the defendant. Before the VOP determination, the defendant was found guilty of being a mope. Given the notion of any mope being lazy, the prosecutor verbalized that losing a job was "typical" of his kind, with no acknowledgment that probation and punishment were the causes of this job loss—a cruel endgame of sorts. The court record proceeded with the formal exchange and without any record of the social exchanges that were the focal point of the hearing. Two hearings were taking place at the same time. One hearing, for the record, documented legal facts about the defendant's possible violation of probation. The second hearing was concealed by being off the record and focused on the racial degradation of the defendant for working in a white suburb. Despite the fact that the defendant was working and exhibiting the type of moral achievement valued by the workgroup, his racial violation of working in a white community overshadowed such attributes, and in fact amplified his racial immorality. He was damned for doing what he should be doing—working.

The case proceeded to a conference in the judge's chambers, where the public defender was outnumbered. It was the public defender in a room with three prosecutors, two probation officers, and a judge. The PD began by explaining that the defendant could not report to his probation officer because the reporting time conflicted with his work schedule. While the PD talked, the probation officer mocked the defendant by pantomiming the playing of a violin for his "sad story." The judge and Marie both laughed, and then focused on their work again. Another probation officer responded to this defense.

> Probation Officer: Your Honor, he was supposed to report between 4:30 p.m.
>   and 7:00 p.m. We gave him time. He never showed up.
> John (SA): Why doesn't that surprise me?

As in open court, the prosecutor punctuated the unreliability and laziness as "typical" to the nature of a mope. The judge concentrated on the defendant's file and then turned to the prosecutors:

> Judge: John, what do you recommend?
> John (SA): I recommend that you don't ask me 'cause I think this guy is a bull
>   shitter.

Marie (SA): I agree.

Judge: I have a problem giving him IDOC.[24] He'll lose his job.

Marie (SA): Well, he's had five different ones . . . he'll get another. Maybe even one in Winnetka . . .

She positioned working in Winnetka as an achievement to be earned, as though the defendant was trying to be a doctor without a college degree. There was little consideration of the difficulties of sustaining employment while on probation in an unskilled job where the defendant had little control of his work schedule. Finally, there was the cruelty in mocking the working poor's need to have more than one job, a fixture of life among many impoverished people.

As the laughter died down, the judge gave her decision. She would wait until the gallery cleared so as to avoid the public oversight of the case, a strategic way to create a secret court with impunity:

Judge: If I give him intensive probation, he won't report . . . I'd rather see him do some County time; ten months CCDOC [jail]. He'll lose his job . . . let's do this when the court gets empty. I want this off the call.

Given the moral violations of the defendant, the public defender remained quiet until she was able to capitalize on the judge's desire to get the "problem" off the call.

PD: I have to go sell this to DeShawn [defendant]. Can we get anything in the single digits . . . Nine months? . . . He won't take it unless it's in at least the single digits . . . You want it off call, so I need to be able to sell this . . .

Judge: There isn't much of a difference in a month.

PD: There's a psychological difference with the single digits . . .

Judge: I'll give him nine months, and three weeks . . . Is that better for a psychological sell?

Like private attorneys, the public defender worked modestly to shave off time from the defendant's sentence. Because the defendant was perceived as morally unredeemable, the benefit of these small favors was positioned as a workgroup "win." In this case, the judge considered the defendant's job only because she thought the defendant might cause trouble in the court. With defendants dehumanized from a cultural and bureaucratic standpoint, the judge could not see the difference in being incarcerated for an extra month. With such a perception, the public defender had to conceal her sympathy by positioning the idea of less time as a "psychological" sell—a mental manipulation of the ignorant defendant merely to make it easy on the workgroup.

DeShawn waited and waited in the gallery, sitting obediently. He waited until it was empty of any people of color, until the only people left were the white professionals. If DeShawn had hope, he likely lost it in the two hours of watching the gallery empty one by one. Really, that waiting in the gallery is where his sentence began. Two hours of waiting on empty hope was likely torture. Torture to watch and certainly worse to live.

A Path of Resistance:
Leveraging Class Markers as a Defense

There are two paths to a defense. The previous examples represent defense attorneys "going with" the racialized frames wielded against their client. This is the path of least resistance, so to speak. But there are more rare instances where a defense attorney asserts an affirmative defense. In these cases the attorney tries to muster some redeemable moral features of the defendant's personal background, features that the workgroup will recognize as worthy of some merit. Defense attorneys affirmatively yet carefully leverage their clients' biographies in order to gain leniency from the workgroup.[25] In creating biographies for their defendants, public defenders often construct the defendants' behaviors as "better than" those of the larger underclass of defendants that is processed through the system. Any positive attribute of the defendant is benchmarked against the racialized caricature of defendants as mopes. While the individual defendant is constructed as redeemable, this tacitly reinforces the entire category of mope as an undeserving, racialized underclass because that is the normative reference group.

This tactic was pursued by a seasoned public defender representing a defendant who had two prior felonies on his record. The defendant, at nineteen, committed residential burglary and at twenty-one was convicted of possession of a controlled substance. The most salient detail of this criminal record is the charge of residential burglary. Residential burglaries are a type of charge that has racial resonance. If the defendant is black, the charge triggers historical fears and tropes about the dangerous predatory black man leaving the ghetto and invading an imagined white space. These fears are coupled with the stereotype of the black "brute," or the historical notion of the black man as a savage, animalistic fiend that would seek out a victim conceived as the most vulnerable and morally sacred—the white woman. Here, George T. Winston vividly describes this lasting trope like a horror film:

> When a knock is heard at the door [a White woman] shudders with nameless horror. The black brute is lurking in the dark, a monstrous beast, crazed with lust. His ferocity is almost demoniacal. A mad bull or tiger could scarcely be more brutal. A whole community is frenzied with horror, with the blind and furious rage for vengeance.[26]

This deep historical context situates the case. The white female judge notes that she does not like "res burgs" [residential burglaries] with little investigation as to the circumstance or descriptive features of the crime, what the defendant stole, how much, or whether any harm was caused to the homeowners. The charge alone marks and reveals the defendant as a lurking "monster" among mopes despite the defendant's having had twelve years without contact with the criminal justice system. The defendant's current charge was possession of marijuana. The conference proceeded in the judge's chambers.

> PD: Judge, this guy's not a bad guy. He's got a job. He supports a wife, and a
>   little boy. So far, he hasn't done anything in about 12 years. If he does
>   time, he'll lose his job.
> Judge: I don't like these res burgs . . . this disturbs me.
> PD: That was twelve years ago, Judge. Is there a way you can give him some
>   type of probation?
> Judge: Eric, if he goes and robs someone on my probation then who are they
>   going to blame? They'll wonder what I was thinking. Now, I have to sen-
>   tence him as a class X offender and that is IDOC.
> PD: Judge, look where he is from. He lives in the Greens and he's been good for
>   12 years. He's practically a saint.
> Judge: Sorry, Eric.

Against the moral rubric of the criminal justice professionals, even a "saint" cannot win. The public defender highlighted several elements of the client's background that addressed the assumptions that the defendant was not just another "bad guy." The PD constructed the defendant as a supportive husband and father with a dark past but a reformed future. He also constructed the defendant as employed and having avoided a felony for twelve years. He stated that the consequences of a felony conviction would mean the defendant could not work—a violation of the cultural values of hard work. In many contexts, the achievements of being employed, supporting a wife and son, and avoiding a felony are basic expectations. But this public defender compared these minimal achievements to others from the "Greens"—the most impoverished area of Chicago, a place considered one of the most notorious ghettos in the nation. Saying that he was from the "Greens" was like deploying a racial slur to denote where he lived.[27] This made him "saintly" versus others in the offender pool.

While this affirmative plea bargain leveraged the defendant's achievements and is within the cultural parameters of racialized justice, defenders are less able to gain concessions with this strategy than if they just "sell out" the client and position concessions as "rewarding" the workgroup. Ultimately, the judge considered how "others" would view her behavior. Much as the "three-strikes" laws curbed judicial discretion in a formal manner, the rigid moral rubric applied broadly to offenders limited the scope of discretion even in a case where a mope was moral. The judge was governed by an invisible "other" who would "wonder what she was thinking" if she made an exception for a mope—an example of how racialized governance disciplines both the governed and the governor.

"Playing" Prosecutor and Revealing the Defense

As an ethnographer, you are constantly balancing the appropriate amount of engagement in your field site. You want to be embedded in its culture, earn trust, but you do not want to tamper with the culture you are trying to capture. There is an abundance of studies focusing the ethnographic lens on marginalized communities in a way that sensationalizes their lives, and perhaps interferes. Some well-intentioned researchers transform their ethnographies into what sociologist Victor Rios calls "jungle book" tropes, where as in Joseph Conrad's *Heart of Darkness*, ethnographers adopt the delusion of their own racial grandeur and perceive themselves as embedded and influential.[28]

When you are studying those in power, such delusions are easier to manage. Given the "us" versus "them" dynamic in the courthouse, I was always conscious of the need to be on the "right" side of moral divides. If I had to "play prosecutor," it meant laughing at racial jokes and ignoring their abuse of defendants. Often, it meant remaining silent and obedient. Also, I realized that as a person of color, if I made eye contact too long with anyone in the public gallery, it would invite a swarm of questions and requests for help. To maintain my street cred, I had to meet these responses with hostility that would match that of a real prosecutor. It was more merciful to play prosecutor by ignoring the public gallery, the cases, the victims, and averting my eyes from the gallery.

It was actually when I stopped "playing prosecutor" by ignoring the people, cases, and files required of the ceremonial charade that I inadvertently interfered with my field site. I changed a man's fate and exposed his public defender's defensive strategy. It all happened because of my ignorance.

At the time, I actually believed that the job of the prosecutor was to read copious files and engage in a legal strategy for the many cases on the cart that I wheeled into court every morning. As a young clerk, doing participant observation, I marveled at how little the prosecutors actually interacted or engaged with the case files that they spent so much time organizing, archiving, and disposing as a bureaucratic duty. The ceremonial charade described in Chapter 2 showed how little legal engagement prosecutors exerted with the mopes that defined the docket. As the previous plea bargain examples illustrated, prosecutors merely reminded the room that the defendant was a "bum," a "liar," or a "bull shitter." There was no citation of case law and little discussion of the types of legal issues that would be worked out *if* the case went to trial. As I would find out, the defense attorneys knew this and used it to their advantage.

When I was tasked with organizing the next day's cases on the cart, I understood this task as reading the content of the files that I created. I pulled them out of enormous file cabinets, thumbed through the evidence, read the police reports, and familiarized myself with the cases that might go up for a plea bargain the next day. I envisioned clerking for a federal judge. I did not understand that the prosecutors had merely instructed me to organize and manage the bureaucracy—not engage in the law.

On one particular day, I sat in the prosecutor's office for an hour stretch and read a file that was on call for the next day. In fact, I stayed late because I was captivated by the victim, a grandmother who was nearly beaten to death by her grandson.

The defendant was a young man named Jerome Harris. He was twenty years old and charged with attempted murder. When his grandmother refused to give him money (presumably for drugs), he beat her with a bat over the head. I read the details of the arrest report and the rap sheet. I thumbed through the gruesome photographs of the elderly victim, the medical records, and the victim/witness report. The medical report detailed the grandmother's permanent hearing damage that resulted from the beating.

In addition to these standard materials, there was an updated victim statement written by the grandmother. She explained how she had parented her grandson, given him love, support, and money. The beating was how he "repaid"

her. She had had enough of the addiction and violence and wanted him prosecuted to the fullest extent of the law. The letter was dated only a few weeks earlier. In prepping this case for the next day, I made the rookie mistake of studying
the legal facts of the case while I managed the bureaucratic organization. I wrote
notes on my legal pad adjacent to the scribbles that would be my field notes.

When the Harris case came on call the next day, the PD asked for a 402 conference on his client's behalf. I was interested in how the PD's strategy would take
shape. The crime carried a sense of stigma, so leveraging class markers or positive appeals did not seem viable. Instead, the PD took on a different approach,
capitalizing on the prosecutors' lack of legal engagement in the case or, even
worse, the lack of concern for another black victim, an elderly grandmother.

The PD began the conference with sleight of hand, sounding causal and
matter-of-fact. He constructed the case as a "sensitive" issue, a family ordeal
because it involved a grandmother and grandson.

> PD: We don't know for sure the extent of the grandmother's permanent inju-
> ries or if she even wants to pursue this to the fullest extent. I talked to the
> mother, and she said the grandmother was doing better.
>
> Judge: David, what are you looking for?
>
> PD: Seven years. We don't know the grandmother's condition now.

The public defender reiterated the lack of knowledge the professionals had
of the case. Three prosecutors sat there with the first chair fingering through
the "guts" of the file—a colloquialism for the "messy" contents of the file—
contents that were too messy to engage with as a matter of habit.

I put my hands in the guts and I would get messy. In fact, I could see my
handwriting on the file inserts that organized the file. Perhaps seeing that writing pour from that file gave me a sense of ownership that I likely should have
surrendered. The prosecutors had missed the victim's permanent damage and
the victim's statement. The public defender was lying by omission and depending on the silence swinging in his favor. It almost did until I decided to plead
the case on behalf of the grandmother.

> NVC: I don't want to interrupt, but I organized the file and in the evidence
> folder, the victim made an updated report about her condition. She has
> permanent hearing loss and she also noted in the last paragraph that she
> wants him tried to the fullest extent of the law. With the permanent dam-
> age, he's got 85 percent of the sentence.[29]

I violated several norms: I spoke. I negotiated. I advocated for a black victim. I caught the public defender in a lie. I exposed my supervisors' apathy and perhaps their negligence. The resulting silence hung in the room.

The PD did not look through the file. He pursed his lips and stood there like a child caught with his hand in the cookie jar. He waited for the prosecution to catch up. The judge leaned back in his chair, put his pen down, and waited for the prosecutor, who thumbed through the file frantically. The victim report emerged and released the knot in my stomach. The judge shot eyes at the public defender for the tactic that seemed but moments away from being successful. The first-chair prosecutor asked for fifteen years in prison, more than double the prison time the public defender was seeking. The judge became incensed at the room and said exactly what I wanted to express.

> Judge: This guy beat grandma . . . but for the grace of God, she didn't die . . .
> I'm giving him 17 years. And, with the permanent physical damage, it's 85
> percent of 17 years which is 14 years, 5 months and 12 days.
> Prosecutor: Go to jail, and don't pass go.

The prosecutor looked back at his protégé, and again I found myself feigning a smile to fit into the room. Humor still punctuated the exchange and minimized the seriousness of the lives affected. In one moment, the judge went beyond the prosecutor's recommendation and added another decade to the sentence, punishing the defendant and the public defender. The judge was invigorated. It was unclear whether he was overtly punishing the public defender for trying to pull a "fast one" on his courtroom colleagues or whether he was giddy to actually be discussing the law rather than simply engaging in the common name-calling and banter that defined most plea bargains.

As an outsider, I muddied the cultural waters, accidentally exposing the rules of the space for a brief exchange where prosecutors came "prepared" with simplistic moral rubrics ready to pursue the mope rather than legal evidence to pursue the case. Always the dutiful student, I was interested in performing for the judge. Yet my arrogance cost a man a decade more of his life.

While the morally reprehensible nature of the crime and a sympathetic victim may make it seem like a clear victory, I was shocked at how emotionally hollow I felt in the aftermath. If not for me, there was no one to care about and advocate for the victim. No one to read her statement, understand her medical conditions, or bear witness to her face contorted by a baseball bat repeatedly bludgeoning her head. This case revealed the little regard that prosecutors had for black lives, and the legal cases that were literally a matter of life and death.

Likewise, the ten-year sentence that I hustled in the back room of the judge's chambers did not feel like a victory. At only twenty years old, I was the same age as the defendant. I was emboldened to play with his life like it was an undergraduate class project. What was worse was that the prosecutors responded like it was a game of Monopoly, *Go to jail, and don't pass go*. Sure, I played prosecutor for a day, but what did it win?

I learned more about the defense that day and how they had to survive in this culture. If the Cook County Court was a game of ceremonial charades, then sometimes defense attorneys needed to capitalize on the prosecutors' lack of regard for the law and the cases they managed. Was it their job to make the prosecutors pay attention to the cases? To care about victims? Did zealous advocacy all but require that defense attorneys manipulate such calculated ignorance? Once I turned to clerking for the public defender's office, I was not surprised by a public defender pursuing a motion to suppress evidence despite the Illinois law broadening the scope of search and seizure. The attorney said she was hoping the judge and prosecutor did not know the new law. She was not hoping the interpretation of the law was in her favor but that the prosecutor and judge did not *know* the law. Yes. Public defenders were fighting dirty. But they were fighting a dirty game where they did not claim to make the rules; they just had to play by them.

As for me, I realized that there was no way to do a study of these courts without getting my hands dirty or feeling dirty after the fact. I played in the guts of the file and thought about the consequences. Even the term "playing in the guts" made it sound like I was an accessory to a crime where you revel in a gory tragedy of your criminal act. At the time of this plea bargain, Jerome Harris and I were both twenty years old. While I was writing this book, Jerome Harris was languishing in a downstate prison. We are both now thirty-eight years old.

4

THERE ARE NO RACISTS HERE

Prosecutors in the Criminal Courts

Prosecution, Post-Racialism, and the "Real" Injustice in the System

A photo of a mother reenacting the murder of her baby, the image of a man arguing his innocence in a murder, and the close-up picture of a dead man's hand. My supervising prosecutor had tried these cases and then hung the artifacts on her wall. All the photos were of black subjects. Two of the photos dramatized the intense anger, fear, and uncertainty of being photographed by police officers just before arrest. The third photo was a picture of the hand of a dead man, with the body barely visible in the background. I marveled at the skill of the evidence technicians who took the shots. Each photo was vivid, saturated with color, and emotionally dramatic. While the gang unit was like a wall of corpses, these pictures were tragedies in motion, distilled to a single moment in time.[1]

Mug shots, crime scene pictures, and even post-conviction jail intake photos are strange and bitter fruits; they migrate out of case files and become the repurposed artifacts of the Cook County Courts. On the surface, these pictures are ubiquitous features of the case files that I so dutifully organized. They are assumed to serve a utilitarian purpose; the pictures verify the identity of subjects, document crime scenes and other facts of the case. The mug shot is also a type of pose. To submit to it is to "internalize the protocols of discipline; it is to agree to act like you are already a corpse."[2]

Regardless of how long I spent studying in the courts I never could acclimate to repurposing these objects as trophies, souvenirs, and conquests.

Even the file folders were fair game. Particularly disquieting was the repurposing of evidence photos. Some of the images were literally of corpses.

While the subjects of these photos are fixed, both the viewer and the displayer of the photo imbue meaning in the image—perhaps a new meaning not intended by either the photographer or the subject. To frame the photo is to heighten its importance, perhaps its artfulness, or to signify something poignant in the world of the person who displays it. It could reflect the type of person who did both the framing and the hanging. The framing and the hanging become particularly poignant when done by a supervising prosecutor and the subjects of the photos are those she prosecutes.

By discussing these artifacts with attorneys, I began to understand the complex and fractured cultural perspectives and practices in the courts, where racism reigned despite an era of colorblind niceties. In particular, in the office of a supervising prosecutor, I asked her to clarify the morally ambiguous photos that she had framed and repurposed as art on her wall.

The three framed images invited me into her office on a daily basis. Yet it took the duration of my clerkship for the owner of that office to extend a real invitation. The prosecutor was a graceful white female attorney in a big-boys' world. Her name was Jane. With a stack of files in my hands, I walked by her office. She called out for me to grab another file to give to my supervisor. As she handed me the file, she paused and said the case was interesting. I should read it. She asked me if I wanted to see what a starved baby looked like and began opening the file. Apparently, this is a common offense and there is a signature texture to their skin. I lied. *Jim already showed me on a similar case*. Because she was about to trade postcards from the edge, I decided to ask her about the postcards she had framed and hung on her office wall.

The first picture showed a black mother and a baby doll. The mother looked so young that the doll made her more child-like than adult-like and made her offense of murder all the more shocking. Jane narrated her version of the defendant's biography. She explained that the defendant had four children from four different fathers. When the defendant gave birth to her fifth child, she decided that she could not keep it. In the hospital, she cradled her baby next to her body. The body that gave the baby life slowly took it away. She smothered the newborn and it died.

This picture was snapped at the police station. Jane explained that the officers asked the mother to reenact how she had killed her child. To comply, she lay in a bare corner of a cement room that looked like a mental asylum. I wrote in my notes: *all was white behind her; her black skin and her dirty brown jacket was a stark contrast to the empty background.* The young mother's eyes pierced the lens; her pose, a silent confession. She lay on the floor in the fetal position, cradled a doll with its face pressed gently against her breasts and swollen stomach. The crime photographed more like an act of love or an expression of grief than an act of violence.

The second picture showed a black man standing against a similar white background in the police station. He was facing the camera, wearing a bright electric blue satin shirt and pants. His white socks were pulled to his knees and he was scowling at the camera.

Jane explained that the man had committed a murder in broad daylight. She laughed as she recalled that he maintained his innocence. He told the officers that many people in his neighborhood were wearing this exact electric blue outfit. According to the defendant, it could be any number of people who actually murdered the victim. To Jane, the idiocy of the story, the outlandish attire that presented as the man's Sunday best, and the scowl on his face promoted him to her wall of fame.

The last picture was focused on a cash register. The lifeless hand of a black man was lying, palm up, on the open drawer. The hand was contorted and gripping a wad of cash with bills falling and crumpling in different directions. The picture allowed the viewer to see part of the dead body—up to the shoulder. Jane explained that the man held up a convenience store and put his gun down to grab the money. The owner picked up the gun and shot the man dead in the store.

These three adjacent images are unified by their racialized features. Each image dramatized a stigmatizing racial trope. Jane's account of the mother was told like a welfare trope: a sexually insatiable Jezebel who not only had too many children but was promiscuous enough to have them with four different men. The defendant is the caricature of a "loose" "welfare mother" whose fertility is not just reckless but deviously criminal.[3] This narrative has no connection to her crime, but it is useful in understanding this defendant's character or supposed nature through the eyes of the prosecutor.

In the case of the man wearing the blue suit, he was described as the caricature of the mope and an example of normative justice—how the system *should* work. In the same manner that the judge and prosecutors mocked black names, this prosecutor used the image to mock a black aesthetic while commenting on the foolishness of the man claiming to be innocent. Because he was a liar and a fool with a moronic excuse, the picture was a comical portrayal of a mope and a monster as one and the same. His conviction was an example of the criminal justice system working as it should—truth is exposed, killers are caught, and mopes are mocked.

With regard to the picture of the dead black man's hand, cultural historian Harvey Young's work on the performance of racial violence is instructive.[4] He examines how whites used the black body as a type of lynching souvenir or keepsake after the violent act. Keeping the body parts—mutilated bone, fingers, ears—commemorates the "performance" of violence as well as the beliefs that condoned the killing. The keepsake fetishizes and dramatizes the violence long after the event is over and renders "visible" the racialized body upon which the violence was unleashed. Likewise, the act of framing and displaying this photo of a dead black man's hand places the white prosecutor as participatory in the continued dramatization of this man's death. When Jane describes this photo, she is clear that she is not paying homage to a death but instead is honoring the drama that resulted in the shooting.

On the surface, these vivid pictures act as the artistic aesthetic of the Cook County Courts. The elements are found in the Gang Crimes Unit, the bulletin board of "first wins" and even the micro-guillotine that sat on my boss's desk. However, these racialized narratives are interspersed with conflicted ideas about justice. While racialized justice and ceremonial charades are one prevailing way of doing the business of the courts, it is not the only way justice can or should be done. Jane emphasized an ability to see the human context in the situations despite racializing the photographed subjects. This was especially powerful in her account of the mother reenacting her crime. Beyond the welfare narrative, Jane explained that the law at that time required pursuing natural life or death for this young mother. She remarked that the law was intended to protect children who were brutally tortured to death. In her mind, this defendant did not deserve a death sentence. She was not the proverbial monster; rather Jane described her with the coded meanings of a mope—lazy, neglectful, and irresponsible, perhaps, but not a "true" monster. In Jane's view, the law did not account for the defendant's personal circumstances. According to Jane, justice was elusive and the law cruel and without context.

Constructing the defendant as a human being with complexity—although racialized as a caricature of the welfare mother—was a violation of the racialized rules of practice in the courts, which all but dictated that the defendant's circumstances should be eliminated from consideration. Here, commentary about substantive fairness of the law and the consideration of the defendant's humanity acted as an alternative narrative that existed alongside racialized understandings of the defendant.

In contrast, the photo of the black man's hand in the register provided another notion of justice. The prosecutor described a narrative of the justice and fairness that was a type of "deserved" vigilantism. The photo dramatized a twist on justice where the victim was vindicated by playing judge, juror, and executioner in the streets rather than the courts. Paradoxically, vigilantism undermined the prosecutor's monopoly on pursuing justice on behalf of the state and demonstrated the contradictory forms that cultural repertoires about racism and justice assume. Ironically, in other contexts, prosecutors pursued "gangbangers" for the same brand of street justice; yet, in the case of an immigrant storekeeper shooting a black man dead, it was perceived as substantively just.

Racialized justice is pervasive in practice. However, the narratives and storytelling *about* justice and fairness were highly contextual, fragmented, and even contradictory. For instance, this prosecutor can critique the "system" as unjust but simultaneously pursue her duty. She can condone street violence by framing it as victims' rights and she can bridge the monster and mope framework with a singular image that shows the system can work, especially when a monster is also a mope. It is these complex frameworks that are masterfully mobilized by prosecutors and attorneys more broadly, as they try to make sense of a system that they often describe as "unjust" but that is their burden to manage.[5]

Beyond "Bad Apples": The Culture of Racialized Justice

The narrative that attorneys told in the private spaces of their offices or outside the earshot of other courtroom actors revealed that racism in the Cook County Courts was located not only with the prosecutors, judges, and sheriffs. It was an entrenched culture—a legal habitus—and all participants owned and reproduced it, even the defense attorneys. In fact, the racialized culture of the Cook County Courts was entangled with the attorneys' understanding of justice. Perhaps these notions were cultivated in law school, but ultimately they came to be refined, renegotiated, and transformed in practice. This often left attorneys talking in complicated, even contradictory ways to help justify the decisions they made while practicing the ceremonial charade of due process.

From the previous chapters, it is easy to categorize prosecutors and judges as the perpetrators of racialized justice. They seem to be the ringleaders of an entrenched culture ruled by racial violence. Defense attorneys seem like beleaguered players merely responding out of necessity or being bullied into submission by a culture of attorneys "gone wrong." While some scholars categorize these types of practices as *failures* of justice, reflecting incompetence and complacency,[6] I argue that they are carefully erected cultural *features* of a court system—a system comprising and defined by a social arrangement of lawyers whose actions affect how justice and racism are experienced in practice. As they negotiate the meaning of race and the law, they constitute or create the experience of justice for defendants. This negotiation of meaning occurs through reflections, storytelling, creating artifacts, constructing a defense, and explaining these rationales to outsiders, like me, and even to the defendants themselves.

Here, I dispel the assumption that racialized justice is a result of individuals, "bad apples," or even a product of one's vantage point in the system. What we shall see is that prosecutors are often toggling between knowing what is *right* and doing what is *racist* while they practice law.[7]

Cultural theorists suggest that people know more culture than they actually use in any one situation.[8] They often switch between frames—perhaps in mid-debate but certainly in different contextual situations. According to Clifford Geertz (1973), culture is a type of defense against "meaninglessness" and allows potentially incoherent experiences to cohere.[9]

What is incoherent in the criminal courts? Racialized justice is disconnected from our expectations of justice or how the criminal justice system *should* work. Its practices exist within the boundaries of a myriad of due process protections, under the radar of the local bar and media, and out of the sight and mind of the general public. Racialized justice is practiced in what *should* be the sanctuary of deliberative justice with the emblem of the state over the chair of what is imagined as a regal judge in a black robe. Images and symbols of Lady Justice portray her as blind and impartial and represent the law as a type of divine moral power. Furthermore, it is assumed that criminal procedure and basic ethical boundaries are taught in law school. Even the Supreme Court blindly assumes, in its recent decision *Connick v. Thompson*, that attorneys, by virtue of graduating with a juris doctor degree and passing the bar, learn both criminal procedure and the ethical imperative to comply with procedures through law school alone.[10]

However, this normative notion of due process and ethics and the cultural scripts that inform these ideals of justice, fairness, and supposed blind impartiality is undermined by the context where attorneys practice in the margins for the marginalized. Racial divides are everywhere and are easy handles that divide "us" (attorneys) from "them" (defendants). Attorneys who practice law in the racialized terrain of the Cook County Courts must reconcile the incongruity of that dirty work in an era that is purportedly post-racial or colorblind. If attorneys work among mopes, inflict violent abuses against the people in the galleries, and wield lynching language in plea bargains in an era of racism without "racists,"[11] what are the narratives they tell themselves to make this feel justified?

Maya Angelou was quoted as saying, "When you know better, you do better." This is not always the case. Criminal justice attorneys can identify racial injustice in the system, subscribe to the principles of due process, and learn ethical standards in law school all while doing racism in the courts. As we saw in the case of Jane, she could narrate thoughtful critiques of the law and whether it provided justice or not, but practice the law in another manner entirely. She could separate her individual belief system from her doing of justice as a "duty." This disjuncture between *perspectives*, on the one hand, and *practices*, on the other, reveals the complex and often contradictory ways that racism persists in institutions, dispersed in cultural practices, rather than hiding as a few bad apples in the bunch. This also illuminates how people of color could manage, and, in fact, be leaders of a system of racism that is larger than any individual attorneys harboring racist beliefs. The courts are a social system with cultural tentacles despite the racial identity and political leaning of any one person at the helm.

Former federal prosecutor Paul Butler asks a poignant question in his book *Let's Get Free*: "Should good people be prosecutors?" This chapter broadens the scope of the question to ask, "Can good attorneys do justice *without* doing racism?" As Butler describes and we will learn in this chapter, one can be "fair-minded, concerned about economic and racial justice, and even believe that there are too many people in prison. Unfortunately, their bodies and souls are working at cross-purposes."[12] This chapter explains how such a disjuncture between perspectives and practices can occur seamlessly and therefore contribute to the institutional persistence of racism.

Racialized justice is a social and cultural arrangement that is practiced. There are cultural rules, boundaries, decorum of behavior, enforcement, and sanctions—which have been examined in the previous chapters. Yet, how attorneys *express* these rules, rather than *perform* them, is much more fragmented and contextual. Beyond the rhetoric of colorblind racism (which has been explored by scholars like Bonilla-Silva), the divide between how people express their beliefs and how they practice them is another way that new racism exhibits "slippery" features. This dynamic is the lesser investigated way that racism operates and perpetuates within the culture of institutions.

We can think about culture as what we say or express. Or, we can think about it as what we do and practice. In the case of the Cook County Courts, practices speak louder than attorneys' words. What we will see is that attorneys—from prosecutors to judges—are able to speak in sympathetic ways about justice, fairness, colorblindness, and even identify bias in the system, but these words often help rationalize the practice of racialized justice that reigns in the courts.

Like other culture more broadly, racism has staying power; it merges with life so as to be nearly invisible to those embedded in it.[13] The culture that is visible (the world of conscious belief, like the belief in due process, human rights, and equality before the law, for instance) can be seen in part because it is not completely fused with the experience of practicing law in the courts. This complexity is another way that racial disparity and racialized practices seem "invisible" to participants and previous researchers. *Real life*, in the Cook County Courts, is *real racism*. It becomes the unbending way that justice is done. By being culturally versed in frames of substantive, procedural, *and* racialized justice, professionals have a complex set of repertoires or tools to discuss and justify these real-life practices and an alternate perspective to deflect and defer blame about the system. They also have a variety of ways of locating and discussing where they believe bias lies in criminal justice.

Again, few attorneys deny that racial bias must be present in the criminal justice system at large. The stream of defendants is visibly poor people of color. However, for the attorneys, bias is in proximity to their work, but located with adjacent professionals—whether it is the other courtroom workgroup members, the police, or lawmakers criminalizing more facets of everyday lives. Like matters of race that are "everywhere but nowhere," injustice lies elsewhere—adjacent to them but not within them. Professionals are able to place the blame elsewhere by "jumping outside its boundaries, invoking another situation, another metaphor, another symbolic frame."[14] For prosecutors, problems in the system lie with the police, the defense, and even policymakers. For the defense, it is the prosecutors and, to a lesser extent, the judges that look the other way. For the collective workgroup, it is the mope who is to blame for their own failures. Taken together, racialized justice stands as a legal habitus in perfect equilibrium, with all participants shifting the blame to other participants so their own hands remain clean.

It is arduous and contradictory cultural work to keep your hands clean in the trenches and justify your post-racial identity as an attorney who is only doing his or her duty. First, we'll look at how prosecutors view and locate bias in the system. Then we'll see how defense attorneys use racialized frameworks as they craft their defense despite their expressed disdain for such rationales. As a result, all participants, as a culture, reproduce racialized justice despite holding perspectives that often run counter to such practices.

Do as I Say, Not as I Do:
Evolving Perspective and a Duty (Not an Identity)

During my time at the court, one prosecutor cynically asked me why I was studying the criminal justice system. She implied that my efforts were a waste of time. "Justice? . . . There's no justice here," she said, shaking her head and pushing the cart of cases to court. One judge ominously compared his adjudicative role to "being a conductor on a train to nowhere . . . being in a system that doesn't work." These were not the types of intimate confessions that I expected from the same prosecutors and judges who were seen abusing defendants and families in open court. These were the first cues I received that racialized justice was a complex management of culture. This cultural work was a mental armor that helped attorneys function in the belly of the beast, where they often viewed their individual perspective as separate and distinct from their duties to the system.

Prosecutors described an "evolving perspective" as essential to their job. Experienced prosecutors discussed how this prosecutorial "perspective"—their vantage point on their cases and the system—evolved with experience. Rather than just subscribing to the cultural practices of the system, prosecutors distanced their personal beliefs and perspectives as an identity separate from their courtroom duties. Such an evolution allowed prosecutors to reflect on the faults of the system and distance their actions from the practices that defined their "duty" to the state and to their courtroom colleagues. This evolved prosecutorial perspective acts like a piece of clay to fill the holes of contradictions and injustices that they witness on a daily basis. It is through this perspective that they can disperse and deflect personal responsibility for what they construct as a "duty"—a duty that all but requires rigid compliance to maintain your street cred in an insular, racialized culture.

One prosecutor reminisced about his early years in the office, when he possessed a monolithic perspective on the system, "You definitely had the feeling that you were keeping the streets safer." After a while, he said, you start to "see the other side." It is this ability to "see the other side" of justice, through the eyes of your courtroom colleagues or in the context of the broader political arena of criminal justice policies and practices, that is at the heart of this evolved outlook. Rarely did prosecutors assume the point of view of defendants or mopes, their families, or the many poor people of color who found themselves in the courts.

Judge Susan Murphy was an experienced judge, and like many of the judges in Cook County, she had been a prosecutor before being elected to the bench. When we met her in Chapter 2, she was explaining the inside joke of laughing at her impression of black names. This mockery occurred during plea bargaining, and she even admitted to me that she shared this courthouse norm with her daughters by gossiping about what she saw as the most idiotic names that came through her courtroom. Names like Uniqua, Johntae, Loveeric, and other "ghetto" or "black" names were often the butt of her jokes. This judge was fluent and complicit in the racialized practices of the court, and even took these racialized narratives outside of the court and into her North Shore home.

However, in subsequent discussions, she described her practice of law and the doing of justice in Cook County as separate from her individual "perspective." After one trial, Judge Murphy allowed me to interview her and discuss her ruling of "not guilty" in a felony drug case. She explained why a particular witness for the defense was compelling and believable. For this judge, the testimony of a black mother was compelling. I told her that the prosecution described the same witness as a "liar."

> Judge: Well, that's the prosecution's perspective. They're so used to thinking in
>   "prosecution" perspective and making strategy in that way that it became
>   ingrained. It's not surprising to hear that they disagree. Talk to the PD
>   and you'll hear a completely different story. . . .
> NVC: If it's all a socialized way of perceiving and interpreting the law, then
>   how do you remain neutral given the years you were a State's Attorney?
> Judge: In my years as a State's Attorney, I wasn't always in agreement with
>   the officers or a certain witness, but I saw it as an obligation or duty to
>   the State like the PD feels a certain obligation to protect the defendant's
>   rights. It's a duty, but for me, it wasn't necessarily a perspective.

As this judge and former prosecutor describes, an evolved perspective allows you to change "teams" or vantage points like changing hats on your head. You can do a duty, on the one hand, while holding an alternative "perspective" that more adequately describes your identity as an attorney. In this case, she even alludes to looking the other way when she disagreed with the police—an entrenched practice that will be explored later in more detail. This divorcing of perspective from practice allows attorneys to keep their hands clean in a racialized system of justice, where they sharply delineate their practice of law as separate from their perspective of law.

In their first years in the system, young prosecutors subscribe unilaterally to prosecutorial perspective as they pick teams on the right side of justice (as we saw in Chapter 2). An evolving perspective is analogous to attorneys' incorporating new repertoires or frameworks for understanding justice—adding more "tools" to the toolkit, so to speak,[15] as they learn the "game" of criminal justice. For a new prosecutor, this initial conception includes a "win-at-all costs" notion of victims' rights or putting away "monsters." It means disposing, en masse, of mopes that bombard the system. This cultural vantage point is institutionally supported through organizational incentives like promotions based on winning trials rather than "seeking justice" as the law and professional ethics dictate. Their perspectives and practices are tightly coupled or aligned.

As attorneys gain experience, their perspectives evolve and the divide between what they do in the courtroom and what they believe individually begins to widen until what they do becomes a "duty"—a type of institutional practice that they do not consciously subscribe to but nonetheless perform. "Evolving" requires a lowering of expectations of what the justice system is able to offer victims and defendants alike. It also involves accepting, ignoring, and turning a blind eye to the everyday practices required of the racialized courts. Turning a blind eye to police officers becomes a way that prosecutors embolden abuse of power by police.

As a result, practicing law in the racialized courts is accepted as a "duty," not a vocation or calling that reflects one's actual beliefs. Attorneys therefore have a clean conscience. This evolved perspective allows prosecutors, for instance, to hold a sharply critical view of the criminal justice system at large, and its capacity to provide justice for any defendant or victim.

Everyone (and No One) Is to Blame

In interviews for this study, prosecutors were asked to reflect on the criminal justice system, its shortcomings, and its capacity for reform. Their answers were strikingly reminiscent of the critiques lodged by defense attorneys. Although they contended that the system was colorblind, they were able to identify a system riddled with incompetence, lying, intense social needs of offenders, and a lack of resources to manage those needs. They could see the system as causing harm rather than mitigating it. Prosecutors agreed with defense attorneys that drug laws were overwhelmingly "draconian" in nature and that many of the low-level felony drug cases were treated as "glorified misdemeanors." If an officer did not show up, prosecutors sometimes would drop the charges entirely (Chicago Appleseed 2007). Prosecutors detailed a strong awareness of the pitfalls of addiction and mental illness gone untreated as well as a larger systemic need for education, social services, and rehabilitation. As one prosecutor explained:

> You don't find highly educated offenders, they are usually lower-income, there are breakdowns in the family. [Probe by interviewer: How would you change this in the court system?] One of the things is alternative treatment plans, which have a really good success rate, with regards to recidivism; you get them into treatment plans, early, and often, because sometimes [they need to go more than once], with job training and education; [we need] more money to go into rehabilitation and continued education.

Another prosecutor criticized the criminal justice system as a type of "factory mill" concerned with case disposition. This critique insightfully described the workgroup's efficiency paradigm that pushed attorneys to "dispose" of people as quickly as possible. Rather than referring to defendants as mopes, he discusses defendants as people with needs:

> In large part there are way too many repeat offenders, way too many of them, if we handled fewer . . . We've become a factory mill, just concerned with the disposition of the case. There is not enough consideration of if the person needs prison time or needs an extra attempt at rehabilitation.

The content of these responses sounds remarkably similar to the earlier accounts of defense attorneys. However, prosecutors have a systemic view, in which blame is cast upon larger, macro-level phenomena like the war on drugs, poverty, lack of education, familial breakdown, and lack of rehabilitative options once a person enters the criminal justice system. Their perspective examines the system from 30,000 feet and such a macro worldview distances prosecutors' complicity in the daily institutional practices that require the system to function efficiently. If the system is viewed as endemically affected by social contexts that are larger than the criminal justice system itself, there is reassurance that blame does not reside with one type of participant. Blame is seen as dispersed among all players, and even across the aisle of the workgroup.

Attorneys have a saying that "former prosecutors know that police lie, while former public defenders know that defendants lie." This "everyone is to blame" notion of the criminal justice system is the evolved perspective that allows criminal justice professionals to reflect upon and criticize the system at large and even the work they do within it. One prosecutor was asked to suggest ideas that could improve the criminal justice system and he described all attorneys as complicit in the system:

> The adequacy and competency of the defense bar (both public defenders and the private bar). You have private defense attorneys who are just in it for the money, they are not interested in their client's best interest; on the other hand, there are public defenders who have potential psychiatric issues, who are completely disorganized, or completely lazy, and they are not reprimanded . . . [Probe by interviewer: You mentioned problems with quality of prosecutors?] There's one prosecutor, a first-chair, who comes in about 5 times a month; everyone knows about it [but nothing gets done; when you have that type of behavior that's tolerated, there is space for other people to mess up or not do their job well].

Another prosecutor used the topic of prosecutorial misconduct as a springboard for shifting the discussion of professional ethics to defense attorneys. While prosecutorial misconduct is seen as rare, this prosecutor describes defense attorneys' unethical conduct as a daily occurrence:

> There is a lot of focus on the prosecution for prosecutorial misconduct. It is rare—there should be more focus on the defense counsel who are unethical on a daily basis.

Culpability is evenly dispersed on both sides. The distribution of guilt to all participants means that no type of attorney is to blame. Much like the issue of race, which is everywhere but nowhere, a view of attorneys as a source of racial bias is difficult to see. As cultural sociologists describe it, culture is like the air we breathe, "an amorphous, indescribable mist."[16] However, because prosecutors most often discuss system-wide problems (rather than the daily interactions that define justice), one must look beyond the courts to find what prosecutors view as the real bias in the criminal system—where bigotry presents as a sharp shade of blue.

Boundary Work and a Thin Blue Line of Bigotry

Many of my days in the prosecutor's office started with my supervisors corralling police officers. The cops, in plain clothes, would walk into the office with a rolled-up newspaper under their arm like they were walking into a men's bathroom rather than an office. They would ready themselves for a long wait to testify in a motion or trial. By 9:00 a.m., the office looked like a circus of cops, laughing, talking, drinking coffee, while the prosecutor served as a frantic ringleader trying to manage the chaos.

In my role as the law clerk, I was often tasked with matching officers to cases as my supervisor prepped another officer or two by her desk. This task gave officers the opportunity to transform the prosecutor's small office into a speed-dating exchange. As I asked about cases, charges, and defendants, they asked me: my name, where I went to school, whether I was a North Sider or a South Sider, and how I liked clerking for the judge. Then more questions followed. *Are you Greek? Mexican? Italian? No, Puerto Rican? Did you know a Ralphie Martorano from Portage Park? How about his brother, Paul?* This interrogation would end with the inevitable question: *Are you single, a pretty girl like you?*

While the Cook County Courts were already a boys' network, the boys in blue instantly shifted the gender dynamics in the room so that *I* was a type of suspect to be questioned. I was no longer the law clerk from Northwestern (as I was in the court), but instead, a potential new conquest to be pursued. One officer even left his number for me. After the end of court call, I returned his call only to realize that he was calling to ask me on a date rather than to inquire about the status of an upcoming trial. I responded with the type of tough-nosed, North Side, take-no-bullshit snark that was necessary for thriving with the police officers who passed through the office: "Officer, when I was born, you were already twenty years old. I think we are done here, no?" He laughed and I knew that I had earned favor with both the officers and the prosecutors. To the officers, I wasn't a snobby rich girl from Northwestern but a girl from the North Side, one who happened to get into that rich-girl school. To the prosecutors, I had followed through with what they had trained me to do, keeping the officers at arm's length, exactly as they had instructed. And even better, I did it while maintaining the tough exterior required for my street cred.

Of course, during my clerkship I learned many of the basics of practicing criminal law, plea bargaining, and the processing of case files. But there is also the kind of training that wafts in hallway whispers; prosecutors warned me to stay away from the police officers. In fact, this message was delivered to me almost like a threat. As if to say, *Listen to us and if you don't, we won't save you.*

Two prosecutors told me of a female prosecutor who became an "urban legend" among the women (and some of the more sympathetic men in the office). After working with a certain police officer on several cases, the prosecutor went on a few dates with him. When she didn't want a relationship, he stalked her and marginalized her in the office by tarnishing her reputation among other police officers and some of the good ol' boys in the prosecutor's office. My supervisors asked a rhetorical question: *How can you call the police when your stalker is the police? No one is coming for you.* I was terrified and found a new reason to keep my head down.

Intermingling with the police was to be handled carefully. In the lore of the office, police were constructed as being a brutish culture unto themselves—distinct and separate from prosecutor's work as attorneys. It took months of field notes for me to understand all the reasons why many prosecutors constructed the police as so unsavory, but a particular exchange made the dynamics more clear.

My supervisor and I were sitting in the office with two Chicago police officers regarding an upcoming case of theirs. As we have seen in previous chapters, storytelling in the trenches of justice assumes an important role for attorneys as they make sense of their work. In the Public Defender's Office, they used a packet of sugar as a prop to tell and retell the injustice of drug laws. That packet of sugar was the amount of powder cocaine that could get a poor defendant three years of their life taken away. On this day, I heard the police officers' tales of life in the trenches as they shared their worldview with a prosecutor—a story that started in the office, finished in the court, and ended just short of the word "nigger."

As the story went, the police officer was working at the station when a thirty-year-old black man came up to the desk and said: "I've done something very wrong." The man confessed to a burglary. He was high on drugs and was trying to get money to feed his addiction. When he came down off his high, he realized what he had done and walked immediately to the police station to confess.

Though I had worked months in the courts by that time, I had not heard a case with the drama of a confession and a defendant painted as making the moral choice. This story was an outlier. I walked with the prosecutors and officers to the courtroom for the start of the court call, and I asked the officer if the judge had been more lenient on the defendant because he confessed. He told me that the judge had berated the defendant in court and set a huge bond to keep him in the lockup. At my question, the officer went from friendly to terse, as though he wanted to set me straight. This quick exchange seemed to indicate that even a "moral" mope was unredeemable and deserved punishment.

Once the officers were out of earshot, the prosecutor pulled me aside. Whispering as though we were being surveilled, she told me that the judge in that case allowed a two-time white offender to get away with a reduced sentence on the same day; for the black defendant who confessed, the punishment was not just a berating and an exorbitant bond but a harsher sentence than a white defendant with a dirtier record received. This prosecutor candidly described a white-black bias in substantive justice. Two defendants, same charges, a white-black difference in outcome. The prosecutor looked around again to see if she was still out of earshot of the police officers and shook her head, as a way to punctuate her disapproval of such bias.

Her effort to distinguish herself from the police and the racial bias was made more poignant because she was the same prosecutor who had angrily instructed me to stop sympathizing with defendants; as she said at the time, "As long as there is a McDonald's 'Help Wanted' sign in the window, there's a job for them." However, in the face of blatant racism, even a mope deserved better. More importantly, such bias undermined the system that the prosecutor was tasked to uphold.

Once we were in court waiting for the judge, I organized the set book (case calendar) and made small talk with the officers to find out their view of the "confession." Now, the officers were out of earshot of the prosecutors, and I had an opportunity to understand how they viewed what the prosecutor saw as clear racial bias. I feigned ignorance and asked a question that played up my inexperience in the system.

> NVC: Wasn't that amazing how that man confessed? That's a great story. I have
> a lot of respect for him.

The cop leaned toward me a little and in hushed tones said:

> It's not often they confess—a black guy—most of them are dogs. He even had
> a good job.

Like professionals, the police applied the rubric of work ethic and the assumption that a black man would not work to the defendant, but they did so in a more blatantly racist manner. According to the officer, most black men are "dogs."[17] This one "even had a good job"—as though the expectation was that he was unemployed or working in unskilled labor. While police officers spoke in traditionally racist ways, attorneys kept their "hands clean," dancing around race with coded language that leveraged the immoral standing of the defendant and the criminal label that affirmed their conclusions. There was little concern on the part of prosecutors that the police officers who held these beliefs were the same ones handing them the cases like an assembly line of racism.

As Bonilla-Silva describes, the language of colorblindness is a "rhetorical maze" of racism without epithets.[18] The moral logics that underpin that maze are shared by both police and prosecutors. For both, black men lack a work ethic and are immoral to the point of criminal. However, the expression and practice of those beliefs differentiate prosecutors from police in ways that allow prosecutors to perceive themselves as "colorblind" and race-neutral. Identifying bias in the system (as in the prosecutor's condemning the sentencing disparity between a black defendant and a white one, or prosecutors' avoiding the police's crass war stories about a black "dog") plays an important role in affirming the moral integrity and race neutrality of prosecutors' work. It creates a boundary between the prosecutors and the police.

Prosecutors' complex array of cultural tools—that evolved perspective—allows them to collaborate with police and share a belief system about morality while distinguishing their identity as separate, colorblind, and race-neutral in comparison to the police. It is through distinguishing themselves and their beliefs as separate from police that prosecutors are able to ignore the racial bias that links them in practice, and compartmentalize when law-bending versus law-breaking is allowable or when they are better off just looking the other way.

As prosecutors reconcile their role in the Cook County Courts, their adjacency to police officers is a crucial reference point as they locate racial bias and abuse as *adjacent to them* but *not emanating from them*. Prosecutors are quite prolific at identifying police misconduct, but they admit to having a "duty" to comply with the cultural rules of the courts. In the same way that prosecutors corralled the police in the mornings, creating order out of the chaos, police represent a cultural dissonance or disruption in what *should be* race-neutral courts. The proximity of prosecutor and police creates strained dynamics between them. This tension is heightened when the prosecutors ignore their own practice of racialized justice and instead seek comfort in their evolved perspective—a perspective that is particularly attuned to deliberatively identifying injustices in the system.

Law-Bending and Law-Breaking

The fall 2014 shooting deaths of eighteen-year-old Michael Brown and twelve-year-old Tamir Rice and the strangulation death of Eric Garner created a symbolic triad. Three vivid examples—a black child, a young man, and a middle-aged father—all killed by police officers on American streets. In the cases of Brown and Garner, rather than indicting these police officers and holding them accountable through the American criminal court system, grand juries—perhaps guided by entrenched local prosecutors—dismissed the cases, erring on the side of police power. In the case of Tamir Rice, a year has passed since the boy's death, and it is still unclear whether the officers that pulled the trigger will be held criminally culpable.

Both the hesitancy and the failure to indict the officers sent a strong message: the killing of an unarmed black citizen is not a criminal act when the killer is a police officer. Despite the Supreme Court's ruling that the death penalty in a criminal sentencing is "qualitatively different" from all other types of punishment and requires extraordinary procedural safeguards, the local prosecutors in these cases pushed policing and punishment—in the form of death—to the streets. They circumvented the court system entirely.[19]

Long before these most egregious cases came to the forefront, Cook County–Chicago was known for its own brand of police brutality—not always in the form of death but instead in the form of systematic torture in an inaccessible area near the courts. A torture ring was led by Chicago police commander Jon Burge, and these practices stretched across three decades (1970s, 1980s, and early 1990s). Special prosecutors alleged that on Burge's watch, more than 120 African American men were tortured and terrorized to coerce confessions.

During Burge's trial in 2010, his victims assumed a lineup, not to be identified as suspects but to be heard as victims. One by one, they described the modern-day atrocities that they endured during torture sessions. Their testimony revealed that suspects were suffocated with plastic bags and cattle prods were used to shock their genitals.[20] Anthony Holmes was one of Burge's first victims. Arrested in 1973, Holmes was taken to a South Side police station where Burge's fellow officers hooked him up to an electrical box, forced a bag over his head, and shocked him until he confessed to a murder that he denies that he committed. As the *Chicago Tribune* reported, Holmes recalls Burge "in his ear, calling him the 'N' word and warning him, 'Don't you bite through that bag.'"[21]

While Holmes spent thirty years behind bars for a crime he was tortured into confessing, Police Commander Burge never faced criminal charges for what reads like three decades of wartime atrocities in an American city—atrocities that were widely known within poor communities around the Cook County Court but ignored by local state prosecutors. Instead, Burge was charged in the federal system with two counts of obstruction of justice and one count of perjury for lying about the torture. He was sentenced to four and a half years in a federal prison. All of his legal representation and pension costs are paid for by the citizens of Chicago, including the victims and the communities that he tortured, a type of welfare program for police.[22]

A crucial yet mostly unexamined part of this story of police brutality was the culpability of local prosecutors who proceeded with criminal cases handed to them by Burge and his officers. How much did they know about such abuses of power and violations of human rights? Given the boundaries that prosecutors create between themselves and police officers, one would predict that prosecutors are not only capable of identifying such egregious acts but also have a vested interest in keeping their hands clean.

An examination of prosecutors' closeness to the police is necessary in order to assess how prosecutors understand racism in the criminal justice system. To understand how prosecutors can identify and condemn racism in some contexts while doing racism themselves in other contexts, one must examine the shared cultural logics and structural codependencies that link and differentiate prosecutors from law enforcement, codependencies that create a dangerous foundation for abuses of power.

As Paul Butler argues, prosecutors expend significant effort fighting in favor of police power. They ask judges to "adopt pinched interpretations of the Constitution and individual rights." Prosecutors are the driving force behind the Supreme Court's approval of racial profiling, camera surveillance, police lying to suspects, and pretextual stops.[23] To put it bluntly, when police say that a defendant consented to a search and the defendant says he did not consent, it is the prosecutor's job to prove the defendant is not just lying, but *is* a liar.

While it is assumed that prosecutors are united in this cause, that assumption ignores the unspoken ways that prosecutors and police are aligned as strange bedfellows. First, as discussed in Chapter 1, criminal justice attorneys have a problem with "prestige," not among the public but within their profession. Prestige is diminished by attorneys mingling with the "human complexities" of non-lawyers. An unspoken boundary exists between prosecutors and the boys in blue. Prosecutors are attorneys with juris doctor degrees. In contrast, police officers, in some cases, have only a high school education and are adjacent to and not part of the legal profession. Given this status divide, prosecutors see officers as separate and distinct from the work they do with other legal actors. Police are accessories to the attorneys' job, but they are not part of the courtroom workgroup or their collegiality with other attorneys or the judge. Thus prosecutors can rationalize themselves as *law-abiding* while police officers are *law-bending* and in some cases *law-breaking.*

The issue of police perjury is emblematic of this point of view. Of the attorneys interviewed for this study, most believed that police perjury sometimes occurs. Not surprisingly, all twenty-four public defenders responded that perjury occurred. Twenty of twenty-seven judges said that perjury occurred, six did not directly respond, and only one said that it did not occur.[24]

Among prosecutors, the variability of their answers showed their evolved perspectives but also revealed a hesitancy to admit a practice that their courtroom colleagues widely confirmed. Twelve of twenty-seven prosecutors said that police perjury sometimes occurred, seven did not directly respond, and eight said that it did not. What was less clear from these interviews was whether the silence, on the one hand, and the denial, on the other, were due to an unwillingness to talk or to a fear of talking. It might also have indicated a flaw in the specificity of the interview question.

While those outside the Cook County Courts would undoubtedly think of lying or fabricating details of any case as perjury, the insular culture of the courts has gradations of truth that map nicely to the construct of a mope. Lying presents in shades of gray where half-truths for certain types of defendants or offenses are not socially constructed as perjury but as part (though an unsavory part) of the everyday features of cases flowing into the courts from the police.

Understanding these "shades" of truth-telling and the context and cases when prosecutors find certain grades of lying to be problematic show: (1) the boundaries created between police and prosecutors and (2) the evolved perspective of prosecutors that allows them to ignore what are seen as small breaches of the law (a signature of due process as a ceremonial charade) while recognizing and distancing themselves from the most egregious offenses. In those cases, the entrenched institutional culture of the courts, where racism is part of culturally erected features, keeps prosecutors from being able to resist the most overt and egregious acts of violence and abuse of power by police. Despite being able to identify overt abuse of power, name it, and see it, prosecutors become enmeshed in a code of silence so that they are complicit in the practices.

Perjury in Shades of Gray

Illustrative of the many grades of truth-telling endemic in the courts was attorneys' use of the word "shading." The word sounds like an artful, delicate, intentional technique used in constructing a picture—a picture of reality painted by the artist. In this case, the police were the creators and the prosecutors were the viewers. "Shading" connotes a learned technique, honed over time and developed with great skill and training. The word "shading" (rather than "lying") illuminated the cultural subtleties required for understanding perjury. It also revealed why you could not just ask a prosecutor whether perjury did or did not happen. The answer may come in the form of more questions: *Maybe? Kind of? Sometimes? In what context?*

Defense attorneys were adamant that "shading" by officers was a widespread practice. One defense attorney described it best as a systematic practice whispered in hushed tones in a loud bar over a drink or two. But the defense attorney never mentions lying; rather he uses the term "fudge," a euphemism for a practice that sounds like poking a hornet's nest:

> You talk to them [the police] in a bar and they'll admit . . . they'll swarm the
> neighborhood and make all the guys line up on a fence and they'll search all of
> them, and they can get away with that in Englewood; 80 percent of them do it,
> not huge fudges.

While words like "fudging" or "testilying" (a hybrid of "testifying" and "lying") were other euphemisms for this practice, "shading" was the most widely used to describe how officers frame information in reports or testimony to make a case more convincing and persuasive for conviction. Such practices could range from modifying the weight or height of an offender on a police report to fit a particular description to flat-out misrepresenting the way evidence was obtained. At best, these practices stacked the deck in favor of prosecutors and transformed due process from a ceremonial charade to a rigged game. At worst, they violated state and constitutional law.

While attorneys and judges developed a relative consensus about these practices occurring, there were conflicting ideas as to the frequency. According to defense attorneys, it was endemic. Many responded that more than half of narcotics cases were a result of shading. Judges, a sample that included many former prosecutors, responded with more classical colorblind rhetoric. They used evasive language and danced around the existence of racial bias in the system. They admitted that some police witnesses lie, but qualified this candid

admission by reminding interviewers that all types of witnesses have the ability
to lie. Rather than discussing the problem as an institutional practice of policing, prosecutors describe police perjury in terms of "some bad apples."

Despite these interviews that were conflicted about the prevalence of police
perjury, my ethnography revealed what some of the attorneys were withhold-
ing from outside interviewers. As we saw in Chapter 3, the judge trained me
in a genre of "cookie cutter" cases, where police would reproduce the same
police report for a parade of different defendants. Drugs would "fall out" of
defendants' pockets as they "fled on foot." For experienced attorneys, the rep-
etitious scenarios (and even language) of the "drugs falling out" of pockets and
so on was a clue to courtroom insiders that the police had likely violated lawful
search and seizure protocol. It was especially suspicious when this epidemic of
cases erupted in patterned ways and in low-income neighborhoods.

Most attorneys agreed that police perjury served one of two functions:
either to act as a code of silence to protect the police after they (or their partners) messed up or to "get the bad guys." The quest to "get the bad guys" is a
parallel cultural theme reminiscent of prosecutors' preoccupation with disposing of mopes by the most efficient means necessary. In this context, one can
think of this shared cultural logic between police and prosecutors as facilitating
an inter-institutional fast track or speed lane for mopes, where two criminal
justice adjacencies (police and prosecutors) work in concert for institutional
efficiency and to serve a larger institutional mission of disposing mopes.[25] The
police use their local knowledge to frame the kids in the community who are
deemed "bad guys"—kids who are guilty of being mopes. The prosecutors
streamline their conviction by reducing due process to the minimum legal
compliance. These small indignities seemed appropriate for charges that signaled a defendant's status as a mope—a delineation that all but guaranteed one's
need for punishment within the racialized rubric of the Cook County Courts.

Bigotry and Abuse in Shades of Blue

Despite their similarities to police officers, prosecutors are more than simply
an extension of the police officers' case-shading pipeline. Their "evolved perspective" allows them to recognize and distance themselves from what they
view as the police's capacity for overt abuse and racism. So far, we have seen
how prosecutors located racial bias as being adjacent to them rather than as
originating within them. This pattern extended to how prosecutors viewed

issues of perjury and abuse of power. For them, if perjury was a shade of gray, then bigotry and abuse were a shade of blue.

Former prosecutors were most candid. One former prosecutor describes the blurred line between law enforcement and law-breaking and elaborates on the unwillingness of management to protect rank-and-file prosecutors. Here, he reflects on what he viewed as practices that could lead to the loss of a legal license, an insight that illustrated attorneys' awareness of the professional consequences of working with many police officers:

> They lie, they cheat, they steal. It's not all, or most, but there are people I didn't trust. I'm not going to lay my license on the line for a lie.

Another prosecutor stated blatantly that all police lie and placed blame with the judges who did not intervene. As a result, some prosecutors were left with little recourse or protection if they came forward to whistle-blow such activity:

> SA: 100 percent, maybe more so now, apparently it is now acceptable and judges don't have the guts to say anything.

Despite this evolved perspective, structural codependencies between prosecutors and police exerted a strong influence. From a structural standpoint, police officers are prosecutors' star witnesses, making police officers central to the prosecutors' ability to earn the convictions that are so essential to their promotion. Paradoxically, prosecutors may be depending on witnesses—law enforcement—who may actually be breaking the law. In an environment of rigid moral divides, where morality is like picking teams, where there are good guys and bad guys, "us" and "them," and a "right" side of justice, these contradictions create cultural dissonance for prosecutors. They are standing side by side with police officers who are potentially breaking the law rather than enforcing it. In a sense, they are standing adjacent to the "monsters" that they pride themselves on putting away. These were the intense structural codependencies that held them accountable to the officers who were key to earning convictions.

Such codependencies pushed prosecutors into passive complicity. Prosecutors described a system vested in a code of silence and fear. This was not unlike the street cred that governed attorneys, who needed it in order to participate in the courtroom workgroup. From a cultural standpoint, in a space where street cred and reputation are important currencies in delineating attorneys (us) from defendants (them), police wield considerable power among attorneys. Attorneys who question the word of an officer or the legitimacy of a report could find themselves with tarnished reputations, being gossiped about as too sympathetic to defendants, being the targets of tacit resistance from officers. This is the institutional equivalent of New York officers literally turning their backs on Mayor Bill de Blasio in protest when he publicly condemned the use of force that killed Eric Garner on the streets of Staten Island.[26]

The cultural practices and structural codependencies between police and prosecutors create a dangerous dynamic. If prosecutors do not comply with the police officers' version of the truth on cases, they face cultural consequences—shunning, tarnished reputation, and the types of humiliation that keep the Cook County Courts in check. However, in addition to attacking reputational currency, police have an additional lever to bludgeon prosecutors into submission. Not only can they ruin reputations, they can ruin the prosecutors' cases—cases that are the only currency for promotion. Such leverage forces prosecutors to look the other way even when they identify injustices. Perhaps this explains how the Burge abuses could continue for three decades while most prosecutors remained silent and dutifully pursued the cases that came their way.

Imagine the cost of police officers' turning their backs on a prosecutor on a daily basis. Perhaps all officers on the prosecutor's cases started "forgetting" their appearance dates. In fact, when I was a young clerk, it did not take much time with the police for one of the officers to lean over and talk disparagingly about a judge in his own courtroom; the officer told me the judge was too lenient. Actually, he used the words "fucking liberal" to describe him.

The judge would rule critically on shaded drug cases, offering not-guilty verdicts more often than other judges in the courthouse did. I had seen one of these cases. A twenty-one-year-old defendant was charged with possession of a controlled substance. The police had a search warrant and tore up the house looking for drugs. They ultimately found the drugs in the defendant's bedroom—a room that he shared with his seventeen-year-old brother. They also found drugs in a closet in a common area of the house.

There were lots of holes in this case, the types of holes that the ceremonial charade all but required you to ignore. With two brothers in the house, sharing a room, it was unclear who knew about the drugs and who possessed them. Regardless, the police charged the twenty-one-year-old brother with felony possession. There were reasons that he was an attractive target. Unlike his brother, at twenty-one he was eligible for adult, felony court. He also had a longer criminal record, making him more vulnerable to conviction and a lengthy criminal sentence. These factors made him a good target but not necessarily the right one. In addition to the confusion between brothers, there were two closets where drugs were found. The closet in the bedroom was a shared space and highlighted the broad discretion in charging. In a shared room, how did the officers know which brother to arrest? Did it even matter to the police? Taken separately, neither closet contained a sufficient quantity of drugs to support a felony drug charge. But if the two amounts were added together, the result was sufficient for a felony charge. It was only by combining the illegal contents of the two closets that the officers were able to push the drug case to the felony courts.

Drug cases, as a general rule, were supposed to be an easy conviction. What was clear to prosecutors and the police was that this judge was making it difficult. The judge found the defendant not guilty, and when he did so, it only fueled his reputation. Two weeks later, as I managed the courtroom books, two police officers sat in the jury box waiting for their case—a highly symbolic seating placement that created the impression that the police officers had the ear of the judge. The officers did not bother to whisper in the judge's own courtroom. Instead, they gossiped out loud, within earshot of me and other prosecutors.

> Police 1: He's such a fucking liberal. We bust our ass . . . he flushes our work
> down the toilet with the crap.
> Police 2: He used to be the State's Attorney here.
> Police 1: Waste of our time.

Such gossip and rumors exert a tacit threat on the workgroup; it brazenly communicated to other attorneys the reputational costs of resisting police cases. Even the judge could be undermined in his own courtroom, among his colleagues, a tactic parallel to the ostracizing of defense attorneys for being "incompetent" mope lovers.

Even in the best of circumstances, when prosecutors are on good terms with officers, they complain that getting officers into court is a logistical nightmare. As one prosecutor described it,

> Occasionally, it's difficult to get reports and some officers don't respond to subpoenas, either because they didn't get them or they ignore them.

Given the punitive tactics used by officers, the ability to tarnish reputations, and make work life difficult, such potentially bureaucratic frustrations amplified the perceived power that the police had over prosecutors. As the prosecutor says, it is possible that officers do not get the subpoenas, but it is just as likely that they feel emboldened to ignore them.

As we saw in the officers' description of the "fucking liberal" judge, police officers view cases with territorial ownership. As the officer stated, "We bust our ass . . . he flushes our work down the toilet with the crap." This possessive ownership of cases may explain the little regard or respect extended to complying with subpoenas. Given the authority that police officers wielded, prosecutors respected and passively accepted this ownership in many ways.

To improve police compliance, prosecutors worked to build "trust" with police officers, showing the officers due respect and exhibiting the street cred to show they were on the same "team." Often trust was built by acknowledging through actions and respect that the case was the police officer's first. If the prosecutors demonstrated respect for that balance of power, the police would even pull strings to get things done for their cases.

> SA: Getting the reports is a big pain; it should take a month, but it takes six to eight in big cases; on the other hand, I've had some outstanding experiences with police officers, [who have gone out of their way] to help your case go smoother; [they'll stop by, make phone calls to the right people for you]; it's so much easier, once they trust you with their case, because it is their case first.

This deference led to the unspoken rule that questioning the honesty and consistency of police testimony or reports is a breach of both trust and respect. Such an action was met with severe hostility or consequences. As one prosecutor described,

> SA: I was on a case and spoke with the defendants who confessed and what they confessed to was different than what the police were telling me. When I approached the officer he had a problem with me questioning him.

To be viewed as "questioning" an officer did not require the prosecutors to overtly challenge a police report, as in the above case. Instead, signals of distrust could be any action by a prosecutor that was perceived to be creating a "check and balance" on police practices, power, and discretion. For example, interviewing police officers separately from their partners could be viewed as a dirty move. Such a technique, which seems to an outsider to be a thorough investigative technique to corroborate the facts of a case, could be viewed by officers as a sign of disrespect, a challenge to their integrity. For the police this was equivalent to being treated like criminal suspects who are taken into separate rooms to tease out inevitable fabrications and inconsistencies. Such a "check and balance" on ethics implied an accusation about the integrity of the officers, and therefore questioned the commitment and loyalty of the prosecutor.

To avoid sending such messages and the consequences that might result, prosecutors often stacked the cards in favor of the police, letting them confer with their partners before questioning them and allowing them to "refresh" their memory on police reports. These techniques allowed prosecutors to signal to the officers that they were on the same team and acted as a good-faith gesture that would benefit future cases. One prosecutor reflected on the pressure to engage in this symbolic exchange of good faith and membership with officers. As he describes, a culture of lying is almost an implied standard, but he only drops the cases where the lying is most apparent. Otherwise he admits to going along with the police's side.

> SA: Sometimes the Chicago police detective doesn't like to hear a negative response . . . And there's the whole culture thing that I was telling you about [police regularly bending the truth]. A couple of times, I dismissed cases when it was clear that they were lying, but I was also younger, I didn't have perspective, and I was working on their side, so I'd let them look at their police reports for ten minutes before [questioning them about a case].

Like the pressure faced by defense attorneys to participate in the abuses of the Cook County Courts, prosecutors are expected to pick sides. Morality has a rigid divide, and certain behaviors, whether as rare as dropping cases or as subtle as allowing police to study their reports, signal moral memberships. This membership translates to cultural currency with police, a currency that guarantees a working rapport for convictions—convictions that lead to promotion. In effect, picking the side of the police offers institutional rewards, and therefore perpetuates the system by creating a management team that played by these rules to get to where they are.

Prosecuting with Blinders

Despite a prosecutor's evolved perspective to identify abuse in the worst cases, police expected prosecutors to view cases with blinders on. To both "see" and "say" that abuses occur is the ultimate offense, the equivalent of a defense attorney fighting too hard for a mope and being viewed as a mope lover. Such a breach of unity could be an affront to the codependent partnership of officer and prosecutor. Just as a criminal offense is an affront not only to an individual victim but to the entire state, such an action on the part of prosecutors could be an affront to the institutional bonds that link police and prosecutors.

"Management," or the leadership in the prosecutor's office, a pool of prosecutors who likely had been promoted through this system of loyalty, enforced this codependency through stringent sanctions. Not only did management not support the attorneys who came forward, but they acted as henchmen at many levels of command, thwarting and even threatening whistle-blowers. One prosecutor described a killing hauntingly reminiscent of the shooting death of Michael Brown, or even Laquan McDonald.

> SA: A police officer killed a guy and they said he was shooting at them at the time. I could tell that didn't make much sense, but I put the blinders on. (I got conflicting stories from police officers who came in at two different times.) I told my supervisor, and he asked why I had had them come in separately (I hadn't, they just came in that way) and told me that I should have them get together and straighten it out. He got mad at me. (I went up the chain of command with the complaint, and didn't get a response.) One supervisor told me, "You're a prosecutor, not a defense attorney." One supervisor got so mad that he threw an ashtray against the wall and broke it. They wouldn't let me see Daley about it. They took the case from me and gave it to another lawyer.

Here, this prosecutor's alliances are questioned. While he is not called a "mope lover," he is accused of being on the "side" of the defense once he takes the "blinders" off. As he goes up the chain of command, he is met with ever more-violent resistance. Stage one is a question of his allegiance; stage two is a violent encounter where a supervisor throws an ashtray; stage three is emasculating him as ineffectual in the organization by taking away his case and giving it to an attorney who would cooperate. Despite an individual prosecutor's resistance, the institutional momentum will proceed with or without him. Finally, they denied this attorney the opportunity to speak to the elected state's attorney (Daley), a protective shield against elected power.

It is not surprising that few prosecutors are willing or able to fight the police or even their own management in the face of procedural and substantive injustice. As the above quote illustrates, prosecutors have the ability to "put the blinders on." This analogy is apt; it implies possessing the proper cultural tools to see injustice but ignoring, in practice, overt abuses of power. This relationship plays an important role for prosecutors. Ideological distinctions between prosecutors and police and the boundaries they express allow prosecutors to critique police practices as deplorable and shift the focus of racial bias and abuse to "non-lawyers" outside their professional sphere.

5

RETHINKING GIDEON'S ARMY

Defense Attorneys in the Criminal Courts

IN SOME COURTROOM LOCKUPS, jail bars have been replaced by the same bulletproof glass that cages the public from the court professionals in fishbowl courtrooms. Once I switched to clerking for the public defender, I noticed that entering the lockup unleashed a fury of desperation from defendants. They would rush to the bulletproof barrier, yell questions at the glass, beg to send messages to their public defender, or ask for help on excruciating matters: *The police beat me. They won't give me my meds. Tell the judge I want a 402 and TASC.* The rush of bodies and desperate faces, the struggle to be heard, the fight of the less-aggressive defendants to make it to the front of the crowd. This was the mad rush of starving people in want of human decency, leniency, answers, protection, and even basic medical treatment. The image of these people pushing toward the glass reminded me that not all lives could be saved. How would defense attorneys choose whom to save and fight for as a zealous advocate? Most important, which of the defendants would be sacrificed for another more worthy, more "respectable" defendant?

From what we've already seen, it is easy to view defense attorneys as beleaguered and besieged by the racialized culture of the courts. Unable to resist, they become complicit in their clients' abuse, despite their awareness of the racialized nature of the courts and their disdain for it. However, for defense attorneys, as for prosecutors, culture is a complex toolkit and one's perspectives can contradict one's practices. So far, we have seen how defense attorneys compartmentalize their behavior in front of their courtroom colleagues. They sell out clients in public spaces while commiserating on the dehumanizing nature of the system in private interviews or in the camaraderie of their offices. What happens when defense attorneys are left to their own devices with their clients? When they are outside the purview of the watchful gaze of their abusive court-room colleagues or the interested (and perhaps sympathetic) ear of an outsider, what rationales do they mobilize to decide who to save in the system and why that choice is just? When all the Latino and black defendants press against the bulletproof glass in desperation, how do the mostly white members of Gideon's Army decide which defendants are worthy of their constitutional right to zeal-ous advocacy?

A considerable amount of research focuses on measuring the "zealous-ness" of defense attorneys.[1] What we shall see is that defense attorneys have the capacity for zealousness, whether it is treatment-based advocacy or trial-based advocacy.[2] But these paths are largely contingent upon the perceived "worthiness" of the defendant, a perception shaped by a racialized understand-ing of the defendants. Worthiness is a function of how the defendants measure up against the racialized rubric that evaluates their morality. Defense attorneys must find the "mopes," defend them to the lowest common denominator of zealous advocacy, and dispose of them to get to the small number of defendants seen as worthy of spending their "capital" on in the court.

The Calculus of Defending

Mark was a young private attorney fresh out of law school but with enough years under his belt to complain about the system. In his practice, he repre-sented many low-income defendants for a stream of drug charges and other low-grade felonies—charges that all but defined his clients' "nature" as mopes. When I asked him to talk about zealous advocacy within the context of the criminal justice system, Mark described defending as a process of tough com-promises and low expectations. While all defendants are equal under the law, he described a careful calculus in determining the worth of the client and the amount of street cred or capital that he wanted to spend. As we have seen in earlier chapters, fighting in the Cook County Courts comes with consequences or costs.

Law professor and former public defender L. Song Richardson describes the process of sorting and deciding which cases will get more attention as a type of "triage" system, similar to that employed in a hospital emergency room. Attorneys (especially public defenders with high caseloads) must determine which cases deserve more attention. The caseloads for public defenders in Chicago are well above the national average. In 2005, for instance, the Public Defender's Office achieved resolution (on average) in 229 felonies for each public defender— well above the nationally mandated 150 felonies per year figure. These caseload standards far exceed the annual caseloads for other notoriously busy states, including Minnesota (100–120), Arizona (100–120), and even New York (150).[3]

In effect, representation is not a right, but a scarce resource, with more clients who have more legal and social needs than can be properly managed.[4] Traditionally, the notion of triage focuses on the costs of time and effort for an attorney and examines how the attorneys allocate their effort to some cases and not others. Less attention is given to another type of careful calculus, in which triage is a calculation of consequences and punishment on the attorneys themselves. This consideration of consequences is similar to the careful calculus that prosecutors employ as they consider the costs of fighting the police. The Cook County Courts as an institution can punish the *governors* (professionals) as well as the *governed* (defendants).

As we've learned, fighting too hard could have great consequences. Mark had to consider the "value" of a case, not in terms of his time management but in terms of the punitive sanctions that could be wielded against him by prosecutors and judges. This meant carefully weighing how much capital he wanted to spend. Here, he describes a host of legal maneuvers to zealously advocate for clients, but each act came with a cost, or as he says, a "price"—a word selection that sounds like fear of violence.

> PA: There are all sorts of opportunities to be throwing monkey wrenches into the process or to be especially vocal or taking a very hard line or being unwilling to budge on particular issues. What you discover, though, is that there's a price that comes with those decisions. And sometimes the price is worth it. And other times it's not. And there's only so much . . . capital you can build up to be able to play those cards when you really need to. I think you have to be able to understand in the eyes of both a judge and a prosecutor, what the value of a particular case is . . . That didn't come off very well.

Like a bank account that does not get replenished, capital or "goodwill" is finite and scarce. Placing "monkey wrenches" in the ceremonial charade has to be worth the cost of losing that capital. As Mark describes, sometimes it is worth the costs and other times it is not. Accordingly, defense attorneys must determine whether a defendant is worth the fight.

Mark continued to explain how such values get determined by using the mope construct much like a prosecutor would. He described his client roster as consisting of two types of defendants. First, he described offenders that seemed "native" to the system. In contrast, he described a tiny subset of outliers. Those outliers who are unique deserve the highest level of his obligation.

> PA: There's a routine that exists especially for those smaller level cases . . . The question . . . becomes: when do you . . . put a brake on the process and [for] what purposes? . . . What makes a difference is the particular circumstances of [the] particular people you're representing . . . especially if you're dealing with clients who haven't ever had any sort of past exposure to the criminal justice system . . . The ultimate outcome that the case can have on their lives is significantly different than [for] someone who already accumulated a half dozen felony convictions and they're just going in and out of the penitentiary. I feel a much stronger obligation. I understand that I have to fully represent the interest of both of those sorts of individuals, but I think for the individual who is facing their first felony conviction . . . I'd probably be a little less flexible to consider . . . plea bargain offers that would still create some sort of harm . . . for my client that's unique because they don't have some sort of felony background.
>
> If you compare that . . . to the person who has got several felony convictions in their background and may have the exact charge, same sets of facts . . . I might be more willing to strongly suggest someone to go along with it [the offer] because in relative terms, the outcome for them, is still significant but the magnitude is . . . a different degree . . .
>
> A judge or a prosecutor is going to recognize, if you bring it to their attention, that this is someone [first-time offender] . . . that there's a bit more at stake here. That doesn't mean that they're going to let me have whatever I want but I think they understand that this is more than just your garden variety dime-a-dozen case.

The "garden variety dime-a-dozen" cases Mark described were repeat offenders flowing in and out of the system. Like the notion of mopes that constitute the majority of the court call, he describes the majority of his clientele in parallel terms and similar to his workgroup counterparts. And there is little context about how and why these offenders circle in and out of the system. There's no mention of addiction, hyper-policing of poor neighborhoods, and inadequate reentry services. Instead Mark imports the mope construct to discuss the majority of his clientele and rationalize why he has a lesser obligation to them.

Those clients who are "unique" from the "garden variety" or ordinary defendants are worth putting the "brakes" on the system and spending precious capital with judges and prosecutors. Mark continues, explaining how he thinks about fighting for those "dime-a-dozen" defendants and the severe repercussions that could occur.

> PA: When you're into that dime a dozen, garden variety case, [if] all I'm doing is throwing a monkey wrench into . . . the bigger process . . . that's going to slow down . . . the machine that is your basic court call . . . that may create problems for me in the future in dealing with those same . . . players. If, say, the first case, of those two cases I have, is with the repeat offender and I've sort of used up too much goodwill pursuing stuff with the first guy, particularly where . . . there's really nowhere to go with the case, where the person is guilty any way you look at it. You still have to do it . . . it doesn't mean I'm looking to force someone to plead guilty the first day . . . the case gets arraigned, not investigating, not putting on valid motions but if I'm dragging things out, longer than they need to be, when it comes time for that second person [who's] never had a case, they may still be irritated with me and be less willing to listen to what I'm trying to accomplish. It's an uneasy feeling . . . because you are making trade-offs but these are the sorts of decisions you find yourself having to make as a practical matter because that's the system that exists and [it's] bigger than you.

Although he first discusses the "garden variety case," where the evidence is overwhelming and there is little legal defense he can give, he is also talking about the garden-variety defendant who is seen as native to the system; this is an offender who is not redeemable.

This triage of gauging capital or "goodwill" of the courts and the moral pricing of the defendant requires seeing your clients through the racialized lenses of the Cook County Courts, much like placing a price on slaves and gauging their worth. Each defendant had a going rate, and part of defending was knowing that value in the market of the court.

The defense attorney admits that for some, incarceration is an inevitable consequence, and he is merely fighting for a difference in time, not a difference in outcome. He is going through the motions like arraigning but not investigating, pleading but not fighting, and submitting to the trade-offs rather than fighting a system that is larger than any individual.

If everyone cannot be saved, then the sorting between the deserving and undeserving defendants becomes the nexus of representation, where the haves become the "have mores" and the "have-nots" become the horse-traded casualties of the courts. This was the fate that most defendants see. While prosecutors and judges use race to quickly sort the deserving from the undeserving, defense attorneys must see the nuances within racial categories to sort and create distinctions between defendants. Most of the defendants are poor people of color who are already familiar with the criminal justice system. Similar to the way prosecutors and judges use the performance of whiteness to distinguish a rare deserving white defendant, defense attorneys use a similar measure, beyond the criminal record, to decide whether to invest capital in a client.

Street Law and a "Lesser" Legal Consciousness

How would you break the news to a defendant that he is not getting a "true" defense? *No one is investigating your case. No, your word will not be believed over the word of the police that roughed you up. And, the witness that can verify your story, we won't call them either because it won't matter to the prosecutor.* It is like telling a man he is dying when he is already feeling the pain of death upon him. Defense attorneys often act as "ambassadors of racialized justice," despite their expressed sympathies for defendants and their disdain for being complicit in a system that abuses their clients. After a triage process governed by the racialized rubrics of the Cook County Courts, defense attorneys find themselves applying parallel racialized frameworks to this undeserving set of clients. Rather than translating the law to their clients, defending becomes an exercise of translating the racialized rules of the court, and warning, like a threat, how the judge and prosecutors will punish them through courtroom processes. Here the attorney tells defendants about retribution for exercising rights in a way that leads them to passively submit to the rules of the courts.

In Chapter 2, we saw how due process was reduced to a ceremonial charade for the undeserving. We also examined the logics and narratives that allowed such curtailing of due process to seem justifiable. Procedural justice was reduced to a performance without substance.[5] When I asked a prosecutor about whether defendants understood their rights when pleading guilty, he described a caricature of the defendant [using Ebonics]):

> They probably don't understand . . . they only listen to what matters: "what you can get . . . and what I be gettin'." Somewhere along the line they were trying to protect their rights but yea, most of it's a waste.

While prosecutors use this characterization to justify subversions of due process in general, defense attorneys appropriate a similar narrative to describe their clients' inferior legal consciousness in the criminal justice system in order to curtail and then rationalize their diminished representation.[6]

"Legal consciousness" refers to the perceptions of law that are gained through daily experience, images, and encounters with legal systems. Because defense attorneys admit that the majority of their clients are regarded as "undeserving" or compatible with the mope construct, they underestimate and undermine their clients' understanding of the legal process by characterizing it as "street law"—a term that references a type of ghetto bastardization of "real" legal knowledge. These racialized conceptions shape the type of defense that defendants receive.

Consider a seasoned public defender named Kevin. I shadowed him into the lockup conference room adjacent to the court. A defendant explained to Kevin that he was in a car with three of his friends when the police pulled them over. His friends were charged with misdemeanor theft or what the defendant called "possession of stolen property," while he was charged with a felony. The defendant was describing an accurate nuance about discretion and charging. While his friends were charged with misdemeanors, he was hit with a felony for what seemed to be the same act.

From my experience in the courts, I thought this defendant brought up an insightful observation and apparent paradox about the criminal justice system and wanted insight from his attorney. I had asked a similar question of my supervising public defender. How could four defendants in the same car be charged differently? She responded by explaining one of the rules of shading: pin the crime on the easiest target . . . the one with the worst criminal record.

In this context, I found the defendant questioning the system to be astute, and certainly asking an appropriate question of his legal counsel. However, Kevin, his public defender, had a different impression of his client's knowledge

of the law—especially given the defendant's use of the term "possession of stolen property."

> Kevin: Actually, I don't think that is a real charge. I would have to look it up to
>   be certain, but I hear defendants using the term all the time.
> NVC: Where do you think they got that idea? Of possession of stolen property?
> Kevin: I bet from TV.
> NVC: Overall, it seems like a lot of defendants know the law . . . they know to
>   ask for a 402 conference. What is your impression of your clients' under-
>   standing of the law?
> Kevin: Sometimes [they understand]. But it is "street" law. They understand it
>   on a street-level . . . they understand what a case is worth and what you
>   can get for it.

Kevin's definition is remarkably similar to the prosecutor's quip about
what defendants understand about due process and the law; as the prosecutor mocked, defendants only understand "what you can get . . . and what I be
gettin'." While Kevin left out the Ebonics, his explanation was built on the same
racialized rubrics and caricatures of defendants as the equivalent of children.
Kevin minimized his clients' legal consciousness or lived experience of the law
as "street law." In the same way that the term "ghetto" is used by whites to locate
and demean the cultural features of black and Latino' lives, "street law" is a
term that undermines the depth and complexity of understanding the law by
defendants, the majority of whom were people of color. While the white attorneys learn law in law schools, defendants are seen to have learned the law from
television and from exposure to the "streets"—a logic that assumes a criminal
history or a moral proximity to other "street people."

As Kevin continued to discuss the construction of the defendant's legal consciousness, he elaborated on this idea of learning the law on the streets. As
we will see, some defense attorneys berate defendants for talking with other
criminally accused defendants. They claim that these defendants are getting
legal advice from "criminals" and view this effort as a result of being "bored"
or having "nothing else to do" in jail. Rarely do they consider the defendants'
justified distrust of the system and perhaps the distrust of their attorneys as
true advocates of their interests.[7]

> Kevin: They all talk in the jail. They have nothing else to do. The big thing is to
>   go to the law library. It's a real prestige thing. They get to go once a week
>   and if they want to go more than that, they need special permission.

Within the mope construct, defendants' educating themselves in the law library is viewed as a charade or a game rather than a concerted effort to advocate on one's own behalf; it is analogous to a small child pretending to read. Defendants find themselves in a racialized trap with their own advocates. They are judged for knowing "street law," but when they try to engage as educated equals with the attorneys (by going to the law library, for instance), they are stigmatized or seen as posturing for status within the jail and among "criminals."

The assumption that defendants did not understand the proceedings created a communication barrier between defense attorneys and their clients, a barrier that resulted in defense attorneys not understanding the client's request or ignoring it entirely. In another case, Kevin was representing a defendant named Tyrell, who was charged with theft. Kevin did not start the meeting by talking about the case, questioning the defendant about the police report or other relevant details. Instead, he began by asking the defendant how he wanted to end or resolve the case.

> Kevin: You going to trial on this? Or bargain it? Do you know what you are
> going to do? If you want to go to trial, you can. It's your right.

Tyrell responded by starting from the beginning and reviewing the facts of the case, as he experienced them, as if to take the reins of his defense. As Tyrell explained, he purchased groceries at a Jewel[8] and then went to see his friend who worked as a butcher at another Jewel location. Kevin asked: "What's his name?" The defendant paused and said, "We call him 'Preacher.'" Kevin asked, "What congregation?" Tyrell snapped as though the question was irrelevant, "No congregation. We just call him dat." Kevin stopped writing and the pen slowed in his hand at the mention of a witness with a neighborhood nickname.

Many times defendants had witnesses to their offense or arrest, witnesses named Pookie, Duchess, or Tio, to name a few. These were not their birth names or the names on their identification cards, but they were neighborhood names that identified people, denoting a belonging to the community, and often signaling the qualities or traits of that person. "Tio," for instance, was a term of respect and reverence for an elder, a trusted figure who earned respect—even if he was not your actual uncle. In a sense, he was "everyone's" *tio* (or uncle) in La Villita.

I knew about these nicknames because I earned one in my old neighborhood. When the police broke up a party and started throwing glass beer bottles around the floor to scare everyone, two close friends said, "Get 'Ivy League' out the back." This name spoke to my stature in the community as the one kid who, in their eyes, had a future to lose. It was a name of reverence and respect for the local girl who was getting out. While Northwestern University was not in the Ivy League, the name was not an error. The inaccuracies were intended to mock me and keep me humble. But certainly the name anointed me with respect and denoted to others (especially men) that I should be protected and not pursued.

I stayed silent as I realized that Kevin, the public defender, was missing the details of the case. He was dismissing Preacher as a mope, rather than seeing him as a witness. Beyond that, Preacher's name denoted a type of earned credibility in the community—features that may have made him a reliable witness *if* the public defender could have seen him as a witness. Certainly "Preacher" was a name bestowed on a person with stature and wisdom, someone who was assumed to be on moral high ground among his peers.

Once Kevin stopped writing, the conference ended. It was clear to me that he was not going to call this witness unless Tyrell called the Preacher by a name deemed credible within the court community, presumably a white name that would not be mocked. I leaned over to see Kevin's notes and I saw nothing written there about the existence of a witness. Like the court record that was selectively turned on and off, Tyrell did not have any record of the competency of his attorney and his effort on his case.

With Kevin leaning back in the chair as though he was waiting to leave the lockup, Tyrell persisted with his story, trying to highlight the circumstances of his arrest. Tyrell admitted to having a Jewel bag of steaks in his hand, but did not think to keep his receipt when he entered the other Jewel. Without a receipt, he was stopped at the exit by the store security guard. Preacher tried to verify that his friend did not steal the steaks. He used his employment as a butcher as a way to verify his allegiance to the store. Regardless of their attempt, Tyrell was charged with a felony.

The defendant insisted on his innocence and vented about the absurdity that allegedly stealing steaks would leave him with a felony charge. After the long story of the defendant's innocence, Kevin responded with a single six-word question that summarized how he viewed the case:

Kevin: So, you want to plea this?

The question hung in the air as though the attorney had not heard the defendant's narrative of his innocence.

Defendant: No, I want a conference.

At first it appeared that the defendant did not understand what a plea bargain was. However, this is another example of how attorneys' preconceived notions of defendants as mopes cloud their ability to identify and respond to their clients' requests. In the same way the public defender dismissed a potentially viable (even credible) witness for having a name that sounded like a mope's name, the public defender was missing the subtlety between *pleading guilty* and *requesting a conference*.

A "conference" (also called a 402) is really the first step in pleading guilty. The conference puts an "offer" on the table and allows the defendant to hear the possible sentence that could be imposed. It is like asking for the price before purchasing an item in a store. A defendant can then decide, theoretically, whether to accept or reject the plea. Without a conference, a defendant cannot make an informed decision. The defendant was picking up on the nuance of the law that came from his perspective as a defendant—the recipient of the deal.

Kevin, conversely, was pushing for a plea—meaning a plea of guilty in exchange for a lesser charge. The defendant wanted a conference—where the judge would tell the defendant (through his attorney) the sentence he could expect. In the defendant's view, it was not about pleading and admitting guilt. It was about doing the cost-benefit analysis, which is something like this: *If I plead (even though I am not guilty), then I will get a particular sentence. What is my innocence worth?*

He wanted to know the practical consequences of his options—testing the waters before he made any move. The defendant's view was about minimizing his jail time—not about admitting or acknowledging guilt. It was about submitting to the ceremonial charade while maintaining your personal innocence.

This exchange between Tyrell and his public defender demonstrates how the mope construct informs and clouds the criminal defense, disrupting how the defense attorneys hear the requests of their clients. As a result, defense attorneys disengage in the case, ignore crucial evidence or witnesses, or misunderstand the instructions of the clients. Because the mope construct assumes a type of racialized ignorance, the blame for these representation missteps is placed back on the shoulders of the defendants themselves.

The Racialized Radar for Hustle

With defendants seen as mopes, their attempt to engage in a case was read either as ignorance or as a hustle for prestige. It was never seen as a defendant's attempt at self-preservation. For attorneys, ignorance was something that could be "controlled." This was an expectation of their job in the workgroup, controlling clients out of the ceremonial charade, as we saw in Chapter 2. Ignorance was passive and more manageable for attorneys. But hustling—that could be a ticking time bomb in the flow of the court.

Defense attorneys had a radar for "hustle"—perceiving the client to be one moment away from bullshitting them with the wrong information or an outright lie like they learned on the streets.[9] Again, implicit in this definition is a stigmatized notion of communities of color being inherently from the "streets"—without family, morality, or community, except the "ghetto" elements that were sources of supposed cultural dysfunction. This radar for hustle was so central to the worldview of defense attorneys that public defenders even included "tips" on managing such street hustle in their training manual for new law clerks. The manual, titled "Making Sense of 26th Street: A Guide for Law Clerks of the Cook County Public Defender," warned new law clerks about the nature of defendants. It told clerks, "Do not be naive . . . Do not encourage their flirting or other BS they may try to pull on you."[10]

This was an institutional warning about the cultural nature of their indigent clients, most of them black or brown. As someone who battled the sexual advances of law enforcement in the prosecutor's office and even a sheriff who would come to my courtrooms on his lunch breaks to watch me work, I found such warnings to be paradoxical. Here, those tasked with enforcing the law were the ones creating the harassment in the offices. Conversely, those charged with breaking the law—pretrial detainees languishing in the Cook County Jail—were too desperate to be hitting on me like the police officers and sheriffs did. When defendants rushed to the glass in the courtroom lockup, or yelled for me, it was not to ask me on a date or sexually harass me. It was to beg for answers. To get help. To relay a message to a loved one. To ask for their attorney or figure out who she or he *was*. Despite what I read in the manual, I realized that a desperate man who is fighting for his freedom is not going to waste time harassing you. You can bet he's going to beg for help or be incensed at not receiving any.

Regardless, thwarting the threat of a hustle was the assumed "frame of mind" of mopes and was certainly viewed as a product of "street life."

> Kevin: Sometimes they try not to let you know what their record is. Sometimes they don't want you to know. It may be they are so caught in that frame of mind . . . the hustling, that they lie.

Kevin never considers that defendants may not understand their former convictions, especially if they received felony probation. At times, defendants perceived prison or jail as the true conviction and interpreted the relative freedom of probation as a second chance. Instead, the notion of hustle became a predominant explanation for defendants' actions.

With defendants viewed as only one moment away from a hustle, what actions fell into that category? It could be any move on the defendant's part that could compromise the attorney's insider status within the workgroup. Like deciding not to plead guilty, exercising due process rights, speaking in court, talking to other inmates about their circumstances, comparing their deal with other "going rates" in the courtroom, or concealing (intentionally or not) a criminal record.

For offenders seen as undeserving whom defense attorneys admitted to neglecting or at least not providing their full obligation, this hustling could have been read in an alternative manner: acts of self-preservation. These "defiant" acts are defendants' attempts to help themselves in a system that symbolically, and substantively, appears to be in a vast conspiracy against them—a system in which their only advocate is actively part of the due process charade.

This preconceived view of the defendant's behavior affects how the defendant is treated (or ignored) by his or her attorney. If a defense attorney perceived the defendant's participation as hustling, the attorney would verbally reprimand the client. In the worst scenarios, if the defense attorney was extremely angry, the defendant would be sent back to lockup without any further consultation, only to wait in jail for the next court appearance. This was the client-defense version of the "silent treatment," but given the conditions of the jail, it was no small consequence. While the lawyers did not cross the boundaries of illegality or professional impropriety, the spirit of their actions could be as abusive as the courtroom norms by prosecutors and judges.[11] Their attorneys were inflicting the type of pretrial punishment that almost inevitably led to a plea of guilty.

Ambassadors of Racialized Justice

Given the racialized assumption about the undeserving set of offenders, what does defending look like between defense attorneys and their clients? Clerking for a public defender named Sandra gave me some answers. Like an assembly line of its own, Sandra quickly conferenced with five defendants in about ten minutes. She left the lockup with what seemed like resolutions for her clients. Some would plea, one would get a motion, and others a request for drug treatment.

As the court call resumed and Sandra began working with defendants free on bond, she asked me to go into the lockup to get some basic information from a young man named Montrell. Just outside the lockup, I called for Montrell and five defendants stepped forward—pushing toward the glass in desperation. They were all black. Each one of them had questions that were muffled by the bulletproof glass. Finally, Montrell emerged, passive, unsure, as though he had been pushed forward by one of the other guys. I yelled awkwardly and enunciated so he could also read my lips. "Can I get your Social Security number, phone number, and prison location?"

"Div 1 . . . Sec 2 . . ." Then he turned, looked back at the others, and then at me again—as if I knew. I said, "You know better than I do." He laughed. Once our exchange was over, I was bombarded with questions on other cases. "Tell Ms. Carey [Sandra] that I want TASC. I don't want to plea." Another defendant said that he changed his mind about his agreement with Sandra. Both defendants asked for Sandra to come back and talk to them again.

I did not want to be the bearer of bad news and tell Sandra that discussions with her clients were derailing, so I just simply started by saying that her clients had more "questions." For any public defender, going back into lockup after that initial conference before court call was similar to opening up the proverbial Pandora's Box. Just as Montrell looked back at his fellow defendants before he answered my simple questions, defendants knew to compare notes. This meant that Sandra's offers and agreements with individual clients were now being collectively compared and bargained. Because most of her clients had new requests, the consensus among Sandra's clients was that she could do better. As I broke the news to Sandra, she was visibly frustrated and made a comment about Montrell "going back on his decision" as though her consultation with him was an on-the-record contract in which your initial word was binding.

Mostly, we just focused on an older, outspoken defendant named Ray. For this defendant, Sandra was pursuing a motion to suppress evidence and quash arrest. I thumbed through the file, which had a few photographs taken by investigators from the Public Defender's Office. The photos showed that where the defendant was "loitering" was actually at a bus stop. Sandra was going to argue that the police officers unlawfully searched and arrested Ray for simply waiting for the bus, not for dealing drugs.

For Ray, losing the motion was too risky and, perhaps most important, he would have to wait weeks in custody for the motion, which could mean spending more time in jail than the offense was actually worth in terms of punishment. He requested TASC (Treatment Alternatives for Safe Communities), which was inpatient drug treatment, with a lighter confinement option and better quality of life relative to incarceration. What was clear was that Ray wanted out of the Cook County Jail, even if it meant pleading guilty for waiting at a bus stop.

Sandra gave Ray his 402 conference, which proceeded in the judge's chambers. She made her case to the judge by using an "undermining" strategy to acknowledge that she knew that the defendant did not "deserve" TASC but had to go through the motions. At one point, Sandra implied that Ray is likely a drug dealer:

> Sandra: He really wants TASC. He is self employed as a salesman . . . God knows what he is selling.

She was reading his case file while giving her impromptu appeal.

> Judge: 18 months IDOC. He's not a good candidate for TASC.

The judge did not give a rationale, legal or otherwise. Sandra broke the news to Ray, who was angry. He refused to accept the offer.

> Defendant: I ain't doing time. No, I ain't doing time.

He was standing and shaking his head. Sandra tried to get him to accept the offer. She told him that his time served in jail awaiting hearings and status dates would amount to being out of jail in a few months. He repeated himself.

> Defendant: I ain't doing time. I will be in longer because I was out on parole. I want to do a motion.

Here, the defendant reveals himself as a hustler, and Sandra puts him in his place by screaming and telling him the real rules of the racialized court and what he has coming.

> Sandra: I had asked you if you were on parole! And it is written right here. You answered, "no." . . . Fine, we'll do the motion but it is your word against the cops. I believe you, but the judge may not. Then, if we lose, the judge will look at her sheet and wonder why you didn't take the 18 months. She is going to whack you so you better stop playing games.

Sandra reclaimed the reins of representation by leveraging the frameworks of racialized justice, acting almost as an ambassador or mouthpiece for the workgroup. Basically, she stopped the game playing by telling Ray that he was a mope. She told him that (although she believed him) his word had no significance. He would not be believed. She warned him that he would be punished for not being grateful for the eighteen months rather than what he deserved. And finally, she undermined his persistence and concealment of his parole status, which was now on his permanent file, as "playing a game." Sandra never once admitted that she did not check the defendant's record, so much of this confusion could have been avoided if she had only read the case file.

In general, an informed defendant is seen as more of a problem to attorneys than one who is ignorant or passive and stays in his place. When defendants were more passive and let their attorneys blindly lead their defense, racialized justice had a different tenor and delivery. The next story describes a passive defendant who allows Sandra to lead the defense with little pushback or resistance.

The defendant was picked up on a minor traffic violation. He was pulled over for not wearing a seat belt and was driving on a revoked license. Because of changes in the Illinois criminal code that expanded the scope of lawful searches, driving with a revoked or suspended license is probable cause, allowing officers to search a vehicle for weapons or drugs. At the time of this research, the public defender was just "learning" about the change in the search-and-seizure law, which, at the time, was upheld by the Illinois Supreme Court. Despite the new law, Sandra was planning a motion to suppress evidence, saying that the police unlawfully found drugs on the defendants. Although there was no legal basis for such a motion, there was a cultural basis that was reminiscent of the public defender who tried to pull a "fast one" on the workgroup in Chapter 3, in hopes that the prosecutors were unaware and unengaged with the case and the law. Because this strategy was a risky option, Sandra told him the hard facts: the state would probably push for about three years IDOC.

Defendant: So they'll be looking for "time."
Sandra: Yeah, and the state doesn't like making offers.

The defendant went through the effort of writing a letter to the judge. He passed it passively to the defense attorney as though it would change her opinion of his case. It was on wide-ruled notebook paper and written in cursive with perfectly slanted letters. It looked like it was written with the care of a sixth grader, but anything on wide-ruled paper degraded the content of the letter. Sandra grabbed it and skimmed it while mumbling out loud. I glanced over to see phrases like: "Judge, I am truly sorry," "I am not guilty," and "Thank you for reading this note."

> Sandra: This note is not going to help you.

She did not give a reason, just that statement. She stuffed the note into the file folder, creasing the letter in uneven ways that made it look like garbage rather than pristine homework. After this exchange, Sandra seemed impatient. She talked quickly and more decisively. In defeat, the defendant finally requested a conference. Sandra warned him as follows:

> Sandra: Now if she gives you 3 years and you don't take it, the judge will take it personally. Then, if you go to trial, she will look at the sheet, see that you didn't take her offer and give you twice as much time.

While she was talking to the defendant about his options, she started knocking on the window so we could get out of lockup.

> Sandra: You think about it [whether to plea] for a while, Mr. Turner.

In this quick exchange, Sandra explained the norms of the courtroom: exercising due process is punishable and exercising rights would be read as a personal rejection of the judge's generosity. Retribution would ensue. This communication of the "laws" of court culture scared the defendant into a plea. Ironically, the judge in this court explained to all defendants, including this one:

> Judge: If you decide to reject the offer, I will not hold that against you should the case go to trial.

In this case, where a defendant was passive, the defense attorney assumed the role of cultural ambassador. While the judge publicly stated that she would not hold his rejection of the offer against him during trial, the subtext of the culture was that during sentencing she would. In this context, justice was a place of confusion and paradox—a place where the court record documented the formal rules of practice that contradicted the logics and norms of the interpretative aspects of law. The defense attorneys were the translators who "warned" defendants about this culture, thereby conditioning them into compliance. Analogous to defense attorneys' fear of repercussions for due process, they passed this fear on to their clients rather than resisting on their behalf.

When a Client Is Worth the Fight

There are long-term consequences to short-term incarceration. Short-term incarceration as a pretrial detainee can be debilitating to one's life. For some defendants, even a modest middle-class lifestyle cannot insulate them from the effects of being a pretrial detainee. Awaiting trial and maintaining your innocence can result in missing days at work, then losing a job, then missing a rent payment, and finally being evicted. Even a person with middle-class standing can quickly be cast into poverty and homelessness if he or she doesn't have access to the resources of a social network to sustain him. This fate can be unleashed on a citizen just for being accused rather than convicted of a crime.

Despite the loss of income that could come with pretrial detainment, cultural markers of a defendant's social class were an important way of distinguishing some defendants from the stream of offenders who are mostly poor people of color. While prosecutors see the category of mope as literally black or white, defense attorneys (especially public defenders) must recognize the nuances in their pool of clients. Middle-class markers trigger a better quality of representation, strikingly different from the exchanges previously described.

Consider the case of Marquise Thompson. The circumstances were nearly identical to those of the previous case. He was in a friend's car and did not know his friend had a gun in the vehicle. Both were charged with "unlawful use of a weapon." Mr. Thompson walked into the lockup conference room to speak with Sandra. In the stream of Sandra's clients, he was just another black man who had been sitting in jail for months. He had been stripped of all identifying class markers except one subtle detail: he wore designer eyeglasses. Etched in the dark frames were the words "Calvin Klein."

Sandra introduced me to the defendant as a graduate student studying the court and asked his permission for me to listen to their discussion. In other cases, Sandra did not explain my role to the defendants or ask their permission. In fact, this was the only time she explained that I was not an attorney to any of her clients. Marquise acknowledged me with a hello and claimed control of the privacy of his case.

Defendant: As long as you don't tell anyone about my case, it is fine.

Sandra was spending a significant amount of her courtroom capital on this case. She was going to trial and going to ask for a jury—the most aggressive due process move. She explained the court culture to the defendant. She believed that the jury trial was the best strategy. The jury might be receptive to the "unfairness" of the situation. She contrasted it with a bench trial, where the judge would listen to the evidence, including testimony from the police and the defendant, and determine who was "telling the truth."

> Sandra: In all honesty, the judge is not likely to believe you didn't know there was a gun in the car.

As she explained the courtroom norms, Sandra was engaging the defendant to participate—talking to him like an equal. For the judge, the defendants are all the same, and her disdain for trials and those who pursue them put him at risk for a loss and a high penalty. Sandra was forced to explain, though, that the judge was unlikely to believe him—like any common mope.

Sandra then asked the defendant whether he had any clothes to wear for the jury trial. It is the defendant's right to wear professional attire during the trial rather than the Department of Corrections uniform so as not to prejudice the jury. Mr. Thompson said he lost everything by being in jail. He could not pay rent, so he lost his apartment and all the possessions in it. Sandra asked whether he had any friends or family in the area. He said no. His whole family was in Michigan and he was an only child.

> Sandra: We have a closet full of clothes that you could use if worse comes to worst.
> Defendant: I don't want to use those. They are probably filthy.
> Sandra: Well, we can try to get in touch with your mom.

Despite his dismal circumstances, he saw himself as separate from other defendants. Pride did not motivate his request; it was concern for cleanliness, possibly due to the conditions that he confronted in the jail. He also asked Sandra for a quick date on the trial. Sandra said she would try her best, but the judge's schedule was "heavy" and "this judge doesn't like doing trials."

> Defendant: Maybe if she knew how long I'd been here, maybe then . . .
> PD: She won't care about that . . . not that it's not important.

The conditions at Cook County Jail were so oppressive that detention facilitated guilty pleas. There was a shortage of beds, as well as outbreaks of TB and other diseases. These conditions exhausted the defendants' endurance while they awaited trial. The defense attorney explained that the judge would not see this defendant as anything special—just another one in the system. The judge would probably not believe him over a police officer, and it would not matter how he was "suffering" in jail. The defendant saw himself as different, misplaced in the system by accident, but his race was a central liability that even his social class could not offset.

His only benefit in the system was that his attorney "saw" his social class despite his race—a nuance that her workgroup counterparts did not offer defendants unless they were white and could "perform" whiteness in a particular professional, middle-class manner.

Sandra treated the defendant with considerable care. She reassured him that his suffering was important—but told him that the judge did not care. She said several times that she "sure hoped that she could help him out." She engaged in what Arlie Hochschild (1983) characterized as "emotion work,"[12] or the display of "appropriate or expected emotions by a service agent during a service encounter."[13] Sandra pursued this emotion work with the defendant and, eventually, with his family.

Later in the day, three family members arrived in court; it was Marquise Thompson's mother, grandmother, and grandfather. Mom gingerly waved to Sandra and said they were the relatives of Mr. Thompson. The family had taken a Greyhound bus from Michigan. Next, they took the CTA (subway). After that, they caught a cab to get to court. Despite the journey, they missed seeing Mr. Thompson's quick status hearing. He was sent back to the labyrinthine jail.

Sandra was kind to them as she put her files aside and sat down to talk with them, trying to make their journey worth the effort. She told them about his need for clothes. She gave them tips on how to get home. She authentically appeared to care about Mr. Thompson's family. She seemed disappointed that he did not even know that his family was in court to support him. Before they left to go home, Sandra said:

> He's a nice boy . . . I sure would like to win it for him . . . he's got a good heart.

This case demonstrates that social-class markers were crucial to getting a defense. Social class allowed this defendant to get the best of Sandra's legal effort—an investment of her courtroom capital, and even some emotion. Marquise Thompson's gain came at the expense of the assembly line of mopes who regularly pressed against the lockup glass, waiting to get Sandra to talk to them.

Pro Se: Encroaching on Professional Terrain

In stark contrast to the defendant who can exhibit "middle-class" features is the deviant defendant who disregards professional authority and expertise—the *pro se* defendant. These defendants have chosen to thumb their noses at the powerful cultural institution. They are rejecting representation and are often defiant. Judges punish these defendants, tell them they "must" have an attorney, throw them back into jail (repeatedly), and threaten that they could receive the maximum sentence for their charge. Numbers like thirty years are thrown into the threat. They are severely mocked by the courtroom workgroup. Often they are evaluated for mental fitness, as though their denial of an attorney is a problem with their health. Because the evaluation lengthens detainment, a provision that should protect defendants' rights is changed into a weapon that can be wielded against them. Because it is the defense attorney who must initiate such requests, they are often playing the "bad guy" in these instances.

So, why is the *pro se* defendant so dangerous? First, in a culture that views any participation as a violation, the *pro se* defendant is not just asking to participate but wanting to participate as an equal. Absent an attorney, it is the defendant who will navigate the system. In a cultural world where the judge repeatedly demands that defense attorneys "speak for them" as a way to silence and exclude defendants, the judge and prosecutors are forced to "deal" directly with the *pro se* defendant. This undermines the very core of their moral rubric that casts defendants as separate and unequal.

Second, these defendants create chaos in the system by causing its efficiency to screech to a virtual halt. Given the production ethic, this is a significant violation. For defendants labeled "monsters" who are facing many years in prison for a violent felony, the usual threats and punitive tactics used on mopes are rendered ineffectual. Consider the case of a defendant with a lengthy criminal record who was currently charged with sexual assault. This defendant refused to accept an attorney, and the judge's persistent attempts to send him back to jail seemed to make him dig his heels in more. He mentioned wanting a jury trial—the worst affront to efficient due process. He ultimately demanded a plea bargain conference and as a *pro se* defendant, he negotiated directly with the more senior prosecutor in the courtroom rather than through his public defender. As the courtroom recessed and the public waited, the first-chair prosecutor invited me to accompany him to lockup, emphasizing the novelty and spectacle of observing a shackled rapist in a closet-sized room.

As the plea bargain progressed, the prosecutor verbally gave the defendant an initial offer. In response, the defendant sat in silent defiance, shaking his head no. The prosecutor lowered the offer three times, with the defendant continuing to use silence to negotiate. Finally, the defendant kept saying he would want a jury if the prosecutor did not give him a lower sentence. The prosecutor gave the defendant the lightest sentence possible to get the "problem" off the call. The sentence was so far below the average sentence, or "going rate," for his crime that the prosecutors poked fun at the courtroom's public defenders—who typically did not produce such favorable outcomes for their clients.

From a defense attorney's standpoint, rejecting representation is a challenge to their professional authority and skills. Being mocked by their prosecutor colleagues due to the actions of a mope or a monster is the ultimate insult. It reveals that the defendant believes that the defense attorney is merely a complicit middleman in a racialized justice system, such that the defendant is willing to endure procedural punishment to avoid "help." Similar to the *pro se* defendant charged with sexual assault, these defendants have nothing to lose and everything to gain by rejecting their attorneys. The case of the *pro se* defendant demonstrates that representation or the rejection of such representation is riddled with professional politics about status and stature among professionals who are marginalized in their profession and in the workgroup. When the defendant encroached on a public defender's legal authority, the defendant could be expected to be put back in line.

In one case, in open court, Nina, a public defender, requested a 402 conference for her client:

> Defendant: No, I want a 401 conference.
> Nina: What do you think this is? 401 doesn't exist . . . what do you think a
>   401 is?
> Defendant: I heard it in lockup.
> Nina: Well, that's what happens when you get legal advice from criminals.
> Defendant: Sorry.

It was not just a correction; it was public humiliation, not to mention a public defender admitting that pretrial detainees were actually guilty "criminals" rather than citizens merely charged (and not found guilty) for criminal acts. The public defender yelled loud enough to let others in the workgroup hear the defendant be put back in line. Even for a small encroachment, reprimand was sharp and swift.

Some defendants decided to challenge the competency of their defense post-conviction and do it *pro se*. This could send a defendant back to a courtroom where he or she would have to publicly declare the grievance with their public defender. This was the ultimate act of defiance. By holding the public defender accountable, the *pro se* defendant was also shining the spotlight on the entire workgroup. A challenge to the ceremonial charade was a challenge to all. In one instance, a *pro se* defendant walked into court in his D-O-Cs (his downstate prison jumper). He was already convicted and had been "shipped" from the jail to the downstate prison where he was serving his sentence. The defendant was there to file a motion. He was challenging his conviction on the grounds of attorney incompetence. Specifically, the defendant claimed that the attorney (PD) misrepresented the severity of the sentence in order to get him to plead guilty. The defendant was making a sophisticated argument; these types of issues were reviewed in the 2012 Supreme Court case *Lafler v. Cooper*, where the highest court affirmed that defendants have a Sixth Amendment right to competent legal counsel during a plea bargain. Before this important case was heard by the Supreme Court, this defendant was making a similar argument about his assigned counsel and was coming back from prison to hold the attorney accountable.

As we have seen, defense attorneys often found themselves assuming the role of ambassadors of racialized justice. It was not uncommon to hear public defenders weigh their client's legal options like pick-your-poison threats. But this was one of the few defendants who decided to come back to the Cook County Courts to challenge what was a well-established practice. As retribution, the public defenders teamed up to bully the defendant in open court.

PD #1: I represented him. Now he wants to represent himself.

PD #2: That's pathetic.

This dialogue was spoken loud enough for the defendant and other participants to hear, which is essential to communicating professional authority among colleagues to save face. In most *pro se* cases, there are sanctions, but because the PD was being accused of misconduct or incompetence, the PDs were launching the loudest disapproval. The judge allowed an extension of the motion because the defendant was not allowed to go to the law library in the prison—another not-so-subtle obstacle in the defendant's way. As the defendant left court, the prosecutors jested to the female judge:

SA: I think he just wants to stop by to see you.

The prosecutor compared the defendant's effort to that of a childhood field trip from prison to see the judge. He also sexualized the defendant as an aggressor while positioning the white female judge as the object of this black defendant's "advances."

The *pro se* defendant reveals that compliance within court culture and acceptance of its representation system not only reproduce racialized justice but also allow professionals to reproduce their stature as well. Excluding defendants, minimizing their capacity to participate, and punishing them into submission for their "moral failings" are not only congruent with the logics of racialized justice but create firm boundaries around professional domains that precariously maintain defense attorneys' membership in the base of the profession. In interviews, defense attorneys possess sympathetic frameworks to discuss the plight of defendants, and provide critiques about substantive justice and the abuse of defendants by prosecutors and judges. But advocacy is largely informed by the rubrics of racialized justice and like a fractal, it mimics the patterns, norms, and sanctions of the racialized Cook County Courts.

CONCLUSION

Racialized Punishment in the Courts:

A Call to Action

THE INDELIBLE MURAL IN THE GANG CRIMES UNIT was where this study began in 1997. My first awareness of the racial divides that defined the courts was in the mug shots of young defendants of color acting as wallpaper for an all-white cast of attorneys. Over time, I realized that each conquest represented many deaths: the defendants, certainly the victims, and the families of both the defendants and the victims. This web of suffering was not just a result of the defendants' actions but was part of a system of racial punishment that defined the Cook County Courts and governed all the participants who found themselves stuck there.

This study is primarily focused on the professionals who ran the Cook County Courts. But like the backdrop of that mural, the defendants, victims, families, and all the people of color who were mistreated in the courts were impossible to ignore. The attorneys and judges often rendered the public, the victims, and the defendants invisible, but perhaps I never was fully immersed in my field site because I never lost sight of their humanity. My hope is that now none of us will be able to look away.

As one of the few people of color among the professionals, I had survivor's guilt. My skin is light enough to pass, and with that came privilege, access, and the ability to leave the courts and head back to Northwestern University. What's more, studying the courts as a researcher required a level of psychological distance that protected me from the emotional toll of observing an assembly line of constant victimization. However, this distance as a researcher was not infallible. As I wrote this book, I looked at the stacks of field notes and court-watching forms. Collectively, in their binders, there were nearly forty pounds of narrative data. Many of these narratives never made it into the book due to a lack of space. For each defendant and person profiled here, there were numerous others whose cases also fit the same pattern of abuse. On the cutting-room floor was a tremendous amount of suffering, and any number of them could be my brother, sister, cousin, or neighbor.

After I left the field site, I went through a mental process of imagining . . . *what if? What if these defendants or victims were my family?* Then I no longer had to imagine. What I had not known back in 1997 was that one of the conquests in that gang mural was my first cousin, my own family and blood. He was charged with first-degree murder, spent two years in the Cook County Jail fighting his case, and ultimately served seventeen years of a thirty-five-year sentence. At one point, when a prosecutor did not give him an attorney in the police station, he feigned suicide by cutting his wrists in order to buy time and beg the doctors in the psych ward to help him get an attorney. He thought that telling an outsider (any outsider) would help him exercise his rights. He was wrong.

I looked back in my field notes and read the description of myself walking reverently, like I was scanning a memorial of the dead. Upon reflection, it seemed like I was unknowingly attending my cousin's funeral. Rarely can we ever prepare ourselves for the consequences of having our intellectual passions collide with our personal lives in the forum of our fieldwork. What is often the case is that many ethnographers have personal motivations or inspirations for going into their field sites. Perhaps they want to understand their old neighborhood, make sense of tragedy, or lend voice to a population. In these cases, the personal becomes the sociological. My journey was different. I understood the sociology of the courts, the social arrangements of racism that fueled its efficiency, and the toll it took on populations of color. Now, the sociological was deeply personal because the collateral consequences were leading to my own life and lineage.

While we think about issues of human rights as occurring on a global scale, they truly begin in our own backyards. As Eleanor Roosevelt describes, human rights begin "in small places, close to home—so close and so small that they cannot be seen on any maps of the world. Yet they are the world of the individual person; the neighborhood he lives in . . . the factory, farm or office where he works. Such are the places where every man, woman and child seeks equal justice, equal opportunity, equal dignity without discrimination. Unless these rights have meaning there, they have little meaning anywhere." The Cook County court system was the local place where I saw violations of human rights in my own city. While it is America's largest unified court, it is located in the city that I call home, in the neighborhood where my father, aunts, and uncles were raised. Now, in the cruelest irony, my eldest cousin was one of the nameless, faceless defendants processed by the courts. How else can you respond except by shattering the code of silence that governs the courts?

While this is a heroic stance, such hopes for justice need to be appropriately tempered. While I was writing this book, word traveled fast through my old Chicago neighborhood that I was writing about "Crook County." Most of these local social networks were supportive, and encouraging. *Tell 'em the shit that goes down. It's time for the city to find out what's happening in there.* Other folks offered warnings. *You're doing a really brave or crazy thing . . . I'm not sure which one. Thank God you're not in Chicago anymore. Watch your back. They will come after you, you know?* These warnings spoke to the fear that resonated in the communities that have been touched by the Cook County Courts. To talk publicly about the abuse that occurred in that complex of punishment was to be at risk and meant you should be on guard.

Then I met Mario.

Mario was neither concerned about the good that would come with breaking the code of silence nor did he care about my personal safety. I met him through a childhood friend who was bragging that I was writing a book. Once we were introduced, Mario made small talk with me. Often, small talk about the criminal justice system leads to unimaginable confessions of surviving personal trauma. I realized very early into my work on the courts that defendants, victims, and family members wanted to be heard. They needed it. Like all trauma, the stories need to be told and re-told to make sense of what happened. I was often on the listening end.

Mario had gone through the Cook County Courts with a few nonviolent felonies. He suffered from bipolar disorder and found that the effects of bipolar and self-medicating on alcohol and cocaine left him hot-wiring cars and dealing drugs, often for the pure exhilaration of it. In 2001 he posted bond on a nonviolent felony and his mother came to pick him up at the Cook County Jail. After she waited two hours at the jail, she asked the guards how long it would take to get her son. She believed that they were *not* getting him despite the posting of his bond. One guard looked at her and simply said, "I'm too busy." The guard remained standing, laughing with his colleagues. Later, the sheriff's officer brought out a black defendant (instead of a Latino) and asked Mario's mom, as a joke, "Is this your son?" This was a cruel gag on his mother, who thought she was actually going to see her son. It was also a cruel prank on the black detainee, who for a few seconds thought that he would be free; instead, he was reduced to the punch line of a joke.

Mario's mother simply asked the sheriffs where her son was. This was enough to invite punishment. There was the initial punishment, and then there was the punishment that lasted for two days. Mario became "lost" in the system.[1]

> NVC: Wait, what do you mean? Where were you?
>
> Mario: I was lost in the system in the Cook County Jail for two days and they would be like, "I don't know where he is. He's here but we don't know where" [said with an inflection as if the guards were taunting].
>
> NVC: Do you think they legitimately didn't know where you were?
>
> Mario: They were punishing both of us and they were showing the power they had over me. "Oh, you don't want to wait, well now you're going to wait twice as long." Asking someone to do their job was enough to get me in jail 48 hours instead of the six or eight I had to do. And I had made bail.
>
> NVC: So you had already gone to bond court, the judge had set bond, and you had paid the bond, and they jailed you for two more days?
>
> Mario: For two days, in Division 1, and they made me work in a kitchen.

Perhaps this experience makes it less surprising that Mario was more indignant than supportive about my work. Like many abuse victims, he questioned what good could come from rocking the boat. Better is the devil you know.

> Mario: What good's gonna come from this? What's going to happen to everybody? The prosecution could get worse. They are going to lash out on everyone more . . . they are going to come down with harder justice on people in retaliation for being the scum that they are. It's going to be more isolated and they're going to keep themselves away from any type of interference from anybody.

For Mario, "justice" *was* "punishment," and he used the words interchangeably. He also talked about retaliation as a consequence of exposing the court's practices. He even anticipated that the culture in the Cook County Courts would become more secretive and isolated as a response to having its cultural rules exposed. Perhaps this would be a protectionist reaction to any type of reform or oversight. Before any talk of reforming the criminal courts and the complex of punishment can begin, breaking the code of silence is a first step in cultural disruption. Accountability and oversight of this court system is the only way Mario and others with similar stories will have the protection they need in the courts. The law, due process protection, and even the Constitution are not enough.

Racialized Justice

Mario's story captures an important theme of this book. Justice in the courts is punishment, racial punishment. In the classic studies of criminal courts, scholars examined the courts after the "Due Process Revolution" and showed that despite a host of due process protections, case pressure and production norms were so intense that professionals engaged in "bureaucratically ordained or controlled 'work crimes,' shortcuts, deviations and outright rule violations" to meet caseload requirements.[2] Malcolm Feeley argues that professionals created a "sense of justice that is compatible with their concerns for speed and efficiency."[3] In the Cook County Courts, the "work crimes" are the racial punishment doled out by court professionals, the ceremonial charades required of licensed attorneys, and a notion of justice built upon racial stigma.[4]

While we've seen how these dynamics work in the criminal court, it is only one of many locations where mostly white professionals are charged with vetting, sorting, and judging the morality of a racialized population. Like criminal courts, probation officers, parole officers, police officers, jailers—to name a few—are making similar distinctions as they exercise discretion. Understanding how racism is mobilized in courts —despite due process protections—is merely a starting point for understanding how the ideologies of professionals reproduce racism and racial stigmas at numerous contact points in the criminal justice system.

Mass Wrongful Conviction

Broadly speaking, there are high costs to this practice of law. First, it is likely that the ceremonial charades endemic in the Cook County Court are producing mass wrongful convictions. When we think about the scope of mass incarceration, we rarely question the legitimacy of the convictions that these numbers represent. We assume that those in jails and prisons received adequate due process as required by the law. The skirting of due process, the lack of engagement in cases, and the fast-paced production ethic are undoubtedly resulting in the conviction of factually innocent people on a scale that is largely unknown and certainly ignored. While there is robust activism around the most egregious cases of defendants who are wrongfully convicted of murder and other high-stakes crimes, there is little interest in the everyday miscarriages of justice where people are serving shorter jail sentences under oppressive conditions or even five or ten years in downstate prisons. As we know, any felony conviction (even crimes that receive only probation) marks offenders in ways that are tantamount to receiving a life sentence with dire consequences for employment, education, and the like.[5]

In addition to the possibility of mass wrongful convictions is the toll these convictions take on the communities they impact. Many works have examined the toll of mass incarceration on communities of color.[6] We've seen here how state-sanctioned legal processes can induce trauma. Lives are belittled; victims are minimized or ignored; and defendants view professionals as street hustlers and "crooks" who manage a rigged, racist system—a White Castle with drive-thru justice for the poor. In appraising the system, one needs to consider a new standard for justice: measuring the system and its legitimacy through the eyes of its consumers, be they defendants, victims, witnesses, or families.

Dismantling New Racism

The current scholarship on race assumes that modern racism, new racism, and colorblind racism are, in fact, different from the traditional racism of the past. As we've seen in the criminal courts, however, this supposed new brand of racism is just as punitive and abusive as traditional forms associated with the Jim Crow era and the like. Colorblind ideology is not "racism lite" nor a kinder, gentler form of institutional racism.[7] Imbued with legal authority, power, and institutional legitimacy, the doing of colorblind racism transforms into state-sanctioned racial degradation ceremonies. The "governors" can claim their behavior as "colorblind" through coded language, mimic fairness through due process procedures, and rationalize abuse based on morality—all while achieving the experience of segregation and de facto racism.

The legal practices in the Cook County Courts have striking parallels to what David Garland refers to as "popular justice."[8] Popular justice was carried out in local communities. It acted on uncorroborated allegations, confessions induced under torture, and the infallible word of white victims or witnesses. It was designed to enact punishment with speed and efficiency, mostly on people of color, and included the degradation and humiliation of the offender. Sometimes the punitive fury of popular justice extended beyond the alleged offender to his family and neighbors.

White citizens who participated as judges, jurors, and executioners took souvenirs from the scene, took pictures of the convicted, and retold these violent moral victories to friends and family both near and far. Beyond the retribution unleashed on a single offender, popular justice governed entire minority populations through terror and fear and mimicked a gross caricature of procedural justice and the rule of law. That is, the cultural sensibilities of American legal processes informed a vigilante version of racial violence.

For Garland, the term "popular justice" refers to the organized "ceremony" of lynching.[9] If this is part of our penal and racial history, then it is apt to compare the symbolic continuity between popular justice of the past and racialized justice of the present. While some of the overt violence and public spectacle of racial violence is gone, the racial and punitive character that underpins today's justice system has unsettling links with our past. Certainly, in the criminal courts, the mug shot murals, the images of suffering defendants, dead victims, starved babies all hark back to popular justice. The cord wrapped around a defendant's chair, the lynching language used in plea bargaining, the jail as a tool to induce a plea bargain, the berating of defendants, and the racial degradation ceremonies all invite this comparison.

Recent media accounts of police violence in American streets invite this comparison too. There were the police shootings of unarmed black men and women, the choking death of Eric Garner, and the police violence used to break the spine of Baltimore resident Freddie Gray. And then there was the violence committed against black children: the shooting death of Tamir Rice and even a case of a pool party in a Dallas suburb where an officer threw a fourteen-year-old girl in a bathing suit onto the ground like a rag doll, pinning her down with the entire weight of his body. And, in Chicago, there was Laquan McDonald. Sixteen bullets riddled the teen's body—the head, the shoulders, the torso, the neck, the arms—as though he was target practice for Officer Jason Van Dyke. These are only the few cases that made the news. What the poor and people of color will tell you is that these are the everyday racial degradation ceremonies exacted in the streets on behalf of the state. These recent events demonstrate that the historical analogies to popular justice are not just symbolic; these incidents are a type of "political theater"[10] that extends from the streets (through the police) into the courts (through judges and attorneys).[11]

David Garland argues that popular justice arose at a historical moment of social transition when formal legal institutions no longer communicated cultural understandings of race. Lynchings became a public forum to express views about race that were no longer officially allowed under the law.

Perhaps the forced niceties and norms of colorblind racism unleashed a similar cultural fury in the United States. It is no longer socially acceptable to express overtly racist sentiments. Instead, Americans speak in coded racial language to conceal their racial ideology. Likewise the due process revolution created procedural safeguards to supposedly ensure equal treatment under the law. America's racial politics cannot be expressed formally—not in conversations and certainly not in the forum of laws and legal institutions.

While racism cannot be publicly discussed, the criminal justice system can enact it; racial degradation ceremonies become a type of political theater on the state's behalf, whether dramatized in a major urban courthouse or in the streets by police officers. In the court, officials can perform ceremonial charades that create the semblance of fairness while hiding racial abuse with bureaucratization, the courtroom record, and a lack of oversight and accountability. What results is a type of state-sanctioned racial violence, where white professionals can govern and deliberate on the morality of blacks and Latinos, enact punishment on them, and do so under the guise of crime control. While the spectacle of racial violence on the body is no longer present, we must not ignore the symbolic racial violence enacted on communities of color and the poor by a court system that gives new meaning to the "process is the punishment."[12]

It may be a fact that some court professionals harbor racist attitudes. Yet it is more plausible that most attorneys working in criminal justice are motivated by some basic core values: protecting the integrity of the law, keeping the streets safe, and ensuring the rights of defendants and victims, to name a few. But socialization into the practice of law in the criminal justice system subverts these values and replaces them with cultural logics that help practitioners rationalize the gross disparities in race and poverty that they confront on a daily basis. What results is a criminal justice system that limits access to the courts, undermines the integrity of the processes, and paints justice as a ceremonial charade where the color of your skin makes you inherently worthy of punishment. We must challenge theorists who claim that the era of colorblind racism is really different from that of traditional racism. Turn on the news, refresh your Twitter or Facebook feed, or head to the courts to see racial degradation ceremonies performed in the name of criminal justice. Criminal justice is the primary theater where such racism can still be expressed with both violence and impunity.

Breaking the Code of Silence: A Call to Action

The assistance of 130 court watchers was instrumental to this research. From a methodological perspective, this allowed for the anonymous collection of data without changing the behavior of attorneys. One could see how these attorneys act when they think no one else (besides people of color) is watching. It is telling that some of the judges were most offended when they discovered court watchers in their courtrooms, spaces that all citizens are entitled to view. One judge particularly offended by a court watcher who was also a summer associate at a law firm said: "Do they pay you so much at your firm that you have time to watch me do *my* job?" Judges could control (and even manipulate) the court record, but they could not control the observations and notes of outsiders watching them do justice. It was as though a pencil and paper were the worst weapons against their culture. It occurred to me that rather than just collecting data, court watching was a type of activism, a way to lend a conscience to an otherwise unaccountable system.

People often ask me what they can do to rectify the type of racial violence inflicted by the courts. The answer is simple: *Go.* Go to the courts. Bear witness to what attorneys and judges do and bear witness en masse. Don't let them show you trials, sensationalized murder cases, or heroic acts of litigation. Go as an everyday person, wearing jeans, hoodies, and the like, and take some field notes and court-watching forms while you're at it.[13]

For professors or teachers, take your students to the courts as a requirement of their education. Do not take them on a tour of the courts, as some voyeuristic exercise. Replicate my data until you change the findings in Cook County–Chicago and perhaps in other jurisdictions. My guess is that this call to action is likely to induce the most response from the Cook County Courts, a place that thrives on insularity and the brash assumption that few will care about the type of "street law" that happens for "street people." That is exactly why you *should* go. American citizens own the courts; not a small monopoly of attorneys.

For Chicagoans, just take I-55 South from the Loop—as though you are making your way to Midway Airport and exit at California Avenue. The segregated breadline will be waiting; the sheriffs will be yelling, the bulletproof glass will remain. Start voting for judges according to what you see. Write down their names and how they manage their courtrooms. Remember: The U.S. Supreme Court ruled that "justice must satisfy the appearance of justice"[14] and by that metric we are all qualified to watch and lend accountability to the courts and their culture. Also, start serving on juries—rather than wanting off. Cast your verdict on guilt or innocence through a critical lens that acknowledges that witnesses may lie but so do police.

For attorneys, take on pro bono cases and slow down the ceremonial charade. Change it from a charade to a process governed by decorum, dignity, and the rule of law. Honor your commitments to the ethical standards that govern the profession rather than the "boys' club" that will undoubtedly pressure you to conform to their way of doing business in the courts. In all, transform your local island of racial punishment back into an accessible American court by going, witnessing, and disrupting the stronghold on criminal law.

ACKNOWLEDGMENTS

Whatsoever things are true, whatsoever things are honest,
whatsoever things are just . . . if there be any virtue,
and if there be any praise, think on these things.
Philippians 4:8

Philippians 4:8 is the motto of Northwestern University and the primary site where I found the peace, inspiration, and joy to think on many things, at many stages of my life and education. When I wrote my first field notes, I was a college sophomore. A generous scholarship from the Hoellen Family Foundation paid for my Northwestern education. The Gamma Phi Beta–Epsilon sorority gave me a place to call home. The Gamma Phi Beta House Corporation Board paid much of my room and board so I could comfortably live, eat, and have the energy to study. The Women's Center supported me with community and counseling, which was essential to maintaining my well-being in the field. Margaret J. Barr, former vice president for student affairs, mobilized many of these resources on my behalf.

I began as a political science major, and this project flourished under the wisdom and mentorship of Stephen Daniels. He has remained a constant source of support for nearly twenty years. Ira Silver and the Chicago Field Studies Program were instrumental to my love of ethnography. The late Jonathan Casper believed in me. Nicola Beisel found me in her lecture hall and told me to "think" about getting a Ph.D. It was through her eyes that I first envisioned myself as a professor.

I was fortunate to return to Northwestern to complete my graduate work. I enjoyed the collaborative nature of the Department of Sociology. My dissertation chair, John Hagan, was a constant source of encouragement. He strengthened this work and my overall scholarship. I thank other members of my dissertation committee who guided me: Robert Nelson, Laura Beth Nielsen, and Malcolm Feeley. I was also inspired by many faculty members who were not on my committee but who were influential and generous: Bruce Carruthers, Wendy Espeland, Wendy Griswold, Aldon Morris, Mary Pattillo, James E. Rosenbaum, Celeste Watkins-Hayes, and Harvey Young.

I was part of a generation of Ph.D. students that gave Northwestern its intellectual and cultural vibrancy, which I described as "NU swagger." In particular, I am grateful to peers who have been a source of intellectual inspiration. They challenged and cared for me as this project developed, read drafts, listened, and uplifted me: Jean Beaman, Ellen Berrey, Amin Ghaziani, Theodore Greene, Marcus Hunter, Nina Johnson, Jeff Kosbie, Armando Lara-Millán, Zandria F. Robinson, Brian Sargent, Heather Schoenfeld, Sara Soderstrom, Robert Vargas, Jill Weinberg, and Queen Meccasia Zabriskie. Other NU friends were helpful in personal and intellectual ways: Lori Delale-O'Connor, Michaela DeSoucey, Gabrielle Ferreles, Issa Kohler-Hausmann, Shaun Ossei-Owusu, Yordanos Tiruneh, and Marina Zaloznaya.

I am thankful for the support of the scholars who make up the Empirical Critical Race Workgroup (eCRT). In particular, I thank Jeannine Bell, Andrea Freeman, Laura E. Gómez, Angela Onwuachi-Willig, Victor D. Quintanilla, L. Song Richardson, and I especially acknowledge Osagie Obasogie for his support and leadership of eCRT, Paul Butler for generously critiquing an early draft of my manuscript, Mario Barnes for his insights and encouragement, and Kaaryn Gustafson for rigorously engaging in the text of this book.

Thank you to Ruth Peterson, Lauren Krivo, Jody Miller, and the community of scholars in the Racial Democracy Crime and Justice Network (RDCJN). I was a Fellow in the 2014 Summer Research Institute and wrote a large portion of this book while visiting the Criminal Justice Research Center at The Ohio State University. I am especially grateful to my amazing mentor, Marjorie Zatz, as well as to Victor Rios for his detailed critiques. I also thank my entire 2014 SRI cohort, especially Danny Gascón, Lallen Johnson, and Reuben Miller.

The Ford Foundation was instrumental in my completion of this book. I was a 2014–2015 Ford Postdoctoral Fellow, and the American Bar Foundation hosted me as a Visiting Scholar in residence. The American Bar Foundation is a vibrant community of scholars, and my work undoubtedly benefited from their support. In addition, I am grateful to Temple University's Center for the Humanities (CHAT), where I was a Faculty Fellow, and Temple University's Grant-in-Aid Award, which generously supported this research. I thank Elijah Anderson and members of the Yale Urban Ethnography Conference, where I am a junior fellow, and Heather Ann Thompson for her mentorship. Thanks also go to William P. Murphy for his advice and consultation, and to Melanie Newport for her research assistance. For their encouragement, I thank Juwan Bennett and Lauren Mayes.

I owe an enormous debt of gratitude to Chicago Appleseed Fund for Justice, from which I received the Badesch Fellowship. I was inspired by the executive director, Malcolm Rich, whose leadership and commitment to social justice is unbending. I also thank Susan Bandes, Daniel T. Coyne, and Thomas F. Geraghty. While I worked closely with Chicago Appleseed in the past, the analytical conclusions in this book are my own.

I thank Stanford University Press for supporting my vision for this book and especially my editor, Michelle Lipinski, for her deep engagement in this project. I also thank editor Barbara Winslow Boardman, who embraced my love of language.

On a personal level, I thank Pastor Jason Ferris, Rebecca Ferris, and the Old Pine Church. I thank lifelong friends who also engaged in the ideas in this book: Barbara Gorder, Julie Groll, David Harb, Marissa Mazzoncini, Carrie Nelson, Yetu Robinson, Bonnie Solomon, Darren Shulman, and Mark Wiwatowski. I acknowledge my earliest teachers: Bonnie Diamond, Marilyn Frank, Tammy Lathan, Carol Levin, Frank Mattucci, Tori Price, and Mary Roth.

I honor the Gonzalez family: My grandparents: Soledad and Jorge Medina Gonzalez and Esther Rico Morgan. My father, Joel Gonzalez, and my aunts and uncles: Ortencia, Veronica, Robert, Martha, George, and Gina. My cousins: Joel, Joaquin, Valerie, Gina, Samuel, Krystle, Ruben, and Katrina.

I am thankful for the love and sacrifice of my great-aunt and great-uncle Marie and Salvatore Valenziano. I also thank my in-laws, Jane and Roger Van Cleve, for their support and care.

I was blessed to meet my husband, Andrew Van Cleve, at Northwestern University shortly before I walked into the courthouse for the first time. He loved me when it started and was there when I finished. He reminded me to simply write the truth. For all your love and sacrifice, thank you; and thank you for choosing me. To my loving sons, Dylan and Micah: may you do justly, love mercy, and walk humbly through life. Thank you for your unconditional love and patience.

To the families, friends, and neighbors who call La Villita, Chicago, their home and to those Chicagoans most deeply affected by the criminal justice system, it is my sincere hope that this book will lend truth to your story.

METHODS APPENDIX

The research underlying this book presents particular methodological challenges. We know that professionals have learned to avoid expressing racial attitudes.[1] For instance, as compared to the non-college-educated, the college-educated express subtle, rather than blatant, racism, making it challenging to understand how racial ideologies can get entangled in professional practices like the practice of criminal law. Professionals may be particularly sophisticated at hiding and coding racial language in racially sanitized ways.[2] In a colorblind era, how can we measure the influence of race if respondents are unwilling or reluctant to discuss it, or, perhaps, strategic in speaking in racially sanitized ways?

Gómez identifies what she calls a "nascent" field in sociolegal scholarship.[3] This emerging field considers "how law and race construct each other in an ongoing, dialectic process that ultimately reproduces and transforms racial inequality." She argues for a conceptualization and operationalization of race that accurately reflects its complexity and social significance. Legal scholarship has been vulnerable to criticism for its shallow treatment of race.[4] A similar criticism is lodged against scholars of criminal justice, some of whom still deny the significance of race entirely despite the racialized nature of mass incarceration.[5] Many works have conceptualized race in narrow terms—doing so phenotypically and "crudely" via subject self-identification, for instance.[6] The sociological consensus is that race is socially constructed—making its consideration one that should be measured dynamically, longitudinally, and from multiple vantage points within the same social context.

Some quantitative works in law and society that consider race as an independent variable have been fruitful in documenting racial disparity as an outcome of processes. In reviewing the literature on racial bias and sentencing outcomes, this approach has limitations, however.[7] In some cases, quantitative works identify only weak effects of race on case outcomes and fail to capture how racial bias is experienced.[8] Works that empirically identify bias (for instance, research focused on criminal arrests and convictions) often miss how race manifests itself in subtleties of process, discretion, and interaction. Other qualitative works on criminal courts, for instance, fail to address race entirely, advancing the myth that the courts are a race-neutral space.[9] As Gómez argues, whether in quantitative or qualitative research, "researchers should use multiple measures of race within a single study in order to be responsive to the socially constructed nature of race and to our knowledge of its flexible and situational nature."[10] In this study, I respond to this methodological imperative and innovate on traditional ethnography.

In this section, I detail my multimethod approach and explain how I incorporated multiple vantage points on the same site over an extended period of time, which included "thick description" of process and meaning through ethnography.[11] I mitigate reliability errors by supplementing the thick description with additional sources of data, including a large-scale qualitative effort and in-depth interviews designed to shed light on the significance and meaning of cultural practices that define legal processes.

My data were collected with two particular vantage points in mind and with a particular attention to minimizing the challenges of measuring race in a race-blind era. First, I sought to understand the professionals' vantage points on the criminal justice system. That is, how did professional courtroom "insiders" understand their cultural world, their work, and their place and duty in the criminal justice system? Second, I sought to understand the consumer experience of justice—how was justice *read and experienced by outside observers?*

Ethnographic Data

This study relies heavily on extended ethnographic accounts of the courtrooms in Cook County–Chicago. These accounts focus on both the main courthouse and a smaller satellite court that handles excess felony cases.[12] Because this book focuses on racial meaning and everyday practices, an ethnographic approach is particularly useful. My approach is a thick description of shared culture that is acquired through interaction.[13]

I immersed myself as a courtroom "insider." As my introduction described, I was "indoctrinated" into this culture. Over the course of seven years (1997–2004), I completed three ethnographic visits of the field site, amounting to nine months of observations. In order to incorporate both participant and observer roles, I worked as a law clerk for the Cook County State's Attorney's Office (six months in 1997–1998) and for the Cook County Public Defender's Office (three months in 2004). This allowed access to front-stage and backstage environments, including offices, courtrooms, lockups, and judge's chambers.

I observed both open-court interactions and private plea-bargaining exchanges (whether they were in the judge's chambers or in the hallways of the courthouse). I observed the shared cultural meanings of the courtroom workgroup as well as the unique vantage points of prosecutors and defense attorneys. In addition to ethnography, I conducted supplemental interviews in private settings, outside the purview and influence of other courtroom workgroup members. These interviews acted as a follow-up to more fully interrogate the rationale for courtroom practices. Because I was a law clerk, using a legal pad and taking notes was viewed as customary for the job. I was able to note dialogue and quotes verbatim. After each day, I would transcribe this material into lengthy field notes that recorded the attorneys' behavior as well as my reflections and reactions to these events.

Interviews

In addition to these data from my own fieldwork and interviews, I contributed to the collection of a larger body of data for a prominent Chicago-based public policy organization, Chicago Appleseed Fund for Justice. In 2006, this organization conducted a large-scale study of the Cook County Criminal Justice System from the vantage point of the professionals working in the courts. As I mentioned previously, two prominent scholars from Northwestern University oversaw the data collection. In the capacity of project director, I had access to the full body of data, which included intensive interviews, written surveys, and observations of courtroom proceedings. White research associates conducted the interviews, which offered the opportunity for white professionals to, hopefully, provide less racially sanitized answers. The 104 structured interviews included 26 judges, 27 prosecutors, 26 public defenders, and 25 private attorneys. Interviews averaged about sixty-five minutes in length. Findings about the viewpoints of prosecutors, judges, and defense attorneys are drawn from this body of data and supplement the data that focus on the behavior of attorneys as they practice law (ethnography and court watching).

Interviews were conducted by young (early twenties) white women who had never practiced law or clerked in the criminal courts in Cook County. As described in the introduction of the book, being a white woman had privileges. The mostly white attorneys and judges were especially inclined to let their guard down and respond candidly to interviewers who were viewed as "nonthreatening" (in terms of gender, race, and age) and were outside the insular culture of the courts.

Supplemental Qualitative Work

Given the nature of my work, I acknowledge my own limitations as a "lone" ethnographer. My indoctrination and participation in the field site changed me into an "insider." I had to be reflexive about how my personal identity—race, education, and other social vantage points—affected my data collection.[14] Finally, while ethnographers often tout the methodological advantage of close personal observations, an ethnographic account of a large organization can lack breadth of coverage and vision.

Beyond providing a deep descriptive account of courtroom practices, my research addresses larger questions that speak to matters of scope and reliability: what are the persistent culture and practices of the Cook County Criminal Courts, across all courtrooms, over time, and how can these be best observed? I addressed these issues by having multiple researchers examine the same setting. This allowed for a larger body of data and a greater social distance between the "Self" (the researcher) and the "Other" (the researched).[15]

My work was conducted in collaboration with Chicago Appleseed Fund for Justice. In all, I oversaw 130 "court watchers" who were sent into all twenty-five courtrooms in the courthouse at 26th and California over the course of two years (2008–2009). The court watchers collected and recorded qualitative observations of courtroom practices from the vantage point of the public galleries and other spaces in the courthouse. Given the large-scale coordination required, this portion of my data began with a pilot study.

Pilot Study

A court-watching initiative was developed as part of Chicago Appleseed's large-scale study of the Cook County Criminal Justice System. While interviews were intended to investigate the views of attorneys reflecting on the criminal justice system, court watching was designed to examine courtroom practices and provide a perspective independent from the views and information gathered through the interviewing effort.

Pilot Effort: Research Instruments and Protocol

At Chicago Appleseed, I trained nineteen law students to conduct court observations in the twenty-five courtrooms at the 26th and California courthouse. These students attended a two-hour training program to learn how to record observations as well as understand the basics of criminal procedure and courtroom dynamics. Court observers were instructed to note their observations on four different forms. The forms allowed them to provide open-ended reports of their impressions and observations in court. The forms also asked more-structured questions of the observers. Court watchers were directed to rank and quantify the performance of the individuals in the courtroom. The four research instruments can be described as follows:

> Form A was a reference form that documented general information on the courtroom: names of judges, prosecutors, public defenders, and private attorneys observed during a particular day of court watching.

> Form B recorded individual hearings. Due to the fast pace of the hearings at the courthouse (77 percent of hearings were five minutes or less), Form B was developed in chart form to allow court watchers to record information about hearings quickly. The form provided space for handwritten notes, and court watchers were encouraged to record any occurrence they thought interesting or noteworthy.

> Form C allowed court watchers to record more-detailed information about the extended hearing or trial. This form included questions on opening and closing statements, the jury composition, information on witnesses and treatment of those parties. Form C also provided space for court watchers to comment on the overall impression within the courtroom and on that particular hearing.

> Form D was developed to provide an opportunity for court watchers to reflect on the totality of their experiences throughout the day. They were asked to quantify the preparedness and behavior of the major courtroom players (judges, prosecutors, public defenders, private attorneys, and sheriffs) and also given room to write open-ended responses.

In all, court watchers collectively spent approximately 160 hours in the courthouse and observed 550 hearings in twenty-five different courtrooms.

Pilot Effort: Critiques and Adjustments

This effort, while yielding insights about court culture and practices, was cumbersome and had a potential for measurement error. Given the speed of court proceedings, and the use of legal jargon, observing "hearings" as a unit of analysis made data collection complex. Court watchers had to study forms in order to use them well in open court, and they had to decide when one hearing ended and the other began. Often, the professionals being observed moved swiftly between cases—switching from plea bargaining to obtaining status dates or even taking a quick testimony from witnesses for a bench trial. With this approach, there was a significant amount of missing data. Some researchers attempted to gather defendants' names and charges from call sheets posted in the hallways in the courthouse, while others did not. Similarly, due to microphone failures, particularly in the "fishbowl courtrooms" with bulletproof glass, observers often could not obtain data on hearing type and outcome as well as note the defendant names. Given the fluidity of workgroup practices, structural obstacles, and the amount of insider knowledge necessary to navigate and train court watchers, there was a high potential for measurement error due to potentially low inter-rater reliability. The pilot effort was essential for purposes of honing the methodological protocol, refining (and streamlining) the research instruments, and anticipating further ways to mitigate issues of reliability.

Court Watching Revised

Court watchers were expected to evaluate the open-court professional practices and conduct their observation in the public spaces of the court. Other criminal court–watching efforts have focused on legal decision making, evaluating the uniformity of case outcomes, or the "fairness" of sentences. Given that court watchers were unable to rigorously observe open-court behavior and record legal factors from case files, case outcomes were beyond the scope of this work. Instead, this research focused on professional standards of practice and how these standards affected the overall impression of the courts as a legal forum.

How do you focus court watchers on a common metric of evaluation? How do you define professional standards? How do you measure a "violation" of standards when you see it? Finally, how do you create inter-rater reliability with 130 researchers? The following material details the protocol of court watching, as well as how I addressed such questions.

Shared Metric of Evaluation

Court watchers needed a common metric by which to evaluate the criminal courts. The rubric had to be a standard that was measurable and agreed upon within the legal community—a standard by which professionals could define their normative manner of professional conduct. The National Center for State Courts and the Bureau of Justice Assistance's Trial Court Performance Standards served this purpose and acted as a common metric by which to define a normative standard of conduct (see Appendix B). The standard promotes "access to justice" as the focal point for evaluating courts. The principle of access to justice extends to "location, physical structure, procedures, and the responsiveness of personnel." Trial courts are expected to "eliminate unnecessary barriers to its services." Barriers can be caused by "deficiencies in both language and knowledge of individuals participating in court proceedings." In addition, "psychologi-cal barriers can be created by mysterious, remote, unduly complicated, and intimidating court procedures."[16]

To obtain agreement on these standards in Cook County, the presiding judge of the criminal courts, Judge Paul Biebel, approved all the data-collection instruments and procedures. In addition, Judge Biebel was interested in the concept of court watching as an opportunity to make the courts more accountable to the public and the chief judge. Thus the concept of court watching as well as the metric for evaluating courtroom prac-tices emerged out of the collaboration with the judicial leadership in Cook County. While these data could also be used for policy purposes, using a professional code that was agreed upon by the leadership of professionals allowed for a common metric by which researchers (outsiders) and professionals (insiders) could find common defini-tions for normative standards of professional behavior. Despite the potential for this type of research to be used for policy and reform, however, no major effort was adopted to change the practices in Cook County by using court watching. Certainly, this tech-nique could be imported into other jurisdictions, and it can be instructive to other legal scholars studying immigrant court, juvenile courts, and the like.

Research Instruments

Research instruments were developed and provided a common lens to evaluate and de-scribe events that the court watchers observed. Court observations were structured and semi-structured, providing the opportunity for researchers to rate professionals on a common numerical scale as well as provide an explanation for their ratings or a descrip-tive account that justified their ratings.

Following the revision of the pilot version of the data collection procedure, court watchers were ultimately given two forms. First, a "court call" form recorded obser-vations of the general court call tasks of the courtroom workgroup, which included the setting of status dates, plea bargains, observations about the demeanor of court professionals and support staff, the courthouse facilities, security, and other environ-mental factors that contributed to the cultural atmosphere of the public gallery, and the professional spaces of the courtrooms and courthouse more generally (see Ap-pendix D for a sample form). This approach simplified observations, in contrast to the pilot study.

The second form used by court observers was called the "Trial/Extended Hearing Form" (see Appendix C for a sample). This form was used to document professional standards during trials (bench or jury), motions, or jury selection. Because trials are not as prevalent, there was less documentation of trials or motions. Often, the culture and features characterized in the general court call form were reflected in the Trial/Extended Hearing Form as well.

Beyond this more structured period of observation, court watchers were required to include written explanations of their ratings and were encouraged to create thick descriptions of their accounts. In the spirit of ethnographic observation, they were in-structed to move beyond the forms and provide field note–like descriptions of their experiences, scrutinizing the experience of justice, the ease of navigating the courthouse, and the "events" and incidents they encountered even while waiting in the public gallery during recess.

All written notes on their experiences, including documentation of small interactions in hallways, security lines, and interactions with court professionals, were collected with their formal court-watching forms. When court watchers submitted their forms, they were given an "exit" interview or debriefing session. They were asked the following questions:

Do you think your appearance affected your experience in court?

What was the response of court professionals to your presence?

What was the most unexpected thing you saw?

Did you feel that your court watching training prepared you for your experience?

If yes, what was most beneficial? If no, please explain . . .

What is one improvement you would suggest to improve quality of the courthouse?

Did you find the forms easy to use? Any improvements that you would recommend?

Please confirm your hourly total for court watching.

These qualitative accounts were telling testimonies of the consumer experience of justice. In this respect, researchers were observers as well as "consumers"—critiquing what they saw and experienced. I recruited researchers of varying racial backgrounds and dressed in "plain clothes" rather than professional attire to blend with the general public. As a result, this study takes a cue from Devah Pager's work examining race.[17] I capture the everyday "experience" of justice by "testing" to see how the researchers of varying racial backgrounds, dressed in plain clothes, were treated within the courthouse.

Given the richness of these accounts, during the second year of this research, court watchers (approximately sixty of them) were asked to write a reflection memo (similar to field notes) to document their reflections on their observational experience (see Appendix B for the debrief prompt).

Training

To ensure consistency of observations and evaluations, court watchers went through training that reviewed the National Center for State Courts standards. All court watchers attended a three-hour training session. (See Appendix A for specifics on how court watchers were recruited and their educational background.) The training covered the following elements: the caseload and composition of criminal courts; the adversarial and cooperative models of justice, trials, and plea bargains; and the organizational dynamics of courtroom workgroups. Court watchers were also briefed on the initial findings of Chicago Appleseed research on Chicago's felony courts. The objective of this training was to educate court watchers on the norms and professional standards of how criminal courts function on a daily basis, offer organizational context for courtroom norms like the prevalence of plea bargaining, and provide a detailed orientation as how to use court-watching instruments. In addition, court watchers were instructed not to narrowly critique specific judicial decisions, but to evaluate all court personnel and their professionalism in court.

In addition to the structured part of the data collection, court watchers learned from my instruction about the descriptive techniques of ethnography. Namely, they were trained to identify and create thick descriptions of social life, how to observe without intrusion, and how to actively interpret ongoing social life, "transforming those experiences and interpretations into texts that could be made available to others as versions or representations of 'what's there.'"[18] Given the numerous observers, the data capture the collective, mundane, and natural social context of culture in action.[19]

Procedure

Court watching was completed over the course of two years. Given the extended time period, and the large number of observers, this method was dynamic and responsive to what was observed in court. Court observing was done in incremental "waves." Initially, court watchers were randomly assigned to the twenty-five courtrooms in the courthouse. Each court watcher was assigned a list of five or six courtrooms for his or her first visit. They were instructed to observe at least one hour of court call. They noted their name, the judge's name (to ensure that rooms were not changed), the date, time, and duration of their visit. In the case of a trial or hearing, they could stay for the duration, or longer if necessary. After one hour, they were to rotate to their next assigned courtroom. If the court was in recess, they could rotate to the next courtroom and go back at a later time to complete their assignment. Court watchers were required to spend at least five hours observing within the courthouse. Some court watchers returned on multiple days and completed well more than the minimum requirement.

The procedure of court assignments takes a cue from multilevel modeling. After each wave of court watching, the hours observed in each courtroom were tallied to inventory an even distribution across all courtrooms. In addition, court-watching forms and comments were analyzed for any initial indication of an "event" or incident that indicated that a courtroom was violating professional standards. An example of such an event was the young African American girl who was taken into a court lockup (see Chapter 2). In some cases, the same event was witnessed by multiple observers in the same courtroom. In other cases, a single observer saw the event. In cases of violation, I considered the correlation of ratings by the single observer, comparing how that person's ratings compared with those in other courtrooms to ensure that he or she was not an outlier. In addition, I compared the evaluation of this courtroom with evaluations by other observers to address inter-rater reliability issues for this courtroom. If a court was consistently rated poorly, or if there were incidents of abuse, more observers were sent to the courtroom during subsequent "waves" of observations.

In summary, inter-rater reliability issues were diminished by requiring open-ended responses for particular ratings, training all observers in a three-hour course, defining a common rubric of evaluation, and sending multiple court watchers into the same courtrooms. Also, by comparing court watchers to themselves, I could examine the correlation of ratings by a single observer to ensure uniformity and consistency of individual observers.

Anonymity of Subjects

As noted in the preface, it is imperative to protect the anonymity of subjects. To protect subject anonymity, I did the following: (1) used pseudonyms; (2) masked branch locations, specific courtrooms, and dates/years; and (3) changed the identifiable features of attorneys, cases, and defendants.

All names in this study, including those of the judges, private attorneys, state's attorneys, public defenders, staff, and defendants, have been changed to pseudonyms. In some cases, distinguishing features of cases have been altered to avoid any possibility of inadvertently revealing the identity of subjects. The features that were changed did not alter the outcome of the case or the findings they illustrated. Please note that I used a pseudonym that stays true to the cultural integrity of the actual subject's name, be it a white, Latino, or African American name.

Because of Cook County's size and its features, it is difficult to identify individual subjects.

Scale and Transfer of Professionals

Cook County processes more than 10,000 cases annually. There are approximately 900 prosecutors and 560 public defenders (representing 23,000 defendants annually). Professional participants often transfer from courtroom to courtroom and sometimes from one branch location to another. The Criminal Division courthouse at 26th Street and South California Avenue handles nearly 80 percent of all felony cases and is often referred to as the "main courthouse."[20] Additional felony courtrooms in six municipal district courthouses are also located throughout Cook County. The professionals in these "satellite" courtrooms were trained at the main courthouse and merely transferred to the satellite locations for periods of time. Observations were conducted in both the main courthouse and a satellite courthouse. This satellite location will not be identified to protect subject identities because identifying the location may inadvertently provide clues as to the attorneys described.

Given (1) the size of the Cook County Courts, (2) the numerous courthouse locations/municipalities, (3) the numerous participants in the pool of potential subjects, and (4) my careful consideration of anonymity, there is minimal risk of identifying any particular case, defendant, professional, or courtroom. Finally, this ethnography was conducted over an extended period of time—which adds further difficulty in identifying subjects, cases, or courtrooms.

Court Watcher Anonymity

As the court-watching phase of this research began, I realized that matching the names of court watchers to their observations of court abuses and ethical violations could pose risks. Additionally, in their reflections, court watchers were candid about their racial privilege or their embarrassment at being mistaken for defendants. As a result, the identity of all court watchers will be protected. In addition, while I tallied the date, time, and location of observations (as detailed above), I did not refer to the date or the court in which the court watchers conducted observations, since that information could compromise their anonymity and that of the professionals they observed.

APPENDIX A

Description of Court Watchers

Court watchers worked on a volunteer basis and were recruited from local law schools, schools of social work and criminal justice, and undergraduate institutions. They were selected through a rigorous process that included the submission of a professional résumé, as well as an application intended to screen applicants to ensure that they would be objective observers and harbor no biases against the criminal justice system. Undergraduate students from six universities (University of Chicago, DePaul University, University of Illinois at Chicago, Loyola University, Northwestern University, and Robert Morris College) were represented. In addition, Chicago Appleseed relied on pro bono support from two law firms in the Chicago area.

APPENDIX B

Court-Watching Debrief

The "code of conduct" delineates parameters of behavior for the professionals at 26th and California, Criminal Courthouse. This code is based upon the National Center for State Courts Trial Court Performance Standards and Measurement and is outlined below.

Standard 1: Trust and Confidence in Public Proceedings

The trial court conducts its proceedings and other public business openly.

The court must ensure that its proceedings are accessible and audible to all participants, including litigants, attorneys, court personnel, as well as members of the public including victims, families, jurors, and the general public.

Standard 2: Safety, Accessibility, and Convenience

Trial court facilities are safe, accessible, and convenient to use for all members of the public, as well as courtroom participants.

Court personnel should not engage in any intimidation or impropriety to visitors including victims, families, jurors, and the general public, regardless of their social background.

Standard 3: Effective Participation

The trial court gives all who appear before it the opportunity to participate effectively, without undue hardship or inconvenience.

The court must accommodate all participants in its proceedings—especially those who have language difficulties, mental impairments, or physical handicaps. This includes interpreters for the deaf, arrangements for the impaired, and translators for non-English speakers. Also, defendants should be able to ask their attorneys questions during proceedings without being reprimanded.

Standard 4: Courtesy, Responsiveness, and Respect

Judges and other trial court personnel are courteous and responsive to the public, and accord respect to all with whom they come in contact.

The criminal court should be accommodating and less intimidating. No court employee should by words or conduct demonstrate bias or prejudice based on a person's social background to other employees of the court, as well as members of the public. Furthermore, victims' and defendants' families should be treated with appropriate tact and basic sensitivity, and their questions should not be criminalized or ignored.

1. Please provide an overall evaluation of your experience at 26th and California against the standards outlined in the "code of conduct." Provide specific examples as evidence of your assessment.

2. Scholars and even courtroom participants often discuss an entrenched "court culture" as an explanation for the persistence and resistance to changes in the felony courts.

   a. To what extent did you observe a distinct "court culture" at 26th and California? From your observations, is court culture a local, court-by-court phenomenon or a "macro"-level feature of 26th and California? Please provide examples and observations from your court watching.

   b. In terms of court management, what responsibilities do judges play in managing or contributing to court culture?

3. Based on your training and observations, please provide a recommendation that would improve the access and quality of justice at 26th and California.

APPENDIX C

Trial/Extended Hearing Form

*PLEASE COMPLETE IF HEARING IS LONGER THAN 5 MINUTES
(i.e., Probation Violations, Motions, Trials, etc.)

1. Time of Observation: _____am/pm to _____am/pm

2. Were you able to witness the entire proceeding?   Yes   No

3 **Prosecutor**: How many participated in hearing/trial (how many were at the table)?

Describe Professional Demeanor	Sex (M/F)	Race

4. **Defense Attorney**: How many participated in hearing/trial (how many were at the table)?

Describe Professional Demeanor	Public Defender (Y/N)	Sex (M/F)	Race

5. Type of Hearing or Trial:
   (Please circle)

   Jury Trial   Bench Trial   Jury Selection
   Other (If possible, please specify_____)

6. If there is a jury, please describe the composition:
   Gender
   > Men _____
   > Women _____
   Race
   > African American _____
   > Asian _____
   > Caucasian _____
   > Latino/Hispanic _____
   > Other _____

7. Witnesses Composition:

Called By	Cross Examined? (Y/N)	Relationship to Defendant	Did the Judge Address Witness? (Y/N)

8. Treatment of Witnesses:
   In general, how were the witnesses treated?

Poor	Inadequate	Acceptable	Good	Excellent
1	2	3	4	5

9. Was the defendant able to ask questions of their attorney during the proceeding?

   Yes   No

   If no, please explain.

   _____
   _____
   _____

10. If you observed a trial, was the defendant's appearance/attire appropriate and professional?

   Yes   No
   If no, please explain.

   _____
   _____
   _____

11. Did you understand what was going on in the courtroom?

　　Never　　　　　　　　Sometimes　　　　　　　　Always

12. Please give your overall impression and comments of the proceeding. Please explain.

　　Poor　　　Inadequate　　Acceptable　　Good　　　Excellent

　　_____

　　_____

　　_____

　　_____

　　_____

　　_____

　　_____

APPENDIX D

Court-Watching Court Call Form

Judge Presiding _____ Observer Name _____ Courtroom Number _____

Entrance into the Courthouse:

1. *Please describe how you and/or others were treated upon entrance into the court (mark once per day). Please include details of the environment of the court (the ease of parking, passing security, the length of lines, interaction with courtroom personnel.)*

   _____

   _____

   _____

   _____

   _____

Time of the hearings:

2. *Were you in the courtroom when the day's hearings began? If so, what time was the first hearing?* _____

3. *Were you in the courtroom when the day's hearings ended? If so, what time did the hearing end?* _____

Atmosphere and facilities:

4. *Please describe the atmosphere in the gallery (general feeling/impressions of whether people understood what was happening, etc.). In addition, how was the public treated by courtroom personnel?*

   _____

   _____

   _____

   _____

   _____

5. *How would you describe the courtroom facilities (cleanliness, security and accessibility of the gallery, acoustics)?*

    Poor   Acceptable   Good

    Please explain. _____

    _____

Ease/difficulty of the hearings:

6. *In general, did you have trouble hearing the parties?*

    Often   Sometimes   Never

    Please specify any person you had difficulty hearing (e.g., judge, defendant) and the specific problem.

    _____

    _____

7. *Was the judge interrupted/distracted by activities in the courtroom while the hearing was in progress?*

    Often   Sometimes   Never

    If so, what were the distractions?

    _____

    _____

8. *Did the judge stop the court record during the proceedings?*   Yes   No
    If yes, why?

    _____

    _____

Defendants:

9. *Did you witness any 402 conferences (pleas)? If so, did the defendant have any outward signs of confusion and frustration with their plea? If yes, please explain.*

    _____

    _____

10. *Were the 402 conferences held in the courtroom or did they occur in the judge's chamber?*

    _____

    _____

11. *If a defendant requested/required an interpreter, was one present at their hearing?*
    Yes   No
    Please explain. _____

    _____

12. *Were the defendants visibly confused by courtroom procedures?*
    Yes   No
    If yes, please explain.

    _____

    _____

13. *Were the defendants able to ask questions to their attorney?*
    Yes   No
    If no, please explain.

    _____

    _____

Professionalism:

14. *In general, please rate the professional behavior of the listed courtroom officials. Professional behavior includes: appropriate attire/neat appearance, use of appropriate language, attentiveness, control of emotions, preparedness, etc.*

a. Judge	Poor 1	Inadequate 2	Acceptable 3	Good 4	Excellent 5
b. Prosecutors	Poor 1	Inadequate 2	Acceptable 3	Good 4	Excellent 5
c. Public Defenders	Poor 1	Inadequate 2	Acceptable 3	Good 4	Excellent 5
d. Private Defense Attorneys	Poor 1	Inadequate 2	Acceptable 3	Good 4	Excellent 5
e. Sheriffs	Poor 1	Inadequate 2	Acceptable 3	Good 4	Excellent 5

15. *If you rated poor or inadequate for any of the above, please explain.*

    _____

    _____

16. *If police officers were present in court, please describe their professional demeanor. Also, where were they seated?*

    _____

    _____

    _____

17. *Did sheriffs assist and/or hinder defense attorneys' abilities to go in and out of lockup? (Please skip if you did not observe this).*
Yes No
If yes, please explain.

_____
_____

18. *Were you required to account for your presence in the courtroom?*
Yes No
If yes, please describe the circumstances surrounding your situation and please identify the courtroom personnel who questioned you.

_____
_____
_____

19. *Are there any other impressions on the courtroom proceedings that you would like to note?*

_____
_____
_____

NOTES

Preface

1. *Offutt v. United States*, 348 U.S. 11, 14 (1954).
2. Alexander 2010, 15, 100.
3. Research anonymity is elaborated in the Methods Appendix.

Introduction

1. Garland 2001; Western 2009.
2. Western and Wildeman 2009, 228.
3. Pattillo, Weiman, and Western 2004; Clear 2007.
4. Pattillo, Weiman, and Western 2004; Chesney-Lind and Mauer 2003; Clear and Frost 2013; Frampton, Haney-López, and Simon 2008; Goffman 2009.
5. For accounts on the ethno-racial representation and stratification of the "professional and administrative U.S. Justice Workforce," see Ward 2006. He reveals limited integration of nonwhites across sectors of the justice workforce. Nonwhites are underrepresented in professional and administrative roles. Also see Butler's (2010) narrative account of life as one of the few black federal prosecutors in his office. For works on how racial identity of professionals affects racially disparate sentencing outcomes, see Farrell, Ward, and Rousseau 2009; Spohn 1990a and 1990b. Also, in a recent study by the Women Donors Network, 66 percent of states that elect prosecutors have no black attorneys in those elected positions. In addition, 95 percent of the 2,437 elected state and local prosecutors were white and 79 percent were white males. To contextualize this lack of diversity, white males constitute only 31 percent of the population in the United States. Clearly, the power to charge, prosecute, and imprison is concentrated in the hands of mostly white males. http://www.womendonors.org/new-wdn-study-documents-the-paucity-of-black-elected-prosecutors/.
6. Bonilla-Silva 2006.
7. Feeley and Simon 1992; Tonry 2011.
8. Goffman 2009; Rios 2011.
9. Bourdieu 1990, 56.
10. There is much debate regarding whether the United States has begun to de-carcerate and reduce the number of Americans in prison. While there are encouraging

signs of decarceration, we should consider the cultural legacy and racial stigmas created by decades of mass incarceration and the institutional practices required to make such a punitive system run so efficiently. This research details the criminal courts' role in that effort and shows the cultural persistence of practices that will likely sustain the punitive tenor of mass incarceration even after we reduce the prison population.

11. "Habitus" refers to socially acquired tastes, preferences, ways of thinking and acting, learned and otherwise acquired from one's family, education, and life experiences. These are the products of deep cultural conditioning. Bonilla-Silva adds that habitus can assume a racialized character. He defines white habitus as a "racialized, uninterrupted socialization process that conditions and creates whites' racial tastes, perceptions, feelings, and emotions and their views on racial matters" (Bonilla-Silva 2006, 104). When a white habitus constitutes an isolated legal institution, this has a dire impact on legal practices.

12. Bonilla Silva 2002, 42. Scholars argue that old-fashioned forms of racism prevalent under Jim Crow have transformed into new forms of racism that focus on moral inferiority rather than biologically based inferiority; Lamont 2000. Often these immoral labels reference the historical stigmas associated with blackness and brownness—the supposed tendency to be lazy, hypersexual, and criminally dangerous, for example. Terms like "symbolic racism" (Kinder and Sears 1981), "subtle racism" (Pettigrew 1989), "modern racism" (McConahay 1986), and "colorblind racism" (Bonilla-Silva 2006) explore this new moral metric that emphasizes core American values like individualism, self-reliance, obedience, work ethic, and discipline. Bobo and Smith (1998) suggest the term "laissez-faire racism" to refer to the new collection of beliefs that includes the acceptance of associated negative stereotypes about African Americans, a denial of racial discrimination as a social problem, and the blaming of blacks themselves for blacks' disadvantage.

13. Haney-López 2014.

14. Bonilla-Silva 1997.

15. Haney-López 2014.

16. Bonilla-Silva 2002; Haney-López 2014.

17. Omi and Winant 1994; Winant 2004; Feagin 2006; Haney-López 2010; Murakawa and Beckett 2010; Lynch 2011.

18. See Obasogie 2013 for a review of the history of empirical critical race theory, which imports the traditional concerns and principles of critical race theory and seeks to measure such claims using empirical methods and data. This book is part of that scholarly trajectory of critical race empiricism (sometimes referred to as eCRT or empirical critical race theory).

19. Accounts of colorblind racism show how whites talk about race through language that appears to be colorblind but in reality uses code words that are racially charged. These studies detail the complex cultural work necessary to appear to hold nonracial ideologies but do not delve into how these beliefs can be mobilized within institutions.

20. See Steffensmeier, Ulmer, and Kramer (1998) for a notion of "blameworthiness"

that constructs sentencing as both a consideration of the severity of the offense and a function of professionals' "views" of defendants' biographical features. Often these professional views (including those of judges) are informed by racialized stereotypes about young black men being prone to crime, deviance, and dysfunction. These stereotypes then influence sentencing decisions.

21. Collins 2000.

22. Garland 2005, 812.

23. Malcolm Feeley's (1979) work situates the criminal courts in their larger social context, arguing that court organizations are acted upon and influenced by larger environmental pressures. This "open system" arrangement includes political influences like patronage, the expansion of the criminal code, and changes in leadership, to name a few. This book revisits the "open system model" by culturally situating the actors who are responsible for case disposition as central to understanding the criminal courts. Like all social actors, professionals are embedded in the cultural context of American life and have an array of cultural tools that they can deploy to make disconnected, even contradictory, beliefs seem coherent in practice (Swidler 1986); Loury (2002, 167) argues that "racial stigma" is cognitively imprinted on the American collective conscience, subsuming the very definitions of who blacks (and certainly Latinos) are understood to be. Racial stigma is part of the American cultural toolkit (Van Cleve and Mayes 2015), and certainly court professionals possess this toolkit. While it may be in line with colorblind ideology to ignore the cultural conditioning of professionals, this book demonstrates that Feeley's "open system" can also be understood as an open flow of cultural meaning that acts upon and is enacted by the professionals as they process cases and people in the system.

24. Pattillo 2013.

25. My last name at the time of this ethnography further complicated how professionals saw my racial identity. While my birth name was "Nicole Gonzalez" and my father is Chicano, my maternal family changed my name to "Nicole Martorano" after a divorce when I was only three years old. Certainly, this Italian surname allowed white professionals to assume a "white" racial identity.

26. The "due process revolution" refers to an eruption of decisions that extended or explicitly defined procedural guarantees for defendants. Among these decisions are *Mapp v. Ohio* (1961), *Brady v. Maryland* (1963), *Gideon v. Wainwright* (1963), *Escobedo v. Illinois* (1964), *Miranda v. Arizona* (1966), and *Katz v. United States* (1967). Such decisions inspired an ample flurry of scholarly literature that attempted to measure whether these rulings affected the experience of justice in practice. The scholarly consensus was that while they were important procedural guarantees, much of the radical legal change that some activists and lawyers anticipated did not change the character of justice for the average defendant. For empirical studies that challenge the facade of justice in practice, see Sudnow 1965; Casper 1972; Eisenstein and Jacob 1977; and Feeley 1979.

27. Feeley (1979) observes a similar racial divide in the lower courts, but he does not incorporate race as an essential variable that can help explain how and why processes can "punish" in practice.

Chapter 1

1. Bogira 2005, 67.

2. Bogira 2005.

3. There are nonwhite legal professionals in some courtrooms as well as some white defendants and visitors, but their numbers are relatively small and do not alter the general patterns that are persistent through an entrenched culture.

4. Because caseloads are not counted consistently across offices, estimates of the percentage of defendants represented by the Public Defender's Office vary. For instance, the State's Attorney's Office reports that the Public Defender's Office represents 53 percent of criminal defendants, while other estimates are as high as 75 percent of defendants (Chicago Appleseed Fund for Justice 2007).

5. Olson and Taheri 2012. Whites account for 13.6 percent of the admissions, but there are no data revealing the features of this broad category of "whiteness." Many white detainees were recent immigrants from Russia and Poland, for example, and were in need of in-court translators. While whiteness often denotes privilege, here this statistic tells little about the other types of disadvantages (like poverty, lack of education, inability to make bond, immigration status, and language barriers) that may affect their experience of justice.

6. Cook County Jail Report 2012.

7. Casper's approach focused solely on the defendants as the consumers of justice. However, the consequences of mass incarceration are far-reaching and extend even to families and entire communities that come in contact with the carceral state—be it through victimization, hyper-surveillance, or the actual commission of a crime. In this book, the notion of "consumer" extends to all who come into contact with the criminal justice system, including victims, witnesses, jurors, defendants, and the general public who seek to access our American criminal courts. It is from their vantage points that we must appraise the appearance of justice and the legitimacy of the system.

8. Casper 1971, 4.

9. There is a robust literature examining the causes and consequences of assembly line justice. In Malcolm Feeley's *The Process Is the Punishment* (1979), most defendants preferred plea bargains to avoid pretrial punishment. Some scholars described plea bargaining as a safeguard against mass caseloads—a type of filtering mechanism that avoids having all cases go to trial (Smith 1993). Other scholars attributed plea bargaining to excessive caseloads, the strain of pretrial incarceration, aggressive prosecutors, and even the perceived incompetence of public defenders (Sudnow 1965; for summary, see Van Cleve 2011).

10. Like a machine, the Cook County Jail that houses pretrial detainees is "programmed to receive" the explosive rate of incarceration. It is like a local entry point to mass incarceration. More than 2 million people are incarcerated nationwide. If this trend were to continue at the current rate, one of every three black males and one of every six Latino males born today could expect to do time in prison ("Report of the Sentencing Project" 2013).

11. The Eagles 1976.

12. Rosset and Cressey 1976; Mather 1979.

13. Eisenstein and Jacob 1977; Van Cleve 2011.

14. Van Cleve and Lara-Millán 2014.

15. Lamont and Molnár 2002.

16. Durkheim 1965.

17. Lamont and Molnár 2002.

18. The advocacy nonprofit organization Chicago Appleseed Fund for Justice noted a recent "R Kelly Effect" that improved the quality of these public spaces. In 2002 R&B singer R. Kelly was charged with crimes associated with having sex with a minor. Reformers hypothesized that this high-profile case, resulting in an acquittal in 2008, forced officials to marginally improve conditions for the outside media that flooded the courthouse in the short term. The *New York Times* noted that the "public spectacle [of] the trial was something of a bust . . . The courthouse is in an inconveniently located neighborhood . . ." which illuminates the "Alcatraz Effect" defusing the spectacle of a high-profile trial. Davis Streitfeld, "R. Kelly Is Acquitted in Child Pornography Case," *New York Times*, June 14, 2008.

19. Children were not allowed in the courts, which is costly to many defendants and victims. Later, we will see cases in which judges respond abusively to the presence of children in court.

20. Auyero 2012. For instance, Auyero's research examines the endless waiting of the Argentinean poor for housing subsidies, identification cards, welfare checks, and court rulings.

21. Auyero 2012, 9.

22. This theme will be explored deeply in Chapter 4.

23. Illinois now has a moratorium on the death penalty.

24. Goffman 1959.

25. See Picca and Feagin (2007) for their exploration of "two-faced racism," in which they examine white-racist activity in the backstage and front-stage locations that define every interaction. In contrast, I show the complete dismantling of the front- and backstage of racism that occurs in a space that acts on behalf of the state.

26. *Pro se* is a Latin phrase that means "for oneself." Defemdants have a constitutional right to represent themselves in state criminal proceedings.

27. Pattillo 2013.

28. While we mostly think about whites wearing "blackface" in minstrel shows of blackface comedy, around the mid-1840s, blacks became minstrels. By the 1860s, they were established performers in this genre but did not alter the tradition of literally "acting out" racial caricatures. Their participation amplified prevailing racist black stereotypes. To participate in minstrel shows, blacks had to "prove" themselves as "real coons" by painting their faces with burnt cork and performing the stigmatized tropes in a manner that whites had done (Krasner 1997).

29. Heinz et al. 2005.

30. Peter Nardulli (1978) characterizes court organizations as "classically" bureaucratic, with power vested in a small group of courthouse participants, calling these court professionals the "courtroom elite" because their decision making has low visibility and

is difficult to evaluate or control. As such, the courts are a monopolistic structure vested in reproducing the court culture. However, despite this monopoly, criminal lawyers occupy a lower status in the profession, according to Heinz and Laumann (1984).

31. The University of Chicago Law School was coded as "elite" while Northwestern University School of Law was categorized as "prestigious." Law schools like Chicago-Kent College of Law, Loyola University School of Law, and DePaul University College of Law were considered "local"—lacking the institutional prestige of the previous categories.

32. This attorney is alluding to Operation Greylord, an investigation by the Federal Bureau of Investigation and the IRS Criminal Investigation Division into the corruption of the judiciary in Cook County. As the *Chicago Tribune* reports, "Nearly 100 people had been indicted, and all but a handful were convicted. Of the 17 judges indicted, 15 were convicted. The tally of convictions included 50 lawyers, as well as court clerks, police officers and sheriff's deputies." http://www.chicagotribune.com/news/nationworld/poli tics/chi-chicagodays-greylord-story-story.html. See also Tuchy and Warden 1989.

33. Heinz and Manikas 1992.

34. In this chapter we will examine how the term "good ol' boys" club is not just an "autonomous set" of lawyers but a reference to their racial homogeneity.

35. Abbott 1981; Heinz et al. 2005.

36. Abbott 1981, 819. For Abbott, high professional stature is the "ability to exclude nonprofessional issues or irrelevant professional issues from practice" (Abbott 1981).

37. Highlighting the status divides between criminal law and the rest of the legal bar was how attorneys in the upper echelon or hemisphere (Heinz and Laumann 1984) of the legal profession related to attorneys practicing in courts isolated like Alcatraz Island. Top law firms in Chicago take their summer associates on courthouse tours to see how the "other half" lives and practices law. Their young associates represent defendants in the criminal courts on a pro bono basis—as a mere training ground to learn trial work. In a sense, the criminal courthouse becomes a tourist attraction and training ground for those at the top of the legal food chain.

38. At times, I noted that being a practitioner required tasks beyond the boundaries of criminal law, and instead encroached on the types of concerns native to a social worker (Van Cleve 2011). Likewise, Malcolm Feeley's study of the lower courts noted: "[L]ower court officials—judges, prosecutors and public defenders alike—feel frustrated and belittled . . . trained to practice law [yet] . . . confronted with the kinds of problems that social workers face" (Feeley 1979, 4).

39. Werth 2015.

Chapter 2

1. This behavior of judges in Cook County was so common that the professionals called them "yellers."

2. Garfinkel 1956, 420–421.

3. Garfinkel 1956, 421.

4. For other accounts of degradation ceremonies, see Gustafson 2013 and Longazel 2013.

5. As we will see, the court processes are transformed into a type of racial theater for mostly white officials to degrade, socially isolate, and denigrate people of color. In the conclusion of this book, I place these ceremonies in the context of other criminal justice locations like policing and argue that criminal justice arenas are the prime locations where whites can ritually denigrate people of color under the badge of the state.

6. Bonilla-Silva (2006, 233) defines the notion of "white habitus" as a "racialized, uninterrupted socialization process that conditions and creates whites' racial tastes, perceptions, feelings, and emotions and their views on racial matters." He argues that white habitus promotes in-group solidarity (also see Bonilla-Silva, Goar, and Embrick 2006). From an empirical standpoint, these claims are measured through surveys and interviews in which one can understand rhetorical expressions and viewpoints. In contrast, this work shows how a racial habitus exists as a social system where racism can be practiced in daily interactions, culture, and congeal in institutions.

7. Feagin and Hernan 1995; Feagin 2006.

8. Bogira 2005.

9. Bogira 2005, 69.

10. For more information on interview techniques, the decision to use young white women to conduct these interviews, and other details on methods, please see the Methods Appendix.

11. Bonilla-Silva 2006.

12. Seven of the 23 private attorneys interviewed were former prosecutors.

13. Prosecutors are ranked as first-, second-, and third-chair attorneys. Each courtroom has a first chair that supervises both second and third chairs. One gets promoted by winning trials that are often handed down through the ranks.

14. Haney-López 2010.

15. Van Cleve 2011.

16. Lamont 2000; Bobo and Smith 1998.

17. Kipling 1929. In later sections, I will discuss the pride that professionals feel in processing offenders that characterize the "half devil" persona. But here I discuss the construction of the mope as the offender who is "half child" but occupies (and wastes) most of the space and resources on the court docket.

18. Roberts 1997, 18.

19. This incident occurred before Cook County's ban on electronic devices, including cell phones and tablets, which went into effect on January 13, 2013. Chief Judge Evans banned these devices to avoid their potential use to videotape and then intimidate jurors, judges, victims, and witnesses. However, the ban exempted "current or former judges; licensed attorneys; all law enforcement officers; all government employees; persons reporting for jury service; jurors (subject to the authority of the trial judges); building and maintenance workers, equipment repair persons and vendors; and anyone authorized by order of court." Again, this ban demarcated separate and unequal treatment of privileges and practices by literally putting in writing the exempt groups that comprise mostly white attorneys and professionals while those most affected tend to be people of color. http://www.cookcountycourt.org/MEDIA/ViewPressRelease/tabid/338/

ArticleId/2094/Chief-Judge-Evans-enters-order-which-prohibits-cell-phones-in-court
houses-where-criminal-matters-are.aspx.

20. The nation saw a similar racial degradation ceremony at a 2015 Texas pool party
where an officer violently threw down a fourteen-year-old black girl in a bikini and
used his body weight to pin her to the ground. The girl was unarmed. Astoundingly,
few women's advocacy groups rallied in protest of this blatant display of violence against
a female. Instead, the forum of criminal justice "revealed" the girl not as a vulnerable
child but as a common criminal and perhaps even as a sexualized threat.

21. Garfinkel 1956.

22. "Sheriff's Women's Justice Programs," Cook County Sheriff, accessed March 12,
2011, http://www.cookcountysheriff.org/womens_justice_services/wjs_main.html.

23. I recorded in my field notes that the judge added the disrespectful term "Miss"
rather than "Judge" when mocking the defendant. In open court the defendant used the
respectful term "Judge."

24. According to historian Patrick Huber (1995), "For approximately the last one
hundred years, the pejorative term *redneck* has chiefly slurred a rural, poor white man
of the American South" (145). "The origin and early usage of the slur suggest that it ridi-
culed not only the sweaty, drudging labor of white farmers and sharecroppers but also
their perceived deviation, at least a limited one, from a pale white complexion. From its
earliest usage then, the pejorative term *redneck* reflected clear connotations of both race
and color difference" (147). Some researchers cited by Huber suggest that the term came
about because whites refused to wear hats when they worked alongside emancipated
blacks who continued to wear large straw hats associated with slaves during the 1870s,
choosing to get a sunburn rather than look like a slave (147).

25. Bonilla-Silva 2002.

26. This refers to plea bargaining a case—where defendants plead guilty in exchange
for a more lenient sentence.

27. Kipling 1929.

28. For an early account of how attorneys simplified legal categorizations, see Sudnow (1965), "Normal Crimes," where attorneys looked at criminal charges and other
extra-legal factors like age, race, and ethnicity to determine which cases were "normal"
and which cases exhibited unique features that were worthy of legal attention. What is
notable is that since Sudnow's study, the categories have simplified and become more
racialized into black/white distinctions.

29. The focus on "winning" trials contradicts both the law and the ethical standards
of the American Bar Association. The Supreme Court and the American Bar Association's
ethical standards sharply dictate a different calling toward justice. The Supreme Court
case *Berger v. United States*, 295 U.S. 78, 86 (1935), ruled that "[t]he United States Attorney
is the representative not of an ordinary party to a controversy, but of a sovereignty whose
obligation to govern impartially is as compelling as its obligation to govern at all; and
whose interest, therefore, in a criminal prosecution is not that it shall win the case, but
that justice shall be done." Likewise, the American Bar Association's standard reinforces
this definition by emphasizing the professional obligation of prosecutors: "The duty of the

prosecutor is to seek justice, not merely convict." See American Bar Association, "Prosecution Function, Part 1, General Standards, Standard 3–1.2c. http://www.americanbar. org/publications/criminal_justice_section_archive/crimjust_standards_pfunc_blk.html.

30. Chicago Appleseed Fund for Justice 2007.

31. On Cook County's status as the most overburdened court system in America, see Gershowitz and Killinger (2011), Spangenberg (2001), and Chicago Appleseed (2007).

32. While these tactics are used to maintain segregation in the court, here I show how these norms are incorporated into the practice of law.

33. Steen, Engen, and Gainey (2005) describe how criminal justice actors import global stereotypes about race and incorporate these stereotypes into local organization norms. Here I focus on how racist tropes act as efficient categories to sort and manage a docket of offenders and are part of the local legal culture and practices.

34. Many legal scholars incorrectly assume that felony "cases are serious . . . defendants are well-represented, procedures are enforced by judges, prosecutors and defense counsel [and] . . . law and evidence matters" (Natapoff 2012, 105). Here we will understand the rationales for why that is not always the case. In fact, many attorneys are trained in misdemeanor courts and bring some of the same cultural practices and assumptions to felony courtrooms, even viewing drug cases as "glorified misdemeanors."

35. An ignorant outsider was important to the prosecutors as well. In the jury selection process, during the voir dire (questioning of potential jurors) my supervisor chose one juror by just asking her name and where she lived. She noted that she selected the juror based on the juror's spelling error on the form. I was confused as to how the prosecutor knew this juror would be an asset to the prosecution. The prosecutor told me to look more closely at the juror form. The potential juror had misspelled her job as "waitres." The prosecutor taught me that a juror *that* "dumb" was one that she could easily persuade.

36. Rather than the judge, prosecutor, or even defense attorney investigating the claims of this defendant, they forced the defendant to plead guilty. These practices supported the police's ability to alter and even lie on police reports and do so with impunity.

37. As an example of how pervasive this practice is, a General Administrative Order (No. 2013–11) was issued in the summer of 2013 by the Chief Judge of the Cook County Circuit Court to curb the denial of indigence hearings.

38. Anytime there are two or more defendants on the same case, the court calls on this unit of attorneys to ensure proper representation and avoid conflicts of interest in the sharing of resources among public defenders from the same office.

39. Subsequent chapters address in greater detail how defense attorneys "defend" their clients in this culture, but this example demonstrates how in *due process for the undeserving*, there is little "law" in practicing law.

40. Boot camp is a military-style alternative to incarceration in Illinois.

41. It was unclear what dialogue was "for the record" and off the record. Many court reporters know when to stop typing (i.e., the mocking phrase).

42. *Wabash, St. Louis & Pacific Railway Company v. Illinois*, 118 U.S. 557 (1886).

43. Heimer 2001.

44. Feeley 1979.

Chapter 3

1. "Gideon's promise" refers to the landmark decision *Gideon v. Wainwright*, 372 U.S. 335 (1963). This historic decision ruled that indigent defendants in state courts have the right to appointed counsel if they cannot afford an attorney. While this ruling was significant progress for the criminally accused, it guaranteed only the assignment of counsel. In practice, the quality of compliance and representation varied by state and county, leaving many to question whether *Gideon* merely offered false hope for fair representation.

2. Blumberg 1967; Van Cleve 2011.

3. Duneier 2011.

4. Davis 2007.

5. Blumberg 1967; Uphoff 1992; Van Cleve 2011.

6. Public defenders represent between 22,000 and 23,000 indigent defendants each year in Cook County–Chicago.

7. The basic duty the defense counsel owes to the administration of justice and as an officer of the court is to serve as the accused's counselor and advocate with courage and devotion and to render effective, quality representation. ABA, *Standards for Criminal Justice: Prosecution and Defense Function, Standard 4–1.2(b)*, 3d ed. (American Bar Association, 1993).

8. "Management" was the term used for a supervisor who may critique or evaluate the rank-and-file public defender.

9. Class was included as a proxy for race because Americans are more inclined to admit class bias than race bias. The free-response aspect of the question allowed attorneys to elaborate their responses about class and race.

10. Bonilla-Silva 2002, 42.

11. Ibid.

12. Lamont 2000.

13. Van Cleve and Mayes 2015.

14. U2 2004.

15. Swidler 1986.

16. In Chapter 5, I demonstrate the complexity of defense attorneys' cultural toolkit (Swidler 1986) and show how racialized rubrics may be deployed independent of prosecutors.

17. The attorney's negotiation gained the defendant one less year in jail.

18. "IDOC" is an acronym for "Illinois Department of Corrections (prison)."

19. The judge initially added a year to the defendant's sentence, which pushed the sentence to a total of nearly 24 months in prison. Ultimately the total sentence was reduced to 18 months—a small win for the defense.

20. "Ex parte communication" refers to a one-sided, off-the-record discussion with only one party of a proceeding and a decision maker on matters relevant to the case. In the *Model Code of Judicial Conduct*, Canon 2, Rule 2.9 defines "ex parte communications" in the following manner: "A judge shall not initiate, permit, or consider ex parte communications, or consider other communications made to the judge outside the presence of the

parties or their lawyers, concerning a pending or impending matter." http://www.ameri
canbar.org/groups/professional_responsibility/publications/model_code_of_judicial_
conduct/model_code_of_judicial_conduct_canon_2/rule2_9expartecommunications
.html.

21. Anderson 2012, 9.

22. Winnetka is a wealthy suburb located in the North Shore area of the Chicago
metropolitan area.

23. For clarity, the dialogue of the participants is labeled either "SA" (for "state's attorney") or "PD" (for "public defender").

24. The judge was considering whether this defendant would go to prison (IDOC)
or jail (CCDOC) for violating his probation. Prison (what professionals called IDOC)
was used for sentences over a year in duration. Jail (CCDOC) was used for sentences
under a year (or for defendants awaiting trial).

25. Heimer 2001.

26. Winston 1901, 108–109.

27. See "How Section 8 became a 'racial slur'" for an example of how places begin
to embody racial meanings such that *where you lived* is conflated with *who you are* racially and morally. http://www.washingtonpost.com/news/wonkblog/wp/2015/06/15/
how-section-8–became-a-racial-slur/. In the case of Cook County, Cabrini-Greens was
constructed as notorious in the popular psyche of white Chicagoans and Americans. It
was dramatized in the horror movie *The Candy Man* (1992), which stars a white heroine
(a graduate student from the University of Chicago who is doing fieldwork) as she goes
deep undercover in the "Greens" only to be overcome and killed by a mythical predatory black man who is part urban legend and part reality.

28. Rios 2011.

29. In Illinois, permanent damage to a victim required serving 85 percent of the
total sentence—diminishing the chance for early release.

Chapter 4

1. In creating a case file for trial, evidence technicians take detailed, professionally
lit pictures that have the unintended consequence of appearing artful and dramatic.
This allows for a vivid dramatization of a crime scene and a proper documentation of
evidence.

2. Jeannene M. Przbylski, quoted in Jackson 2009, 8, n. 2.

3. Roberts 1997; Collins 2000.

4. Young 2005.

5. Ann Swidler's book, *Talk of Love*, similarly examines the fractured way that people can hold contradictory beliefs about love and make them coherent as they speak
about their belief system regarding love and marriage. Similarly, discussing "justice"
requires complex cultural work and, certainly, context.

6. Bach 2009.

7. Chapter 5 will address this dynamic among criminal defense attorneys.

8. Dimaggio and Powell 1991.

9. Professionals do not monolithically express the rubrics of racialized justice. Rather, they wield cultural ideas or schemes about justice, fairness, and due process, like a complex "toolkit." They draw from a "repertoire of meanings to frame and reframe experience in an open-ended way" (Swidler 2001, 40). This is the type of cultural work that allows attorneys to reconcile the cultural dissonance of what they do in the trenches of justice.

10. *Connick v. Thompson*, 563 U.S. (2011).

11. Bonilla-Silva 2006.

12. Butler 2010, 103.

13. The work of cultural theorist and sociologist Ann Swidler is instructive to understanding this complex terrain of *practices*, on the one hand, and *perspectives*, on the other: "Often our ability to describe a cultural perspective, or to see it at all, comes only from our skepticism about it. The culture we fully accept does not seem like culture; it is just real life" (2001, 19).

14. Swidler 2001, 40.

15. Swidler 1986.

16. Ghaziani 2009, 581; Van Cleve and Mayes 2015.

17. This is reminiscent of the Jim Crow image highlighted in the preface: "No dogs, No Negroes, No Mexicans."

18. Bonilla-Silva 2002, 48.

19. *Furman v. Georgia*, 408 U.S. 238, 286–289 (1972).

20. Trymaine Lee, "Jon Burge, ex-Chicago Cop Who Ran Torture Ring, Released from Prison," MSNBC, October 3, 2014, http://www.msnbc.com/msnbc/jon -burge-ex-chicago-cop-who-ran-torture-ring-released-prison.

21. Jason Meisner, "Ex-Cop Burge Leaves Prison, but Torture Victim Is Left Seeking Reparations," *Chicago Tribune*, October 2, 2014, http://www.chicagotribune.com/news/ ct-jon-burge-prison-release-met-20141002–story.html.

22. It is estimated that the City of Chicago spent more than $100 million on legal fees and settlements related to the accusations. The 120 victims received only $5.5 million in reparations. http://www.usatoday.com/story/news/2015/04/14/chicago-to-pay -reparations-jon-burge-police-torture-victims/25766531/.

23. Butler 2010.

24. Myron Orfield's survey of the Chicago criminal justice system (1987) found that defense attorneys, prosecutors, and judges estimated that police perjury at Fourth Amendment suppression hearings occurs in 20 to 50 percent of the cases. Also see Slobogin 1996, 3, and Dripps 1996, 698.

25. Van Cleve and Mayes 2015, 415.

26. In order to contextualize this fear of police officers, note that Illinois is famous for the notorious case of Drew Peterson, a former police officer from Bolingbrook, Illinois (a Chicago suburb), who was convicted of killing his third wife. During sentencing, Peterson was quoted as telling the prosecutor (James Glasgow) to look him in the eye and "Never forget what you've done here." In prison, Peterson made good on his word by, allegedly, hiring a hit man to kill Glasgow. Peterson is currently charged with one count of solicitation of murder for hire and one count of solicita-

tion of murder. While in prison, Peterson still collected his police pension despite being a convicted murderer and allegedly plotting to kill a prosecutor. Jon Seidel, "New Charge Is 2nd Time Drew Peterson Accused of Trying to Hire Hit Man," *Chicago Sun-Times*, February 9, 2015, http://chicago.suntimes.com/crime/7/71/355506/drew -peterson-tried-hit-man-prosecutor-james-glasgow.

Chapter 5

1. Blumberg 1967; Skolnick 1967; Uphoff 1992; Van Cleve 2011.

2. Van Cleve 2011.

3. Chicago Appleseed 2007; Spangenberg Group 2001. Nardulli (1978) studied the effects of high case volume in our criminal courts with a concern for variables like the decision to plead guilty, the decision to pursue a trial, and the type of sentence given in a guilty plea. The results showed that no variables were statistically significant with caseload pressure. In contrast to these organizational concerns, I focus on the rhetoric that rationalizes due process practices. In addition, I note that these studies were completed in the late 1970s at the advent of mass imprisonment—when the incarceration rate was still growing.

4. Van Cleve 2012.

5. Goffman 1959.

6. Nielsen 2000.

7. Casper 1971.

8. Jewel is a local chain of grocery stores in Chicago.

9. Imagine if this logic were extended to the relationship between medical doctors and patients. Every mispronunciation of a medication or an ailment or any missing information on the patient's part could be read by a doctor as a "hustle" and an attempt at deception. This analogy reveals the toxicity of racialized assumptions and how these assumptions compromised the chance for low-income people of color to receive zealous advocacy.

10. While certainly it would not be wise to give out personal information to any defendant, or even to a law enforcement officer (as we have seen), this quote illustrates that the word of the defendant was viewed as unreliable. Prosecutors also called defendants "bull shitters," and here we see the language and viewpoint appropriated by public defenders.

11. During the ethnography, a defendant turned the tables on this strategy. He was aware that he was not getting out of jail. He decided to get on the "early bus" back to jail so as not to have to talk to his attorney. It was a protest, of sorts, and the sheriffs were happy to comply. The PD responded, "Fine, it'll be a long month."

12. Hochschild 1983.

13. Ashforth and Humphrey 1993, 88.

Conclusion

1. I observed other offenders being held, unnecessarily, in the Cook County Jail. During my field work, a defendant came to court from the jail with a new charge. He pleaded to the judge, "How could I get a new charge if I've been in jail?" The judge

looked closely at the file and said, "Sir, you were supposed to be released a week ago?" Apparently, this defendant had already served his sentence and was begging the sheriffs to believe that he was done. The public defender sympathetically gave the defendant the number for the public defender's office and said she would help. What I wondered was, *If the sheriffs would not cross-check or believe his release date, why would they let him use the phone to get help?*

2. Blumberg 1967, 22.

3. Feeley 1979, 283.

4. One particular exception was David Sudnow's (1965) work on how public defenders coped with such organizational priorities. He argued that public defenders developed proverbial characterizations of the types of defendants (social identity, race, or ethnicity) who typically committed certain crimes. For instance, burglaries were "normally" committed by repeat offenders who were African American and "lower class." Public defenders then coach their clients as to the proper defensives strategy (Skolnick 1967). In contrast to Sudnow's work, the categories used by professionals in this study are notably simplified. While Sudnow and others discovered professionals' complex use of ideas about crime, race, ethnicity, and social class in the effort to meet organizational demands, this multifaceted rubric does not apply to today's offender population, which tends to be male, people of color, and those who are extremely poor.

5. Pager 2007. While there is much scrutiny of mass incarceration and the scale of imprisonment in the United States, there is little introspection on the processes or ceremonial charades that led to these convictions. This needs to be an additional focus for scholars concerned with mass incarceration: the illegitimacy of the processes that lead to felony convictions and imprisonment.

6. Pattillo, Weiman, and Western 2004; Chesney-Lind and Mauer 2003; Clear and Frost 2013.

7. Bonilla-Silva, Goar, and Embrick 2006.

8. Garland 2005.

9. Historically, public torture lynchings assumed many forms and have been wielded against whites and blacks alike. Garland (2005) refers to lynching as the racial violence of whites against blacks in the early 1890s—thirty years after Emancipation—and argues that popular justice was a collective punishment that is omitted from the "standard narrative of penal history" (Garland 2005, 796).

10. Garland 2005, 819.

11. Foucault is relevant to understanding how the racialized punishment inflicted during due process speaks to the standard penal narrative that Garland describes. In *Discipline and Punish* (1978), Foucault takes us through what he characterizes as a "correlative history of the modern soul" and a new power that passes judgment and wields discipline. He describes in horrid detail the calculated punishment of "torture" that was used for both judicial "truth"-finding purposes and for the operation of punishment itself. This is not unlike the spectacle of lynching—enacting on the body a public spectacle of fury.

At the beginning of the nineteenth century, the great spectacle of punishment left "the domain of the everyday perception" (Foucault 1982). In the modern era, the focus of punishment shifted from the body to the soul. On the surface, punishment, like racism, became more "humane," but with this humanity does not come leniency. Foucault argues that there is a shift in the object and the scale of punishment with new techniques that make punishment an efficient, industrialized endeavor. Punishment is regularized, homogenized, and subtle. A "machinery of law" emerged that was inflexible, absolute, and intolerant of individuals. Through surveillance and a permanent gaze, punishment deterred disorder in ensuring absolute enforcement of the law but had a representational effect on the minds of the people without being cruel to the body of the criminal. In this way, the punishment punishes the criminal and disciplines the social body (Foucault 1982, 95).

In the case of our modern criminal justice system, Foucault's clear distinction between the two types of punishment—of the body or of the soul—is not so distinct or separate. Process is inextricable from punishment. The machinery of law is an instrument of social control but focused directly on the discipline and governance of racial minorities and breaking both the mind and the body of the racialized defendant. A revised conclusion is that both the body and the soul are objects of punishment, with the punishment on the soul through the policing of morality as a public endeavor and the punishment on the body now hidden from spectacle within deplorable jail conditions that house pretrial detainees awaiting their day in our criminal courts or in police brutality that occurs in impoverished, segregated communities.

12. Numerous works discuss the role of mass incarceration in creating the "New Jim Crow," but there is less dialogue regarding how racism is dramatized by the state and within institutions. The criminal justice system is a central forum for this type of political theater.

13. All court-watching forms and instruments appear in the appendixes of this book. They can be scanned and printed for any reader to use. Please copy, distribute, and share these forms and put them to use in your jurisdiction. Also, the court-watching training PowerPoint and forms will be located on Stanford University Press's website as well as on my personal website, www.nicolevancleve.com.

14. *Offutt v. United States*, 348 U.S. 11, 14 (1954).

Methods Appendix

1. Lamont 2000, 73.

2. Lamont 2000.

3. Gómez 2010, 488.

4. Gómez 2004; Haney-López 2007; Obasogie 2007.

5. Van Cleve and Mayes 2015.

6. Gómez 2004, 499.

7. For review of criticisms, see Lee 2009.

8. Hagan 1974; Hagan and Albonetti 1982; Brooks 2000; Hagan, Shedd, and Payne 2005.

9. Mather 1979; Feeley 1979.

10. Gómez 2010, 499.

11. Geertz 1973.

12. The professionals in the satellite court were trained at the main courthouse and merely transferred to that location for periods of time. Their patterns of practice were the same as those of the main courthouse.

13. Mather 1974.

14. Fine and Weis 1996.

15. May and Pattillo-McCoy 2000.

16. See National Center for State Courts, "Trial Court Performance Standards" (2011), http://www.ncsconline.org/d_research/TCPS/area_1.htm.

17. Pager 2007.

18. Emerson 2001, 23.

19. Swidler 1986.

20. Chicago Appleseed 2007.

REFERENCES

Abbott, Andrew. 2004. *Methods of Discovery: Heuristics for the Social Sciences*. New York: W. W. Norton.

———. 1981. "Status and Status Strain in the Professions." *American Journal of Sociology* 86, no. 4: 819–835.

Alexander, Michelle. 2010. *The New Jim Crow: Mass Incarceration in the Age of Color-blindness*. New York: New Press.

Alschuler, Albert. 1968. "The Prosecutor's Role in Plea Bargaining." *University of Chicago Law Review* 36:50–112.

Anderson, Elijah. 2012. "The Iconic Ghetto." *Annals of the American Academy of Political and Social Science* 642, no. 1: 8–24.

Ashforth, Blake E., and Ronald H. Humphrey. 1993. "Emotional Labor in Service Roles: The Influence Identity." *Academy of Management Review* 18:88–115.

Auyero, Javier. 2012. *Patients of the State: The Politics of Waiting in Argentina*. Durham, NC: Duke University Press.

Bach, Amy. 2009. *Ordinary Injustice: How America Holds Court*. New York: Metropolitan Books.

Binder, David, Paul Bergman, and Susan Price. 1990. "Lawyers as Counselors: A Client-Centered Approach." *New York Law School Law Review* 35:29–86.

Blumberg, Abraham S. 1967. "The Practice of Law as a Confidence Game: Organizational Cooptation of a Profession." *Law and Society Review* 1:15–40.

Bobo, Lawrence D., and Ryan A. Smith. 1998. "From Jim Crow Racism to Laissez-Faire Racism: The Transformation of Racial Attitudes." In *Beyond Pluralism: The Conception of Groups and Group Identities in America*, edited by Wendy F. Katkin, Ned Landsman, and Andrea Tyree, 182–220. Urbana: University of Illinois Press.

Bogira, Steve. 2005. *Courtroom 302: A Year behind the Scenes in an American Criminal Courthouse*. New York: Random House.

Bonilla-Silva, Eduardo. 2006. *Racism without Racists: Color-Blind Racism and the Persistence of Racial Inequality in the United States*. Lanham, MD: Rowman and Littlefield Publishers.

———. 2002. "The Linguistics of Color Blind Racism: How to Talk Nasty about Blacks without Sounding 'Racist.'" *Critical Sociology* 28, nos. 1–2: 41–64.

————. 1997. "Rethinking Racism: Toward a Structural Interpretation." *American Sociological Review* 62, no. 3: 465–480.

Bonilla-Silva, Eduardo, Carla Goar, and David G. Embrick. 2006. "When Whites Flock Together: The Social Psychology of White Habitus." *Critical Sociology* 32, nos. 2–3: 229–253.

Bourdieu, Pierre. 1990. *The Logic of Practice*. Redwood City, CA: Stanford University Press.

Brewer, Rose M., and Nancy A. Heitzeg. 2008. "The Racialization of Crime and Punishment: Criminal Justice, Color-Blind Racism, and the Political Economy of the Prison Industrial Complex." *American Behavioral Scientist* 51, no. 5: 625–644.

Brooks, Richard. 2000. "Fear and Fairness in the City: Criminal Enforcement and Perceptions of Fairness in Minority Communities." *Southern California Law Review* 73:1219–1273.

Burawoy, Michael. 2003. "Revisits: An Outline of a Theory of Reflexive Ethnography." *American Sociological Review* 68, no. 5: 645–679.

Butler, Paul. 2010. *Let's Get Free: A Hip-Hop Theory of Justice*. New York: New Press.

Casper, Jonathan D. 1972. *American Criminal Justice: A Defendant's Perspective*. Englewood Cliffs, NJ: Prentice-Hall.

————. 1971. "Did You Have a Lawyer When You Went to Court? No, I Had a Public Defender." *Yale Review of Law and Social Action* 1, no. 4: 4–9.

Chesney-Lind, Meda, and Marc Mauer, eds. 2003. *Invisible Punishment: The Collateral Consequences of Mass Imprisonment*. New York: New Press.

Chicago Appleseed Fund for Justice. 2007. *A Report on Chicago's Felony Courts*. Chicago: Chicago Appleseed Fund for Justice.

Church Jr., Thomas W. 1985. "Examining Local Legal Culture." *Law and Social Inquiry* 10, no. 3: 449–510.

Clear, Todd R. 2007. *Imprisoning Communities: How Mass Incarceration Makes Disadvantaged Neighborhoods Worse*. New York: Oxford University Press.

Clear, Todd R., and Natasha A. Frost. 2013. *The Punishment Imperative: The Rise and Fall of the Grand Social Experiment in Mass Incarceration*. New York: New York University Press.

Collins, Patricia Hill. 2000. *Black Feminist Thought: Knowledge, Consciousness, and the Politics of Empowerment*. New York: Routledge.

Davis, Angela Y. 2007. "Racial Fairness in the Criminal Justice System: The Role of the Prosecutor Symposium on Pursuing Racial Fairness." *Columbia Human Rights Law Review* 39:202–232.

————. 1998. "Racialized Punishment and Prison Abolition." In *The Angela Y. Davis Reader*, edited by Joy James, 96–110. New York: Blackwell Publishers.

Dean, Mitchell. 1999. *Governmentality: Power and Rule in Modern Society*. London: Sage Publications.

Dezalay, Yves, and Bryant G. Garth. 2002. *The Internationalization of Palace Wars: Lawyers, Economists, and the Contest to Transform Latin American States*. Chicago: University of Chicago Press.

DiMaggio, Paul J., and Walter W. Powell, eds. 1991. *The New Institutionalism in Organizational Analysis*. Chicago: University of Chicago Press.

Dripps, Donald A. 1996. "Police, Plus Perjury, Equals Polygraphy." *Journal of Criminal Law and Criminology* 86:693–716.

Duneier, Mitchell. 2011. "How Not to Lie with Ethnography." *Sociological Methodology* 41, no. 1 (August): 1–11.

Durkheim, Émile. 1965. *The Elementary Forms of the Religious Life*. Translated by Joseph Swain. New York: Free Press.

The Eagles. 1976. *Hotel California*. Asylum, compact disc.

Earl, Jennifer. 2008. "The Process Is the Punishment: Thirty Years Later." *Law and Social Inquiry* 33, no. 3: 737–778.

Eisenstein, James, Roy B. Flemming, and Peter F. Nardulli. 1988. *The Contours of Justice: Communities and Their Courts*. Boston: Little, Brown.

Eisenstein, James, and Herbert Jacob. 1977. *Felony Justice*. Boston: Little, Brown.

Emerson, Robert M. 1983. "Holistic Effects in Social-Control Decision-Making." *Law and Society* 17:425–455.

———, ed. 2001. *Contemporary Field Research*. Boston: Little, Brown.

Emmelman, Debra S. 2003. *Justice for the Poor: A Study of Criminal Defense Work*. Burlington, VT: Ashgate Publishing.

Engel, David M. 1999. "Making Connections: Law and Society Researchers and Their Subjects." *Law and Society Review* 33:3–16.

Farrell, Amy, Geoff Ward, and Danielle Rousseau. 2009. "Race Effects of Representation among Federal Court Workers: Does Black Workforce Representation Reduce Sentencing Disparities?" *Annals of the American Academy of Political and Social Science* 623, no. 1: 121–133.

Feagin, Joe R. 2006. *Systemic Racism: A Theory of Oppression*. New York: Routledge.

Feagin, Joe R., and Vera Hernan. 1995. *White Racism: The Basics*. New York: Routledge.

Feeley, Malcolm. 1979. *The Process Is the Punishment: Handling Cases in a Lower Criminal Court*. New York: Russell Sage Foundation.

Feeley, Malcolm, and Jonathan Simon. 1992. "The New Penology: Notes on the Emerging Strategy of Corrections and Its Implications." *Criminology* 30, no. 4: 449–474.

Fine, Michelle, and Lois Weis. 1996. "Writing the 'Wrongs' of Fieldwork: Confronting Our Own Research/Writing Dilemmas in Urban Ethnographies." *Qualitative Inquiry* 3, no. 2: 251–274.

Foucault, Michel. 1982. "The Subject and Power." Afterword to *Michel Foucault: Beyond Structuralism and Hermeneutics*, 2nd ed., edited by Hubert L. Dreyfus and Paul Rabinow, 208–228. Chicago: University of Chicago Press.

———. 1978. *Discipline and Punish: The Birth of the Prison*. Translated by Alan Sheridan. New York: Pantheon.

Frampton, Mary Louise, Ian Haney-López, and Jonathan Simon, eds. 2008. *After the War on Crime: Race, Democracy, and a New Reconstruction*. New York: New York University Press.

Garfinkel, Harold. 1956. "Conditions of Successful Degradation Ceremonies." *American Journal of Sociology* 61, no. 5 (March): 420–424.

Garland, David. 2005. "Penal Excess and Surplus Meaning: Public Torture Lynchings in Twentieth-Century America." *Law and Society* 39, no. 4 (December): 793–834.

———. 1997. "Governmentality and the Problem of Crime: Foucault, Criminology, Sociology." *Theoretical Criminology* 1, no. 2 (May): 173–214.

———, ed. 2001. *Mass Imprisonment: Social Causes and Consequences.* Thousand Oaks, CA: Sage Publications.

Geertz, Clifford. 1973. *The Interpretation of Cultures.* New York: Basic Books.

Ghaziani, Amin. 2009. "An Amorphous Mist? The Problem of Measurement in the Study of Culture." *Theory and Society* 38:581–612.

Goffman, Alice. 2014. *On the Run: Fugitive Life in an American City.* Chicago: University of Chicago Press.

———. 2009. "On the Run: Wanted Men in a Philadelphia Ghetto." *American Sociological Review* 74, no. 3: 339–357.

Goffman, Erving. 1974. *Frame Analysis.* Cambridge, MA: Harvard University Press.

———. 1959. *The Presentation of Self in Everyday Life.* New York: Anchor Books.

Gómez, Laura E. 2010. "Understanding Law and Race as Mutually Constitutive: An Invitation to Explore an Emerging Field." *Annual Review of Law and Social Science* 6, no. 1: 487–505.

———. 2004. "A Tale of Two Genres: On the Real and Ideal Links between Law and Society and Critical Race Theory." In *The Blackwell Companion to Law and Society,* edited by Austin Sarat, 453–470. Malden, MA: Blackwell Publishers.

Gustafson, Kaaryn. 2013. "Degradation Ceremonies and the Criminalization of Low-Income Women." *UC Irvine Law Review* 297. http://www.law.uci.edu/faculty/full-time/gustafson/.

Hagan, John. 1989. "Why Is There So Little Criminal Justice Theory? Neglected Macro- and Micro-Level Links between Organization and Power." *Journal of Research in Crime and Delinquency* 26, no. 2: 116–135.

———. 1987. "Review Essay: A Great Truth in the Study of Crime." *Criminology* 25:421–428.

———. 1974. "Extra-Legal Attributes and Criminal Sentencing: An Assessment of Sociological Viewpoint." *Law and Society* 8, no. 3: 357–384.

Hagan, John, and Celesta Albonetti. 1982. "Race, Class, and the Perception of Criminal Injustice in America." *American Journal of Sociology* 88:329–355.

Hagan, John, and Holly Foster. 2006. "Profiles of Punishment and Privilege: Secret and Disputed Deviance during the Racialized Transition to American Adulthood." *Crime, Law, and Social Change* 46:65–85.

Hagan, John, John D. Hewitt, and Duane F. Alwin. 1979. "Ceremonial Justice: Crime and Punishment in a Loosely Coupled System." *Social Forces* 58, no. 2: 506–527.

Hagan, John, Carla Shedd, and Monique R. Payne. 2005. "Race, Ethnicity, and Youth Perception of Criminal Injustice: Toward a Comparative Conflict Theory." *American Sociological Review* 70:381–407.

Haney-López, Ian F. 2014. *Dog Whistle Politics: How Coded Racial Appeals Have Reinvented Racism and Wrecked the Middle Class*. New York: Oxford University Press.

———. 2010. "Post-Racial Racialism: Racial Stratification and Mass Incarceration in the Age of Obama." *California Law Review* 98, no. 3: 1023–1073.

———. 2007. Introduction to *Race, Law, and Society*, edited by Ian F. Haney-López, xi–xxii. Burlington, VT: Ashgate.

Heimer, Carol. 2001. "Cases and Biographies: An Essay on Routinization and the Nature of Comparison." *Annual Review of Sociology* 27:47–76.

Heinz, John P., and Edward O. Laumann. 1984. *Chicago Lawyers: The Social Structure of the Bar*. New York: Russell Sage Foundation; Chicago: American Bar Foundation.

Heinz, John P., and Peter M. Manikas. 1992. "Networks among Elites in a Local Criminal Justice System." *Law and Society Review* 26, no. 4: 831–861.

Heinz, John P., Robert E. Nelson, Rebecca E. Sandefur, and Edward O. Laumann. 2005. *Urban Lawyers: The New Social Structure of the Bar*. Chicago: University of Chicago Press.

Heumann, Milton. 1978. *Plea Bargaining: The Experiences of Prosecutors, Judges, and Defense Attorneys*. Chicago: University of Chicago Press.

Hochschild, Arlie R. 1983. *The Managed Heart: Commercialization of Human Feeling*. Berkeley: University of California Press.

Huber, Patrick. "A Short History of 'Redneck': The Fashioning of a Southern White Masculine Identity." *Southern Cultures* 1, no. 2 (Winter 1995): 145–166.

Hurwitz, Jon, and Mark Peffley, eds. 1998. *Perception and Prejudice: Race and Politics in the United States*. New Haven, CT: Yale University Press.

Jackson, Bruce. 2009. *Pictures from a Drawer: Prison and the Art of Portraiture*. Philadelphia: Temple University Press.

Jepperson, Ronald L., and Ann Swidler. "What Properties of Culture Should We Measure?" *Poetics* 22, no. 4 (1994): 359–371.

Kinder, Donald R., and David O. Sears. 1981. "Prejudice and Politics: Symbolic Racism versus Racist Threat to the Good Life." *Journal of Personality and Social Psychology* 40, no. 3: 414–431.

Kipling, Rudyard. 1929. "The White Man's Burden: The United States and the Philippine Islands, 1899." In *Rudyard Kipling's Verse: Definitive Edition*. Garden City, NY: Doubleday. http://historymatters.gmu.edu/d/5478/.

Klein, John F. *Let's Make a Deal: Negotiated Justice*. Lanham, MA: Lexington Books, 1976.

Krasner, David. 1997. *Resistance, Parody, and Double Consciousness in African American Theatre, 1895–1910*. New York: Palgrave Macmillan.

Kress, Jack K. 1976. "Progress and Prosecution." *Annals of the American Academy of Political and Social Science* 423, no. 1: 99–116.

Lamont, Michèle. 2000. *The Dignity of Working Men: Morality and the Boundaries of Race, Class, and Immigration*. New York: Russell Sage Foundation.

———. 1992. *Money, Morals, and Manners: The Culture of the French and the American Upper-Middle Class*. Chicago: University of Chicago Press, 1992.

Lamont, Michèle, and Virág Molnár. 2002. "The Study of Boundaries in the Social Sciences." *Annual Review of Sociology* 28 (2002): 167–195.

Lane, Winthrop D. 1922. "Cook County Jail: Its Physical Characteristics and Living Conditions." In *Reports Comprising the Survey of the Cook County Jail*, edited by George W. Kirchwey, 71–92. Chicago: Calumet Publishing.

Lara-Millán, Armando. 2014. "Public Emergency Room Overcrowding in the Era of Mass Imprisonment." *American Sociological Review* 79, no. 5 (October): 866–887.

Lee, Taeku. 2009. "Between Social Theory and Social Science Practice: Toward a New Approach to the Survey Measurement of 'Race.'" In *Measuring Identity: A Guide for Social Scientists*, edited by Rawi Abdelal, Yoshiko M. Herrera, Alastair Iain Johnston, and Rose McDermott, 113–144. Cambridge: Cambridge University Press.

Lizotte, Alan J. 1978. "Extra-Legal Factors in Chicago's Criminal Courts: Testing the Conflict Model of Criminal Justice." *Social Problems* 25, no. 5: 564–580.

Longazel, Jamie. 2013. "Moral Panic as Racial Degradation Ceremony: Racial Stratification and the Local-Level Backlash against Latino/a Immigrants." *Punishment and Society* 15, no. 1: 96–119.

Loury, Glenn. 2002. *The Anatomy of Racial Inequality*. Cambridge, MA: Harvard University Press.

Lynch, Mona. 2011. "Crack Pipes and Policing: A Case Study of Institutional Racism and Remedial Action in Cleveland." *Law and Policy* 33, no. 2: 179–214.

Mahoney, James. 2000. "Path Dependence in Historical Sociology." *Theory and Society* 29, no. 4 (August): 507–548.

Manza, Jeff, and Christopher Uggen. 2006. *Locked Out: Felon Disenfranchisement and American Democracy*. Studies in Crime and Public Policy. New York: Oxford University Press.

Mather, Lynn. 2003. "What Do Clients Want? What Do Lawyers Do?" *Emory Law Journal* 52:1065–1086.

———. 1979. *Plea Bargaining or Trial? The Process of Criminal Case Disposition*. Lexington, MA: Lexington Books.

———. 1974. "Some Determinants of the Method of Case Disposition: Decision Making by Public Defenders in Los Angeles." *Law and Society Review* 8, no. 2: 187–216.

May, Reuben A. Burford, and Mary Pattillo-McCoy. 2000. "Do You See What I See? Examining a Collaborative Ethnography." *Qualitative Inquiry* 6, no. 1: 65–87.

Maynard, Douglas W. 1988. "Narratives and Narrative Structure in Plea Bargaining." *Law and Society Review* 22, no. 3: 449–482.

———. 1984. *Inside Plea Bargaining: The Language of Negotiation*. New York: Plenum.

McConahay, John B. 1986. "Modern Racism, Ambivalence, and the Model Racism Scale." In *Prejudice, Discrimination, and Racism*, edited by John F. Dovidio and Samuel L. Gaertner, 91–126. Orlando: Academic Press.

McIntyre, Lisa J. 1987. *The Public Defender: The Practice of Law in the Shadows of Repute*. Chicago: University of Chicago Press.

Meyer, John W., and Brian Rowan. 1977. "Institutionalized Organizations: Formal Structure as Myth and Ceremony." *American Journal of Sociology* 83, no. 2: 340–363.

Murakawa, Naomi, and Katherine Beckett. 2010. "The Penology of Racial Innocence: The Erasure of Racism in the Study and Practice of Punishment." *Law and Society Review* 44, nos. 3/4: 695–730.

Myers, Martha A., and Susette M. Talarico. 1986. "The Social Contexts of Racial Discrimination in Sentencing." *Social Problems* 33, no. 3: 236–251.

Nardulli, Peter F. 1978. *The Courtroom Elite: An Organizational Perspective on Criminal Justice.* Cambridge, MA: Ballinger.

Natapoff, Alexandra. 2012. "Misdemeanors." *Southern California Law Review* 85:101–163.

Neubauer, David W. 1974. *Criminal Justice in Middle America.* Morristown, NJ: General Learning Corp.

Nielsen, Laura Beth. 2000. "Situating Legal Consciousness: Experiences and Attitudes of Ordinary Citizens about Law and Street Harassment." *Law and Society Review* 34:1055–1090.

Noel, Joseph R. 1924. *Report of the Committee on New County Jail and Criminal Court Building.* Chicago: Committee on New County Buildings. Municipal Reference Collection, Harold Washington Library Center, Chicago.

Obasogie, Osagie K. 2013. *Blinded by Sight: Seeing Race through the Eyes of the Blind.* Stanford, CA: Stanford University Press, 2013.

Olson, David E., and Sema Taheri. 2012. *Population Dynamics and the Characteristics of Inmates in the Cook County Jail.* Chicago: Cook County Sheriff's Reentry Council.

Omi, Michael, and Howard Winant. 1994. *Racial Formation in the United States from the 1960s to 1990s.* New York: Routledge.

Orfield, Myron W. 1987. "The Exclusionary Rule and Deterrence: An Empirical Study of Chicago Narcotics Officers." *University of Chicago Law Review* 54:1016–1069.

Pager, Devah. 2007. *Marked: Race, Crime, and Finding Work in an Era of Mass Incarceration.* Chicago: University of Chicago Press.

Pattillo, Mary. 2013. *Black Picket Fences: Privilege and Peril among the Black Middle Class.* Chicago: University of Chicago Press.

Pattillo, Mary, David Weiman, and Bruce Western, eds. 2004. *Imprisoning America: The Social Effects of Mass Incarceration.* New York: Russell Sage Foundation.

Pettigrew, Thomas. 1989. "Nature of Modern Racism in the U.S." *Revue Internationale de Psychologie Sociale* 2:291–303.

Picca, Leslie Houts, and Joe R. Feagin. 2007. *Two-Faced Racism: Whites in the Backstage and Frontstage.* New York: Routledge/Taylor and Francis.

Provine, Doris Marie. 1998. "Too Many Black Men: The Sentencing Judge's Dilemma." *Law and Social Inquiry* 23, no. 4: 823–856.

Rabinowitz, Mikaela. 2010. "Holding Cells: Understanding the Collateral Consequences of Pretrial Detentions." Ph.D. diss., Northwestern University.

"Report of the Sentencing Project to the United Nations Human Rights Committee Regarding Racial Disparities in the United States Criminal Justice System." August 2013. http://sentencingproject.org/doc/publications/rd_ICCPR%20Race%20and%20Justice%20Shadow%20Report.pdf.

Richardson, L. Song, and Phillip Atiba Goff. "Implicit Racial Bias in Public Defender Triage." *Yale Law Journal* 122 (2013): 13–24.

Richey-Mann, Coramae, Marjorie S. Zatz, and Nancy Rodriguez, eds. 2006. *Images of Color, Images of Crime: Readings.* 3rd ed. New York: Oxford University Press.

Rios, Victor. 2011. *Punished: Policing the Lives of Black and Latino Boys.* New York: New York University Press.

Roberts, Dorothy. 1997. *Killing the Black Body: Race, Reproduction, and the Meaning of Liberty.* New York: Vintage Books.

Rosett, Arthur, and Donald R. Cressey. 1976. *Justice by Consent: Plea Bargains in the American Courthouse.* Philadelphia: J. B. Lippincott.

Russell, Katheryn K. 1999. *The Color of Crime: Racial Hoaxes, White Fear, Black Protectionism, Police Harassment, and Other Macroaggressions.* New York: New York University Press.

Russell-Brown, Katheryn K. 2004. *Underground Codes: Race, Crime, and Related Fires.* New York: New York University Press.

Sampson, Robert J., and Janet L. Lauritsen. 1997. "Racial and Ethnic Disparities in Crime and Criminal Justice in the United States." *Crime and Justice* 21:311–374.

Sarat, Austin, and William L. F. Felstiner. 1986. "Law and Strategy in the Divorce Lawyer's Office." *Law and Society Review* 20, no. 1: 93–134.

Sewell, William F. 1992. "A Theory of Structure: Duality, Agency, and Transformation." *American Journal of Sociology* 98, no. 1: 1–29.

Simon, Jonathan. 2007. *Governing through Crime: How the War on Crime Transformed American Democracy and Created a Culture of Fear.* New York: Oxford University Press.

Skolnick, Jerome H. 1967. "Social Control in the Adversary System." *Journal of Conflict Resolution* 11, no. 1: 52–70.

Slobogin, Christopher. 1996. "Testilying: Police Perjury and What to Do about It." *University of Colorado Law Review* 67:1037.

Smith, Christopher E. 1993. *Courts, Politics, and the Judicial Process.* Chicago: Nelson-Hall.

Snow, David A., E. Burke Rochford Jr., Steven K. Worden, and Robert D. Benford. 1986. "Frame Alignment Processes, Micromobilization, and Movement Participation." *American Sociological Review* 51:464–481.

The Spangenberg Group. 2001. *Keeping Defender Workloads Manageable.* West Newton, MA: The Spangenberg Group.

Spohn, Cassia. 1990a. "Decision Making in Sexual Assault Cases: Do Black and Female Judges Make a Difference?" *Women and Criminal Justice* 2, no. 1: 83–105.

———. 1990b. "The Sentencing Decisions of Black and White Judges: Expected and Unexpected Similarities." *Law and Society Review* 24, no. 5: 1197–1216.

Steen, Sara, Rodney L. Engen, and Randy R. Gainey. 2005. "Images of Danger and Culpability: Racial Stereotyping, Case Processing, and Criminal Sentencing." *Criminology* 43, no. 2: 435–468.

Steffensmeier, D., J. Ulmer, and J. Kramer. 1998. "The Interaction of Race, Gender, and

Age in Criminal Sentencing: The Punishment Cost of Being Young, Black, and Male." *Criminology* 36, no. 2: 763–797.

Suchman, Mark C., and Lauren B. Edelman. 1996. "Legal Rational Myths: The New Institutionalism and the Law and Society Tradition." *Law and Social Inquiry* 21, no. 4: 903–941.

Sudnow, David. 1965. "Normal Crimes: Sociological Features of the Penal Code in a Public Defender Office." *Social Problems* 12, no. 3 (Winter): 255–276.

Swidler, Ann. 2001. *Talk of Love: How Culture Matters*. Chicago: University of Chicago Press.

———. 1986. "Culture in Action." *American Sociological Review* 51, no. 2: 273–286.

Terkel, Studs. 1992. *Race: How Blacks and Whites Think and Feel about the American Obsession*. New York: Anchor Books.

———. 1974. *Working: People Talk about What They Do All Day and How They Feel about What They Do*. New York: Pantheon Books.

Tonry, Michael. 2011. *Punishing Race: A Continuing American Dilemma*. New York: Oxford University Press.

Tuohy, James, and Rob Warden. *Greylord: Justice Chicago Style*. New York: G. P. Putnam's Sons, 1989.

Uggen, Christopher, and Jeff Manza. 2002. "Democratic Contraction? Political Consequences of Felon Disenfranchisement in the United States." *American Sociological Review* 67:777–803.

Uphoff, Rodney J. 1992. "Criminal Defense Lawyer: Zealous Advocate, Double Agent, or Beleaguered Dealer?" *Criminal Law Bulletin* 28, no. 5: 419–456.

U2. 2004. *How to Dismantle an Atomic Bomb*. Interscope, compact disc.

Van Cleve, Nicole Gonzalez, and Armando Lara-Millán. 2014. "Criminal Justice as a Welfare Handout." Paper presented at The Interplay of Race, Gender, Class, Crime, and Justice symposium, April 26, 2014, University of California, Irvine School of Law.

Van Cleve, Nicole Gonzalez, and Lauren Mayes. 2015. "Criminal Justice through 'Colorblind' Lenses: A Call to Examine the Mutual Constitution of Race and Criminal Justice." *Law and Social Inquiry*, doi: 10.1111/lsi.12113.

Van Cleve, Nicole Martorano. 2012. "Reinterpreting the Zealous Advocate: Multiple Intermediary Roles of the Criminal Defense Attorney." In *Lawyers in Practice: Ethical Decision Making in Context*, edited by Leslie C. Levin and Lynn Mather, 293–316. Chicago: University of Chicago Press.

———. 2011. "The Racialization of Criminal Justice: The Jim Crow Courts in an Era of Mass Incarceration." Ph.D. diss., Northwestern University.

Venkatesh, Sudhir. 2008. *Gang Leader for a Day: A Rogue Sociologist Takes to the Streets*. New York: Penguin Press.

Wacquant, Loïc. 2005. "Race as Civic Felony." *International Social Science Journal* 57, no. 183: 127–142.

———. 2000. "The New 'Peculiar Institution': On the Prison as Surrogate Ghetto." *Theoretical Criminology* 4, no. 3: 377–389.

Ward, Geoff K. 2006. "Race and the Justice Workforce: A System Perspective." In *The Many*

Colors of Crime: Inequalities of Race, Ethnicity, and Crime, edited by Ruth D. Peterson, Lauren J. Krivo, and John Hagen, 67–90. New York: New York University Press.

Watkins-Hayes, Celeste. 2009. *The New Welfare Bureaucrats: Entanglements of Race, Class, and Policy Reform.* Chicago: University of Chicago Press.

Western, Bruce. 2009. *Punishment and Inequality in America.* New York: Russell Sage Foundation.

Western, Bruce, and Christopher Wildeman. 2009. "The Black Family and Mass Incarceration." *Annals of the American Academy of Political and Social Science* 621, no. 1: 221–242.

Winant, Howard. 2004. *The New Politics of Race: Globalism, Difference, Justice.* Minneapolis: University of Minnesota Press.

Winston, George T. 1901. "The Relation of the Whites to the Negroes." *Annals of the American Academy of Political and Social Science* 18 (July): 105–118.

Young, Harvey. 2005. "The Black Body as Souvenir in American Lynching." *Theater Journal* 57, no. 4 (December): 639–657.

INDEX